Jimmy Burns is an award-winn~~and~~ [and] seven other books. He was born in~~...~~ reported for the *Financial Times*, Londo~~n~~, *Observer*, BBC and the *Economist*, and was the *FT* correspondent in South America in the early 80s. His book on Argentina and the Falklands War, *The Land That Lost its Heroes*, won the 1988 Somerset Maugham Award for non-fiction. When not in Spain, or travelling elsewhere, he lives in London.

www.jimmy-burns.com / Twitter: @jimmy_burns

Praise for *La Roja*

'A fascinating, personal and sometimes provocative journey through some of the key men and moments that have shaped Spanish football, and Spanish society.' Sid Lowe, *Guardian*

'Burns tackles his subject with care and enthusiasm. At the heart of the story is the ongoing battle between Madrid and Barcelona, and the struggle – both political and footballing – of the two great citadels.' *Scotsman*

'[A] splendid book . . . *La Roja* is indeed much more than a journey through Spanish football. It is a story of pain, humiliation and ferocious regional rivalry.' *Belfast Telegraph*

'Carefully chronicled . . . a vivid survey of Spanish football.' *Financial Times*

'*La Roja* shows in colorful detail how the traditions and loyalties of one country ended up by giving us the finest clubs and national team of the present moment.' *Wall Street Journal*

'*La Roja* . . . goes beyond the football to explain a country, a society and its transformation through, thanks and despite the beautiful game.' Guillem Balague

'Novel . . . Moving . . . Burns' central concern is not whether David Silva can play as a false nine, but how Spain's football team represent the people (or peoples) found within its current borders. He succeeds in telling that story.' *When Saturday Comes*

'*La Roja* is not just a tremendous book to read. Jimmy Burns' latest book is an educational tool for fans of Spanish football and fans of the game in general.' Simplyfutbol.com

Also by Jimmy Burns

The Land That Lost its Heroes
Barça: A People's Passion
Papa Spy
Spain: A Literary Companion
When Beckham Went to Spain
Maradona: The Hand of God
Beyond the Silver River

LA ROJA

A Journey Through Spanish Football

JIMMY BURNS

**SIMON &
SCHUSTER**

London · New York · Sydney · Toronto · New Delhi

A CBS COMPANY

First published in Great Britain by Simon & Schuster UK Ltd, 2012
This paperback edition published by Simon & Schuster UK Ltd, 2012
A CBS company

This book is copyright under the Berne Convention

All rights reserved

this v ... of Jimmy Burns to be identified as the author of
... with him in accordance with sections 77 and 78
of the Copyright, Designs and Patents Act, 1988

Simon & Schuster Australia,
Sydney

Simon & Schuster India,
New Delhi

A CIP catalogue record for this book is available from the British Library

ISBN: 978-0-85720-654-1
Ebook ISBN: 978-0-85720-655-8

Typeset by Hewer Text UK Ltd, Edinburgh
Printed in the UK by CPI Group UK Ltd, Croydon, CR0 4YY

For Kidge, Julia and Miriam

Contents

Preface

The human wave started in a town in South Africa, watched by a worldwide audience of over a billion people, and gathered force as it swept up the continent, before crossing the Mediterranean and rolling across the stark landscape of Castile-La Mancha and crashing onto the streets of Madrid. The heat and dust of a suffocating local summer was refreshed by sheer human effervescence as over a million Spaniards filled the centre of the Spanish capital, celebrating the return of their heroes, the winners of the 2010 Football World Cup.

After being honoured by King Juan Carlos and Queen Sofia at the royal palace, the players had boarded an open-roofed double-decker bus and begun a slow progress towards the banks of the River Manzanares. The route took them from the palace of Prime Minister José Luis Zapatero and through the Plaza España, the square that has at its centre a monument to Cervantes, creator of Don Quixote. In that short journey, the character of a nation seemed defined.

Throughout its turbulent history, pockmarked with foreign invasions, coups and civil wars, Spain has had its fair share of great and disastrous monarchs and political leaders and failed missions. But while Zapatero was a once-popular socialist leader who was on his way to being politically sunk by his administrative incompetence in the face of Europe's financial and economic crisis, King Juan Carlos endured as a symbol of national reconciliation. For it was this king that had assumed the role of head of a democratic state after the death of the dictator Franco in 1975 and resisted an attempted army coup six years later. This defiance of the army was in startling contrast to his grandfather Alfonso XIII who in the 1920s had passively accepted the bloodless uprising of General Miguel Primo de Rivera.

Perhaps the most significant aspect of the 1981 coup was not that it happened but that it failed. Spaniards woke up to the benefits of democracy and rallied round. Spain had changed irrevocably since the dark days of Franco and there was no turning back. And yet it was the statue of the fictitious literary figure of Quixote that still served as a reminder that this was a nation personified in a 'hero' whose nobility and achievement – so celebrated by Spanish philosophers seeking to place their country on a moral and political pedestal – proved delusional.

In the lead-up to Spain's bloody civil war in 1936, Manuel Azaña, then President of the Second Republic, remarked that in the defeat and disappointment of Don Quixote was the failure of Spain itself. He might have added – with an eye to the future – that Spain's football had for much of its history also mirrored its politics, touched as it was with tales of individual brilliance, occasional collective effort, but ultimate underachievement of the national squad in contrast to the international success of rival clubs.

And yet in that summer of 2010, beyond Quixote's statue thousands lined the streets and avenues, before closing in as the victory bus made its slow progress, each individual citizen stretching out their hands in collective admiration, or rather making sure they were not dreaming.

This was no ordinary homecoming. For a start, the celebrations extended across the country from Seville in the south to Barcelona in the north, a reflection of the rich mix of regional identity represented by the champions. In the Basque Country, where the terrorist organisation ETA was still waging a bloody campaign for independence from Spain, a shopkeeper was beaten up by thugs for celebrating the team's victory, while right-wing Spanish 'patriots' covered a statue of a Basque nationalist politician in the red and yellow of the Spanish flag. In Catalonia, a few radical Barça fans who also wanted independence from Spain refused to watch the World Cup and staged a counter-demonstration. But these were isolated incidents. The pervading image was of an explosion of Spanish flags all over the country, even in the most nationalistic anti-Spanish neighbourhoods, as if the shared and successful enterprise in football had for a moment at least set aside the seemingly irreconcilable political, social and cultural prejudices that had separated Spaniards from different regions and backgrounds for much of their history.

This was not only the first Spanish team to win the World Cup in the tournament's history, but one that had done so with an artistry that many believed represented the best football ever seen. La Roja, the red one, was how the team had been nicknamed. The name was aired almost as a matter of fact in an early press conference given by Luis Aragonés, the national coach under whose command a new creative and winning style of football came to be played by Spain in the run-up to its victory in the European Championship of 2008. Red shorts and shirt had been one of the main colours worn by the national squad for as long as most Spaniards could remember; only politics had seemed to get in the way of accepting it as a brand like, say, the Azzurri in Italy or Les Bleus in France. When he used the word, Aragonés felt that enough water had flowed under Spain's political bridge for Spaniards to call a spade a spade, or a team's kit by its proper colours. But even in 2008 those old enough to remember the Civil War and to have supported Franco found Aragonés provocative. For to be a Roja in the Civil War was to be anti-Franco, and while Real Madrid played in white, Barça had red in its colours and the Catalan flag more red stripes than the Spanish flag. As for Zapatero, Real Madrid fans were not best pleased to have in power the first Spanish prime minister ever to declare himself publicly a Barça fan – even if he was born in the very Castilian town of Valladolid.

The summer of 2008 was the honeymoon period of the Zapatero socialist government prior to the global banking crisis detonated by the collapse of Lehman Brothers. That spring Spain's socialist party had again triumphed in elections, giving Zapatero a fresh mandate to pursue his agenda of sweeping social, political and cultural reform. Despite a bitterly fought campaign, the election victory appeared to endorse Zapatero's boldest decisions such as the withdrawal of Spanish troops from Iraq, the granting of more autonomy to the regions, and the legalisation of homosexual marriages.

The future looked red. To that extent Aragonés stood accused of political opportunism by certain elements of the right. But then Aragonés was not a politician. In fact he had a reputation for saying what he felt like when he felt like saying it, however politically incorrect, for instance when he incensed the English media with his racist jibes against black English players. But somehow La Roja caught on and grew in popularity, not because of Aragonés but despite him (before the World Cup campaign was under way Aragonés had been replaced by Vicente del Boṣque), as if the term appealed subconsciously to a national mood, marking the point at which Spain had moved from being a failed state to a civilised nation, which could also be good at football and find in this a sense of common purpose.

The incisive English traveller Richard Ford rode on horse-back the length and breadth of Spain in the mid-nineteenth century before penning arguably one of the best books ever written on the country by a foreigner: *A Handbook for Travellers in Spain and Readers at Home*. Ford reached the conclusion that one of the fundamental characteristics of the Spanish people was their incapacity or unwillingness to pool their energies for the common good, what he called their 'unamalgamating' tendency.

'Spain is today as it always has been,' Ford wrote, a 'bundle of small bodies tied together by a rope of sand, and, being without union, is also without strength.'

La Roja was the passion that ran through the nation's veins, but, in its modern context, one that was life-giving. This was the colour of a sporting achievement recognised by fans across frontiers, not the red of execution squads that for centuries had set Spain apart from the rest of the world. Football played by players with style, and unity of spirit and purpose. One for all, all for one.

The World Cup tournament in South Africa would be remembered for many things – the deafening vuvuzelas, England's abject failure, the US's relative success, the humiliating exit of France amid a major dressing-room revolt, Maradona's eccentricities, the brutishness of the Dutch, the pervasive good cheer of the local people – but most of all for the fact that the best side won.

I don't know how many football fans around the world remember where they were at the precise moment in extra-time when in Johannesburg's Soccer City stadium Spain's Andrés Iniesta coolly controlled a bouncing ball from Cesc Fàbregas, then drove a beautifully struck half-volley into the Dutch goal. But I will never forget where I was, watching it live on TV, under a starlit sky on a beach in southern Spain near to where a group of Englishmen had played the first game of football on Spanish soil back in 1887. When Iniesta's goal was scored we knew Spain had finally done it and broke out into a collective dance.

The Dutch had played in their traditional orange, the Spaniards in dark blue, shedding their usual red colours for the sake of visual clarity. But the Spanish team stuck to their nickname La Roja – the Reds. It had brought them success, after many years of agony, making them first European and finally World Champions – the Reds had prevailed. *Viva La Roja!*

Introduction

I blame Mendizabal for giving me an enduring obsession with Spanish football.

He was a Spanish boy of Basque origins (I only remember calling him by his surname) who brutally interrupted my first serious attempt, aged seven, at trying to engage with the beautiful game. I had just begun to run with the ball towards the opposite goal, when the venture ended as abruptly as it had begun. Mendizabal, taller than me and twice my weight, hacked me from behind and sent me tumbling onto the frozen turf of a school's sports ground near London's Hammersmith Bridge.

Mendizabal, my classmate from Bilbao, got a cautionary warning from our English PE teacher Mr Atkinson, while I was left nursing a bleeding hole where part of my knee had once been, and clutching one hand in agony. Now in middle age, I wear my permanent scar on the leg and my broken finger like a badge of honour – my rites of passage into a game that was destined to remain an inseparable part of me through childhood, youth and adulthood, although I admit only as a fan and an amateur, not a pro. My dreams of becoming a professional footballer evaporated that day Mendizabal's boot broke my run as easily as the windmill shattered Don Quixote's lance.

I now see that my experience of the game had been defined from birth. I was born in Madrid to a Spanish (Castilian) mother and a father with mixed Scottish, English, Basque, and South American blood in him. It meant that when it came to football, my allegiances and interest were destined to wander between continents and within Spain in its full geographical, cultural and political diversity.

If the Argentine Alfredo Di Stéfano was my first football hero it was because childhood – except the times I studied at an English prep school with Mendizabal – was spent for long periods with my mother in Madrid, during the 1950s. This was a period when Franco's Spain struggled on account of its isolation from the rest of Europe. It was in the days before mass tourism, when Spain, and Madrid in particular, was still regarded by most foreigners as a sinister, backward and repressive place. Spain's national football squad barely resonated beyond the Spanish border but these were golden years for Real Madrid when the club attracted an enthusiastic following that defied political and national barriers. My mum remained a life-long *Madridista* and to her dying day could never understand why my loyalties were never permanently anchored at the Bernabéu. The answer lay in the fact that while the hospital where I came bloodied and screaming into this world was a couple of blocks away from the Bernabéu, my mum never took me to the stadium. She took me to bullfights instead, and my visits to the Bernabéu were dependent on the occasional acts of generosity of an old friend of my grandfather Gegorio, an eminent doctor who had kicked a ball around in his youth, in the early days of Spanish football.

I remember on my first visit looking up at the giant stadium, glowing in the dark like an illuminated cathedral, dwarfing all the buildings nearby, and being touched by the genuine warmth and excitement of the crowd. Of Real Madrid, I remember the dominating presence of Di Stéfano, around which not just a team but a whole game revolved. While most of the players seemed to stick to their positions, Di Stéfano seemed to be all over the pitch, tracking back and supporting his defence or leading endless attacks on the opposite goal. He had extraordinary energy and superb skill and the crowds loved him.

I found the atmosphere of Madrid's main bullring, Las Ventas, and the Bernabéu to be very similar, each as respectful of skill and domination as it was brutally dismissive of blunder and submission. Di Stéfano carried on his shoulders the destiny of a game as surely as did a star *torero* that of a *corrida*. In time I would see other analogies between bullfighting and Spanish football – in the fury and the grace, in the perfect kill and perfect goal, in the scrappy cape movement and failed pass, in the ease with which the emotional pitch of the crowds could switch from a roar of celebration to a litany of abuse, in the sense of life and death, in the precariousness of achievement. Only the use of white handkerchiefs marked a difference. While in Las Ventas they were brought out to petition trophies, in the Bernabéu they symbolised disgust, with a referee's decision, with an off-form Real Madrid, with a game that was played without guts and ended in humiliation.

In adulthood my horizons broadened and I followed Spanish football wherever I felt I could see it best played and that meant continuous visits to the Camp Nou where certain Dutchmen, notably Johan Cruyff, cast their own particular magic spell on Spanish football. And yet to have even a drop of Spanish blood during the 1950s was to be aware that Di Stéfano was the best player there had ever been, and Real Madrid the best club in the world. Real Madrid was a goal factory in those days, and its players fought like lions to score as many goals as they could – and it was Di Stéfano whose stickers I collected on the many days I was left imagining him. To watch him now on YouTube is to barely glimpse the greatness of a player who occupied space and time, dominating a game with his personality and skill. Thank God for the memory of our elders.

I might have spent those early childhood years at some London stadium or become, like Mendizabal, a fan of Athletic Bilbao, the best of the pre-modern Spanish clubs, were it not for the fact that my father, who spent much of his time in England, was never really interested in football – his school days had been spent playing tennis, rugby and cricket. No tribal loyalties there. In adulthood he lost interest in sport alto-gether, partly because he slipped a disc, but mainly because he spent the war years as a spy rather than watching Stanley Matthews, and then spent the rest of his life using up his spare time with books, painting and chess.

But school and holidays in Spain and later work as a journal-ist gave me plenty of experience of seeing how a variety of Spaniards of all ages played and they seemed to play a great deal of football whatever the regime in power.

This is a story about how one of Europe's most impover-ished nations endured political turmoil to become a creative melting pot of sporting talent. Over the years I have reported on football in Europe and South America, and I came to realise how the development of football in Spain could only really be explained within the country's political and social context and its openness to foreign influences from the old and new worlds. This book covers a period of history during which the geograph-ical epicentre of the game, with its early English influences, has moved over the last century from the Basque region, across the Atlantic to South America, and back again to Madrid and Catalonia where two clubs, Real Madrid and FC Barcelona, not only share a majority of local fan clubs around Spain but command a mass global following live, on TV and on the net.

From its early beginnings when the first football was played in the mining towns of southern Spain and near the shipyards of Bilbao by British engineers and sailors, through to the influx of South American stars and other Europeans, the engagement of foreigners with home-grown Spanish talent overcame political adversity and produced football of sublime skill, passion and huge entertainment value. But it proved a long road.

This book takes us on a journey through some of the extraordinary characters, and games, that have defined Spanish football from the early days when a few enthusiasts developed their talent kicking a ball on a piece of industrial waste ground to the emergence of professional native talent groomed by, among others, expatriate Englishmen. The story continues with the cross-fertilisation of Spanish and foreign players and the profound impact on the success of clubs like FC Barcelona and Real Madrid – among the most powerful and successful sporting institutions in the world and major contributors to the first Spanish national team ever to win the European Nations and World Cup.

This is a journey through some of the landscapes, cities, people, myths and real circumstances that contributed to Spanish football's transformation from pupil to master. *La Roja* is about how world football's great underachiever became world football's great champion. It is about the country I was born in, and how its football became beautiful.

Jimmy Burns London/Madrid/Barcelona/Sitges, February 2012

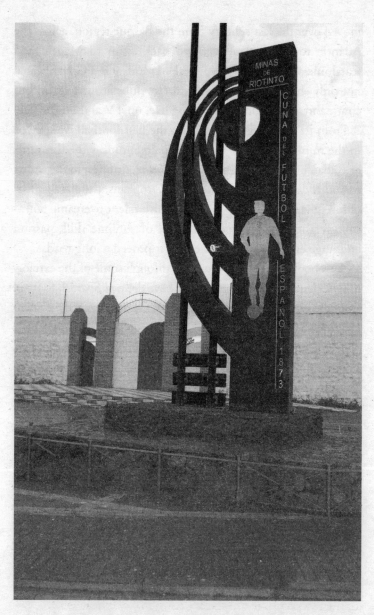

Rio Tinto – a monument to the Birth of Spanish Football

1

La Furia

During Franco's dictatorship between 1939 and 1975, football was a pastime that was actively encouraged by the State – that is as long as it was not exploited by the enemy. And the enemy ranged from communists, Freemasons and freethinkers to Catalan and Basque nationalists, most of them decent human beings whose clubs were rooted in local cultural identities. It gave Spanish football, when I was growing up, its political edge, it separated us football lovers into democrats and fascists.

Franco was brutal on and off the pitch. Far from magnanimous in his hour of victory, he emerged in 1939, at the end of the Spanish Civil War, determined to rule his country with an iron fist. Spaniards were divided between those who continued to support him and his military rebels and those who had fought against him on the side of the democratically elected Republican government. The former were rewarded with jobs, social security benefits and new houses. The latter faced imprisonment, execution and social exclusion, including exile.

Culturally, Spain was reduced to a playground, carefully

controlled. With an increasing number of Spaniards migrating from the countryside to the big cities, in particular Madrid and Barcelona, and the spread first of radio and then TV, football overtook bullfighting as the most popular pastime, tolerated by a regime that saw sport through the prism of self-preservation, a vehicle for defusing antagonisms of a dangerously political ilk. Of those years, one of Spanish football's most eminent native commentators, Alfredo Relaño, has written:

> Football kept growing. The world (Spain) rebuilt itself after the war and there was little to do except work as many hours as possible . . . pick up the pieces from the ruins, and on Sundays go to the football match. These were hard years, of shortages, cold, and few diversions. There was a radio in each house (the invention of TV was on its way), a cinema in each neighbourhood and football. At times there were cycling competitions and boxing fights (and bullfights) but above all football, and not much else.

During the 1920s, when Spain's first professional footballers began to make their mark, it was the direct, aggressive, spirited style of the Basque team Athletic Bilbao that set a benchmark, although the term *furia* (fury) that came to denote their style could not claim originality. Basques played the way they did because they were taller and physically stronger than other Spaniards and because they were accustomed to playing in wet conditions, when much of Spain was semi-desert. In the old days of emergent Spanish football few pitches were covered in turf.

Spaniards at the time were quite happy to recognise that the aggressive, spirited game of football had its roots in Britain, and the English teachers that came to Spanish clubs. Under Francoism things changed and the term *furia Española* (Spanish fury) became part of the regime's militarist nomenclature. *La Furia* was redefined and promoted by the state's propaganda machinery as one of the leading virtues of a New Spain. It was resurrected from the mythology of conquest and glory that belonged to the country's imperial past such as the recovery of Muslim Granada by the Catholic kings and the creation of Spanish America by the early *conquistadores* – conquering warriors. It also drew on the national stereotype mythified in the literary figure of Don Quixote, the incarnation of the spirit of non-compromise, with his hopelessness and failure forgotten beside his nobility of purpose.

As the Falangist newspaper *Arriba* wrote in 1939 a few months after Franco had emerged triumphant from the Spanish Civil War: 'The *furia española* is present in all aspects of Spanish life, to a greater extent than ever . . . In sport, the *furia* best manifests itself in football, a game in which the virility of the Spanish race can find full expression, usually imposing itself, in international contests, over the more technical but less aggressive foreign teams.' In other words football was to be played as if the ground was a battlefield, and the players soldiers. What mattered was courage, sacrifice and above all the physical annihilation of the opponent. Neither skill nor creativity, let alone fair play, was part of the armoury.

Franco liked the phrase *La Furia* because he felt it exemplified the essence of Spanish nationhood. Unsurprisingly it was a Basque-born player sympathetic to the regime that became emblemic of the cause. The occasion was the 1950 World Cup in Brazil when Spain faced England in the group stage, the player in question, Athletic Bilbao's Telmo Zarra. The leading scorer in six Spanish championships, Zarra had already achieved the popular iconic status previously achieved by the legendary Spanish bullfighter Manolete, killed in the bullring of Linares three years earlier. It was popularly said that Zarra played with three legs, the third being his devastating head. Zarra rammed home with his foot rather than headed Spain's winning goal, having beaten defender Alf Ramsey off a cross from Gainza. When the match was over, Spanish football's top official Armando Muñoz Calero told Franco, 'Excellency: we have vanquished the perfidious Albion.' Thus did Franco's Spain get its own back for the defeat of the Invincible Armada. Well, up to a point.

It proved a pyrrhic victory. In a four-team final mini-league, Spain's chances of winning the World Cup ended after being beaten 6–1 by Brazil. This perhaps explains why Franco consoled himself with the thought that the crowning moment of football achievement was when Spain showed a lot of *furia* and beat the Soviet Union in the final of the 1964 European Nations Cup, the only major trophy the Spanish squad won during three decades of Franco's dictatorship.

Long after Franco died, there would be no shortage of Spanish commentators that would blame Spain's failure not on *La Furia* but on the lack of it among certain players in the national squad. And yet bad luck and a dearth of inspired coaching at national level as much as politics lay behind Spain's record of underachievement. With the exception of its gold medal in the 1992 Olympics, democratic Spain had to wait until 2008 before it won the European Championship again, after enduring years of pain and disappointment under a succession of, in the main, lacklustre coaches.

By then Spain's national team had caught up with the

quality of its great clubs, found a decent coach, and forged a consensus around how football could best be played in a way that was not only effective but also wonderful to watch. I myself had become a Barça fan, a conversion that got under way in the 1970s when Johan Cruyff came to Catalonia. Like Di Stéfano, his personality and way of playing influenced a whole generation of players, although his presence proved more enduring. And to fans like me he came to personify in football the best of Spain after Franco. It helped fuel my later enthusiasm for La Roja and the way it refined *La Furia* into a new aesthetic where the nobility of purpose became entwined with creative play as a winning formula.

An abandoned mine in Southern Spain built by English engineers

2

British Roots

The piece of land where the first game of football in Spain was played lies buried underground in an abandoned mine in southern Spain. To find it, I set off one chilly winter morning from London's Victoria station on the Gatwick Express. Four hours later I was in a hired car, driving out from Seville airport, the local *Ole* radio station blaring flamenco music, a warm sun struggling to break through the Atlantic clouds. I drove towards the hills of Aracena, through olive groves and strawberry fields and pasture land where fighting bulls grazed.

Off the main motorway to the Portuguese border, a secondary road took me to the giant opencast mines of Rio Tinto, one of the oldest mining areas in the world – the site, some say, of the legendary King Solomon's mines – where generations of men have carved their enduring and brutal imprint on a once beautiful landscape. It is as the historian David Avery vividly described it more than thirty years ago, 'a labyrinth of strangely sculptured and brilliantly coloured interlocking valleys where hands and machines long ago tore the hillsides apart into gigantic fissures and carved them into a series of deeply descending angular terraces.'

This is not just a multicoloured cavity in a desolate landscape. It is nature consumed by man's advance. Whole mountains, valleys and villages have disappeared, making any sense of orientation that much more difficult. While the rain pelted down, the countryside seemed to subside, and down the hillside and across the fields ran water stained, like the river, blood-red by the oxidised mineral residue.

Thankfully it had stopped raining by the time I reached a magnificent viewing point over the Corta Atalaya. Under fading daylight, the opencast pit presented a kaleidoscope of colours: a pinkish rock face speckled by lines of leaf-green and gold, high escarpments of black and purple slag and the levelled banks of silver-grey pyrites. My guide was José Antonio Delgado, the young bearded former mayor of Rio Tinto, the local town which owes its existence to the foundations laid by British pioneers in the second half of the nineteenth century. Antonio was not a football fan. He was a socialist who knew something about the Spanish Civil War graves recently dug up in the nearby village of Nerva.

One of those buried there was Luis Ruiz, a local veterinary surgeon who had played as a goalkeeper for his local village team in the lead-up to the Civil War in 1936. A year before the outbreak of the conflict, the vet denounced the local butcher to the health authorities for selling meat from diseased cows. The butcher never forgave Ruiz for the fine he had to pay and the lost trade. When the village was taken over by Franco's forces, the butcher accused the vet of being a 'red'. The vet was taken away and summarily executed. I met his niece Pilar in a cramped first-floor apartment near the village square. Chain-smoking and with a face that seemed already at death's door, she told me how her family got their revenge many years later when the butcher was gored to death by a fighting bull. 'The bull was called *Justiciero,* the just one,' she said before she was gripped by a coughing fit.

José Antonio wanted to share with me his concern about more contemporary issues – the decimation of the local environment, the growing youth unemployment, and the local drug trafficking. He pointed to the mine's slag. 'Spain's first football pitch is buried in there somewhere,' José Antonio said.

I then met Rafael Cortes, a sepulchral-looking local historian who knew something about football. 'Football is part of our heritage,' he told me. We sat sharing a bottle of red wine and a large piece of roasted local pork with José Reyes Remesal, the president of the local football club, Rio Tinto Balompié. Remesal was a genial rogue who looked like a man who spent much of his day enjoying himself. Cortes had no doubt that Rio Tinto was the true cradle of Spanish football although he bemoaned the fact it had never received sufficient recognition from the state or from the world of football generally. Part of the problem was that since the mines stopped operating in the early 1990s, Rio Tinto had lost its way. The majority of the local bars had been turned into fan clubs of Real Madrid and FC Barcelona. The only other club in town was Athletic Bilbao because the Basque Country shared a mining tradition. Usually drunk on the local fire-water, the unemployed villagers watched the most popular matches on TV. 'People here follow Real Madrid and Barça because they can afford the best players, win the most trophies,' said Cortes.

Then his friend Remesel took me to the local football stadium. It dated from the early 1930s when the British had built a new town for the workers after gradually destroying the old one. Of the earlier period little remained except a few picturesque houses and an Anglican church from the exclusive British neighbourhood of Bella Vista, named after the panoramic views which only the senior managers and engineers were able to enjoy. The stadium was eerily empty. With its ragged turf and stone perimeter, with standing room for about 3,000 fans, it resembled a giant sheep's pen. It was easy to mistake the two small changing rooms for public latrines. The local club played in a minor regional division. Being its president, Remesal admitted, was more of a hobby than a full-time occupation. But he proudly showed me the 'trophy room'. It was filled with a few cups dating back to the 'glory days' of the early 1930s when Rio Tinto Balompié won an inter-village championship.

Precisely where that first game on Spanish soil was played and who contested it remains a subject of dispute for it is not just a football pitch but a whole town, originally known as Minas de Rio Tinto, that today lies buried under a slag heap. However, early photographs suggest that the most likely playing field was near to where Rio Tinto English Club had its offices in Calle Sanz number 2, near the mayor's office, along a street of whitewashed and red-tiled houses. It was there that the Rio Tinto Football Club gathered its players for their inaugural kickaround on the local feast day of San Roque in August 1887.

San Roque, or Saint Roch as he is known in France, is a medieval saint with a popular cult following on both sides of the Pyrenees. Legend has it that he was struck down by the plague but endured thanks to a piece of bread brought to him by a faithful dog. The saint's image, pointing to an open sore on his thigh, with the dog by his side, was once displayed in practically every Spanish church before falling victim to the ravages of the Spanish Civil War. Nonetheless, that first football game in Spain proved an innovative act in a country that had largely fallen behind the European mainstream since its heyday as the world's most powerful nation in the sixteenth century. Having squandered the immense wealth derived from its American empire, Spanish power in Europe had gone into steady decline thanks to a series of long costly wars and internal revolts. While some parts of northern Spain benefited from a belated industrial revolution and overseas trade, and gathered a growing number of migrants to its major towns, a majority of the country remained a largely rural, semi-feudal society steeped in its mainly Catholic traditions and vulnerable to foreign predators.

It was an investor from the City of London called Hugh Matheson who one February morning in 1873 financed the purchase of the moribund copper mines of Rio Tinto from the Spanish state. At the time Spain was immersed in one of its periodical dynastic struggles between conservatives and liberals after the overthrow of the Bourbon monarchy and its temporary replacement by a republic prior to the restoration of Alfonso XII. Matheson took advantage of the extended period of political instability and financial weakness of the Spanish state and cut a good deal. Of the £3.5m he paid, a first instalment in gold coins was transported by train and bullock-drawn carts. Railways came belatedly south of the Pyrenees so that many parts of Spain, not least the south, remained in a primitive state of underdevelopment.

Matheson then used the capital he had raised in the City to secure not just mineral rights – one of Spain's prime assets – but also powers for the compulsory acquisition of land for the building of railways linking the mines to the sea, along with the absolute freehold in perpetuity of all land and buildings owned by the Spanish state within the Rio Tinto boundaries. On 29 March 1873, the Rio Tinto Company was registered, thus beginning a process that was to transform the run-down works into one of the most profitable and ruthlessly exploitative mining enterprises in Europe.

Over the following decade, the population of Rio Tinto and its neighbouring village Nerva grew from 1,000 to 10,000, with the local farming population swamped by an influx of new migrants from surrounding Andalusia and beyond, including a strong contingent from the northern region of Asturias, where there was similarly high unemployment. The enduring traditions of the nearby *pueblos* or villages were subsumed into a working class subjected to the pressures and tensions of a cash economy driven by ruthless managers. The mining camp coalesced into a community which felt itself subject to rather than part of the foreign presence. The new miners were nicknamed by the old villagers *los mohinos* – a word that has several meanings in English. The most relevant was stubborn, and prone to violence. On the other side of the social divide, the surveyor of the north-lode opencast in those early days was a man called Douglas Gordon, who carried out his inspections astride a jet-black horse, wielding a riding crop. The miners called him Don Diablo.

In 2011 the only native English speakers I had come across in Rio Tinto were a couple of wild boar hunters from some US shooting club in Wisconsin. But then the mines – nationalised by the Spanish state during the 1950s – had long ceased to function, and whatever sense of community that had once resided there had had the stuffing knocked out of it.

But let us return to the time of that first football match in 1887, a time when the poverty and rootlessness contributed to the violence that was rife among the miners. Under the influence of the local fire-water made from potato-spirit, knife fights would easily break out between the men. The feast days of San Roque, patron saint of the sick and the disabled, was an occasion for the local population, however poor or oppressed, to indulge in some collective fun, with an extended fiesta lasting over two days. Daytime entertainment, when the men were still sober enough to keep standing, included a local version of tug-of-war, donkey and mule races, and climbing a greasy pole.

When the British acquired the mines, they extended the railway line through the site of the local bullring but quickly built another one just outside the village, in the style of Seville's Maestranza. It was inaugurated in 1882 with a huge enthusiastic crowd turning up in support of the two stars of the ring, Currito Cuchares and *El Morcilla* (The Black Pudding). While the newly arrived Brits looked down on the fiesta as the activity of an uncouth underclass of local natives, they had the good sense not to boycott it – at least not straight away. Two years after the bullring was built, the company bought it from its Spanish owner and pulled it down, claiming it had become a gathering point for prostitutes and drunks. Within three years, a group of mining staff, including managers, chose to mark the day of San Roque with a football match between two teams picked exclusively from non-Spaniards.

The early kick-around of the English expatriates on Spanish soil almost mirrored the primitive folk years of football in England, the land where it had all first begun. As Hunter Davies records in his social history of the British game, *Postcards from the Edge of Football,* football in its early days in England was usually held on festive holidays, with two teams of unlimited numbers trying to get a ball from one end of a village or neighbourhood to another and reaching a designated goal. 'Kicking each other, fighting, settling old scores, using weapons or any sort of physical violence was allowed, and people did get badly injured and, sometimes, killed.'

The first football match recorded in Spanish history near the mines of Rio Tinto was almost as loosely played, although *Los Ingleses* aspired to bring a culture of civilisation to one of the least developed areas of Europe with its backward feudal economy and endemic political turmoil.

When not forming the focus of a loose scrum, the hard leather ball was kicked as far as possible from one end of the pitch to the other. Heading was a widely used if awkward tactic of a game the British played in cloth caps to protect them from the harsh local sun. Spaniards watched from the sidelines. No written account nor oral tradition survives that might have fleshed out the detail of that particular game on the feast of San Roque. But one can imagine the local crowd being unimpressed initially by the crude physical antics of the foreigners. The game seemed to ape the violence into which their drunkenness occasionally descended. It also lacked both the creativity and brinkmanship of the one popular local entertainment they could claim as their own but to which the company had effectively laid waste – the bullfight.

The myth would have us believe that this first game was born as a gesture of sportsmanship that reached out and engaged Englishmen with Spaniards. The reality was rather different – that these early expatriate pioneers played football much as they might have played polo, rugby, tennis, or croquet, as a way of asserting their differentiation from the natives.

The British who kicked a ball around locally for the first time were watched by the Spaniards like visitors from another planet, the banter of the players – cries of 'hooray' and 'jolly good' would no doubt have resonated round the makeshift football pitch – as foreign to them as the Anglican church, bereft of images, and Victorian Home Counties villas the managers built for themselves in the privileged quarter of Bella Vista.

The faded photographs that survive from the period are evocative of the British Raj of imperial India, with the men and women's uncompromising dress code – white flannels, large hats, voluminous silk dresses and parasols – and tea habits contrasting with the stark surrounding landscape and roughly hewn shirts and trousers of the Spaniards. Other museum pieces that survive to this day remind one of the relative luxury enjoyed by the British: the general manager's private train compartment, its interior resplendently carved in mahogany and furnished in leather, and the *casa grande,* the palatial home, similarly decked out in the style of a colonial governor.

Huelva – monument to the unknown player

3

Spanish Roots

The primitiveness of the poor Spaniards who first set eyes on a football is not difficult to imagine. It was made vivid by Antonio, a local taxi driver from the port of Huelva whose grandfather had been a miner. Antonio told me of an enduring ritual to which a local cuckolded man resorted in order to 'cure' himself of his wife's alleged infidelity. This involved having a local witch identify the wife's lover by smelling her panties after she returned from her latest liaison and then burning them. Along with 'evil spirits' and *brujeria* – witchcraft – it was bull-fighting, flamenco, saintly relics, weeping Virgins, bleeding Christs, and witches that the locals of the villages and towns near Rio Tinto were familiar with, not the site of upright white-skinned Anglo-Saxons and Celts in rolled-up sleeves and variously coloured undershorts kicking a ball around and barging each other on a patch of waste ground marked out with poles referred to as 'doors'. The game was played by the British according to their language and their rules, and when the game was over the players returned to their club house – to which no

Spaniard had access – with its portrait of Queen Victoria, billiard table, and back-numbers of *The Times* and the *Illustrated London News*.

The early history of Spanish football – and its legacy – would have been very different had Rio Tinto Football Club not evolved gradually as a local Spanish club, under native management and recruiting from an increasing pool of players within the mining company. The breakdown of barriers in the region was facilitated by the increased flow of personnel between the mines and the nearby port of Huelva once the railway connection had been built and inaugurated in 1875 with 83 kilometres of track, ten bridges and four tunnels. Football then began to attract the growing interest of much larger segments of the local population, not just as spectators, but also as participants. Small ad hoc teams began to spread across the surrounding villages. Football belatedly took on a Spanish identity.

Rio Tinto Football Club for a while tried to maintain its self-imposed exclusivity, registered as a British sporting entity just as the mining company had been registered as a British company. However in Huelva the British community found itself forming an alliance – out of sheer economic self-interest – with local representatives of the landed and trading classes, several of whom had been educated in English schools and had learned to play football.

From the early 1870s a small but thriving British community made this corner of the southwest coast of Spain – half a day's sail on a good wind from where Nelson confronted the French in the Battle of Trafalgar – their home for much of the year. In early July, led by their women and children, they decamped to Punta Umbria, a hitherto undiscovered beach where they built their well-appointed holiday homes on a stretch of virginal sand. In the 1870s, British investments in Rio Tinto were given protection by a garrison of English soldiers as Spaniards fought Spaniards over the future of their monarchy in the Carlist Wars. 'Marched out of Huelva on Wednesday. Played football with some railwaymen for about an hour out. The only diversion we truly had,' wrote a British officer, Captain W.F. Adams, in September 1874.

In Huelva, as in Rio Tinto, the British tried to monopolise the game for as long as they could. A local newspaper report on a game played near the mines between Rio Tinto and a team of visitors from Huelva on 6 May 1882 showed a majority of players on both sides to be Englishmen and Scots, with names like Brady, Campbell, Stourton, Higgins, Simpson, Crump and Alcock. A journalist from the local *La Provincia* newspaper wrote:

On a beautiful afternoon and before a large crowd the long awaited game between the teams from Huelva and Rio Tinto was played. We may have to wait for some time before we witness another match as well organised and balanced with teams of equal strength. Although Rio Tinto had some tough players, Huelva played with greater subtlety and craftiness. Huelva was on the attack right through the game, but at the last minute it was Rio Tinto that slipped in the winning goal.

Huelva Recreation Club (later renamed Recreativo Club de Huelva) was officially founded in December 1889 by Alexander Mackay, a Scottish doctor employed by the Rio Tinto company. Unlike its rival based nearer to the mines themselves, El Recre, as it came to be known, was quickly registered as a Spanish entity, a move that would eventually lead to its incorporation into the nascent Spanish Football Federation with entitlement to participate in official competitions across the country. The club played its first game a year later in Seville against employees of the British-owned and operated Seville Water Works at the Tablada hippodrome. El Recre passed into Spanish hands in the first decade of the twentieth century and then disappeared from the map of top-flight football as the focus of the sport shifted elsewhere in Spain.

To this day Huelva disputes with Rio Tinto its claim to be the *'cuna del fútbol Español',* the birthplace of Spanish football. Although Recre has floundered, relegated to the Spanish second division in modern times, a large monument to an unknown football player stands at the entrance to the town. It is cast in a similar mould to the one that stands near the football stadium in Rio Tinto.

Both projects display that boldness and foolhardiness that characterised a mining community while risking great hubris, much like the big statue to Maradona which stands defiantly at the entrance to the Boca Juniors stadium museum in Buenos Aires. The province of Huelva, like Argentina, hangs on to its great myths although the reality is that the game was exported years ago.

What is beyond dispute is that by the early twentieth century Recreativo had ceased to be foreign, with Spaniards making their presence increasingly felt in its club administration and its team. Among the most influential of the Spaniards involved with Recreativo's early development was Manuel Perez de Guzman, a land-owner originally from Jerez who moved to Huelva and developed business ties with the British. Perez de Guzman became vice-chairman of the club in 1906, while four of his sons joined as players. Of the siblings, the most legendary was the third-born, José or 'Pepe', who shared his love of football with an equal passion for flamenco and bullfighting.

In the inter-war years Pepe achieved a reputation as a gifted musician, writer and exponent of the local fandango, characterised in its dance form by slow arching and spiralling movements played to distinct guitar rhythms and sung verses dedicated to the beauty of the Virgin of El Rocío. Pepe also liked to bullfight on horseback and developed a close friendship with the hugely popular Ignacio Sánchez Mejías, one of the most famous and cultured bullfighters in the history of the 'sport'. Sánchez Mejías' fame as a bullfighter grew when most of Europe was fighting the First World War and Spain remained neutral.

The bullfighter would later defy the traditional cultural norms which inspired his profession, and forged strong friendships among the so-called generation of '27, a movement of young left-wing poets who experimented with new forms of writing and living in an attempt to break out of the repressive hold the Catholic Church and the military traditionally had on Spanish society. Sánchez Mejías was badly gored on 11 August 1934 in the bullring of Manzanares and died soon afterwards of gangrene, his life and death forever mythified in the moving eulogy written by his friend, the poet Federico García Lorca. Local football fans also honour him as the one-time president of Real Betis, one of the two rival clubs based in Seville.

Before leaving Andalusia, I drove back to Seville and caught up with Sol, an old childhood girlfriend, who was one of Manuel Perez de Guzman's descendants. Although not a great football fan herself, she had agreed to introduce me to some friends who were, in the old gypsy quarter of Triana on the left bank of the coiling Guadalquivir River. She took me down a narrow street, lined with balconies filled with geranium pots. It was midday and a small group of mainly middle-aged men propped up a bar decorated in colourful tiles. The walls were covered with religious icons and football posters. Two images appeared to be the subject of particular veneration. One was the neighbourhood's favourite Virgin, Esperanza de Triana, whose statue is carried across the bridge every Good Friday in a moment of high emotion at the culmination of Holy Week. The other was of the Virgin of the Kings who, legend has it, appeared in a dream to King Fernando of Castile-Saint Fernando, the Spanish monarch who began Andalusia's fight back against occupation by Arab Islamists in the thirteenth century by taking Seville. Every local football fan knows by heart the battle hymn she inspired.

> *A tus plantas se postra Sevilla por rendirte homenaje . . .*
> *Reina aquí, pues tu Sevilla, que Fernando conquisto.*
> At your feet Seville kneels . . . our Queen, for it was this
> Seville that Ferdinand conquered.

Near both Virgins was a giant poster of the Betis team of 1935. It was the only league championship Betis had ever won, and they did it the year before Franco's military uprising sparked off the Spanish Civil War. The next trophy the club won was the Copa del Rey – the King's Cup – more than forty years later when Spain had become a democracy.

'We were given the title royal by the King's grandfather Alfonso XIII in the 1920s but we never owed our victories to Franco,' said Cayetano, a gaunt-looking and somewhat intense school teacher.

Next to him his elderly companion, a long-retired dock

worker with the girth and ruddy face of Sancho Panza, was prompted to share a somewhat contrasting piece of history. He recalled following a Spanish national squad team in Franco's time in the Cold War years to a game behind the Iron Curtain. 'The stadium was full of Russians – all looking rather serious and severe. So I and my mates started singing some flamenco to try and humour them. The Russians thought we were crazy.'

Another member of the group, a young off-duty taxi driver with gypsy looks called José Maria, tried to explain why he was a Betis fan. 'To be a Betis fan means supporting the team even when it loses. It's a sentiment that goes beyond success or failure. Our colours are predominately green, which represents hope.'

One of Lorca's most stirring refrains – and one of my favourites – focuses on the colour green as a powerful image of nature at its most essential and prolific: 'Green I want you green / Green the wind and green the boughs / The ship upon the ocean seen / the horse upon the hill . . .'

I often wonder what might have happened to Lorca had he not ended up being shot and buried in an unmarked grave near Granada after the outbreak of the Spanish Civil War. Perhaps this sensitive and vulnerable gay artist would have detested the whole mythology of *La Furia* and the self-conscious virility of football during the Franco years. On the other hand his presence at the occasional match might have helped counter the macho image of its more radical fans; indeed he helped produce one of the more lyrical rallying chants in football, embellishing still further the sound of rhythmic flamenco that thankfully is the dominant sound one hears these days whenever one or the other Seville club plays – or when *La Roja* play in Seville.

Some Betis fans admitted that their fathers or sons belonged to the city's other club, Sevilla FC – mainly because it was a club that had proved more successful in Spanish and international club football. Sevilla FC won the first ever Copa del Generalissimo after Franco had come to power. Although the losers were Racing del Ferrol, the club from the Galician town where Franco was born, the cup was handed out by the new sports minister General Moscardó, one of Franco's most trusted generals, and in the Montjuic stadium in Barcelona, home to the city's other club, Espanyol, whose loyalty to the new regime was never in doubt. Sevilla FC also won the league title for the first and only time in the 1946–47 season before securing four Copa del Rey and two UEFA championship titles over the next sixty years (2005–06 and 2006–07, won mainly thanks to foreign players).

Tradition has it that Betis was the club of the people, with its roots in a neighbourhood famous once for its poverty and radical politics as opposed to Sevilla FC, the club of the *señoritos* – the upper-crust rich kids. Betis was given the 'royal' title as a way of restoring some social balance between the two rivals and defusing class conflict. Such token patronage proved unnecessary. Social distinctions between the two clubs blurred anyway over the years with shifting patterns of immigration and urban development. Today each have their separate stadiums in up-market neighbourhoods of the city, and class and political divisions between their football fans here are as deceptive as in other parts of Spain.

The Spanish can be very proprietorial over their football, not inclined to acknowledge outside influences. I met Juan, a middle-aged Andalusian shopkeeper who supported FC Sevilla. He was adamant that 'Spanish football belongs to us just like our bullfighting and our flamenco music. It comes from our soul.' When I mentioned the English roots he insisted that it was the 'Basques that owe their football to the English'. He did acknowledge that it was Basque players who made up the spine of Betis's championship team.

Still, I was intrigued by Juan's comments, so I flew to the Basque capital of Bilbao.

Bilbao fans

4

Basques

The Basque people claim ownership of their very own quintessential ball game of pelota. So they say, it came into existence long before the English kicked their first football. Played with the hand or a basket scoop against a wall, it demands great skill as well as strength and endurance to keep hammering the hard leather ball in unexpected directions at great speed. Pelota figures large in local mythology. The *jentilak,* the legendary Basque giants, are reputed to have played their own version of a ball game, kicking and throwing the great boulders scattered by glaciers on upland meadows in the Pyrenees and Cantabrian mountains. Other contemporary myth-makers suggest that the first footballers in the Basque region were Neolithic shepherds. However, the first documentary evidence of pelota in the Basque country is a 1509 prohibition against the sport being played in the Cathedral of Santiago in Bilbao. But it was the coming of the English that was destined to make football even more popular than pelota, even in the Basque Country.

The UK link existed in the sixteenth and seventeenth

centuries when Bilbao's old port of El Arenal was the gateway for the wool trade between Castile, London and Flanders, and for the Basque manufacturing trade. Nearby woodland provided charcoal for smelting iron. Then, when the forests were exhausted, coal was imported from England on ships that exported iron, and later steel, on the return journey.

As in the south of Spain, the British connection in the nineteenth century asserted itself on the Cantabrian coast in the context of political instability and economic underdevelopment. During the Peninsular War of the early nineteenth century, Wellington's 85th Infantry regiment 'liberated' the Basque city of San Sebastián from Napoleon's occupation only to proceed to sack it. The pillage lasted all day and into the night, during which the darkness was dispelled, so bright was the light from the burning buildings. The population felt abused and humiliated at the destruction of the city by their 'allies'. It was, they suspected, a deliberate act to stifle northern Spain's commerce with France.

British troops would make some amends in 1833 when they helped defend the town during the First Carlist War, one of Spain's periodic nineteenth-century dynastic struggles. The war pitted the supporters of Don Carlos, the brother of the late autocratic pro-French King Ferdinand VII, against the regime of the more 'liberal' and enlightened regent Maria Christina, supported by the ill-equipped British auxiliary force.

Many soldiers did not survive to tell the tale. Some of the bodies of the English volunteers lie discreetly in a small cemetery above the city of San Sebastián on the slopes of Monte Urgull. The memory of Wellington's sacking was not easily eradicated from local memory and partly explains why local club Real Sociedad has never claimed to owe anything to *Los*

Ingleses. During the Carlist Wars, British troops also died in Bilbao, but this town they chose not to pillage. Those killed in liberating it from the French were buried on a piece of waste ground on the banks of the River Nervión. The area, today the site of the Guggenheim Museum, is known to this day as the Campa de Los Ingleses (the field of the English) and it was where the British kicked their first ball around in the late nineteenth century. By then, the invention of the Bessemer furnace, which converted low-phosphorous iron – Bilbao's speciality – into high-quality steel, had turned the Basque capital into an industrial dynamo.

As in Rio Tinto, the first games of football in Bilbao were linked to the nearby mines, and the English who exploited them. Nevertheless, whereas Rio Tinto was run like a mining camp set in a Victorian colony, with the natives effectively segregated, Bilbao's industrial development was never fully surrendered to the British and football in its beginnings provided a vehicle for integration between the foreigners and the local Basque shippers and industrialists who formed the vanguard of Spain's entrepreneurial class. Several of the more prominent Basques were educated at English public schools. Bilbao also created an urban working class, who along with their employers refused to submit themselves to the rule of a British colony and whose pay and conditions, while still miserable, were generally better than those down south. To this day the ritual chant that rises from the belly of San Mamés, the stadium of local football club Athletic Bilbao, is '*Aliron, Aliron, Athletic Campeon*'. The Royal Spanish Academy's official dictionary says that *aliron* comes from the Hispanic-Arabic *al'ilan*, meaning 'proclamation', and that is its most common usage in Spanish football – except in the Basque country. At

Bilbao's mining museum you will be told that the word derives from the phrase 'All Iron', which an English mining technician would write in chalk if a mined rock was found to have more than 70 per cent iron content. Such a discovery earned the poorly paid Basque miner a bonus and was a source of some contentment, if not jubilation. Thus did *aliron* make its way from the mines to the football pitch.

The game's Anglo-Saxon roots in the Basque country had to contend from an early stage with a strong sense of local culture and political identity, as I discovered visiting this part of Spain over many years. On a return visit to Bilbao early in 2011, I was invited to lunch by the city's main football fan club in a building they owned in the Casco Viejo or old quarter. The so-called Siete Calles, or seven (narrow) streets, is a tightly knit community of tapas bars and other hidden temples to Basque gastronomy. Ours was no ordinary football lunch over endless rounds of beers and cheap snacks. It began with several glasses of red Rioja at the entrance to a bar and developed into a feast lasting all afternoon in the large basement of an anonymous building equipped with a large kitchen and several dining tables and chairs. This was the fans' private club or gastronomic society, known colloquially as *txoko*.

There was more Rioja to be drunk, along with several bottles of Patxaran, the local Pyrenean liquor made from anis and blueberries. But the focus of activity revolved around the dishes prepared by our host – a fanatical football fan turned in an instant into a master amateur chef. For our meal he produced several plates of tapas, from cured meats and tortilla to stuffed peppers and prawns, and followed this up with a large cod baked in green pepper sauce. Then came the cheeses, and the ice creams, and the cakes.

Food enough to indulge one's culinary tastes proved the perfect complement to our football conversation, this txoko's favourite topic. I began asking my host, Juan Maria Arana, the president of Athletic's association of fan clubs, why he was a fan. He replied: 'I was nine years old when I went to see my first match in our stadium San Mamés in 1946. My father was in the navy and spent most of the time at sea. But my grandfather took me along with my brothers. It was after the war – what we called the years of hunger because of the post-war food shortages. But somehow watching Athletic lifted the spirits. We beat Oviedo 4–2 – the two goals were scored by a Basque player, which felt like a bit of betrayal! We weren't allowed to speak our language then, or wave our flags, but we had our red and white colours and that was the reason of our existence. It still is.'

According to local artist and writer Juan Antonio Frade de Villar – K-Toño to his friends – every hidden street and avenue and bridge and tramline and bus and metro route in Bilbao led you to the San Mamés stadium if you just knew the way – and he did. From the moment I had landed in Bilbao, the inimitable K-Toño with his Quixotic beard, cape and learned head forever covered by a *txapela* (a typical Basque beret) had guided me through the town's secrets. There was not a corner of the city that was unknown to his inquisitive eye. His passion for Athletic and its world was reflected in a book of vignettes and sketches he liberally gave out to his friends like a bible. Early on in the day, K-Toño had taken me to visit the magnificent Ibaigane Palace which houses the club headquarters. Commissioned and owned by the Basque business magnate Ramon de La Sota in the early twentieth century, the palace was turned into a military headquarters during the Franco regime. 'I remember my days as a conscript there, doing night guard duty in the garden, listening to the military governor General Santamaria standing on the balcony in his pyjamas and barking orders before he rode out to exercise at La Campa de Los Ingleses,' he told me.

But it was his beloved San Mamés – named after an early Christian martyr mauled by Caesar's lions – that had endured within him long after General Santamaria had been consigned to the dustbin of history. 'I cut my football teeth kicking a ball in the nearby streets and I've been going to that stadium for more than sixty years. I will always treasure memories of great triumphs and hundreds of games fought by legendary players, and the tears shed, sometimes from disappointment, others from pure joy.'

Others began to chip in, pledging that they would remain fans to their dying day, even though these days the club does not produce teams like FC Barcelona and Real Madrid. Perhaps Athletic needed to loosen up a bit on its Basques-only policy, I suggested. I was told by one of the veterans present that the policy of restricting access to the team only to those born in the Basque Country had been applied only during Franco's time not because the old dictator had any respect for Basque nationalism but because he thought only the Basques were pure Spaniards. Things had changed since democracy and these days you could be born anywhere in the world and join the club as long as you had some Basque blood running through your veins. 'In my humble opinion, the policy is more nuanced and it has changed through history,' suggested Iñigo Gurruchaga, a Basque journalist who lives between Bilbao and London.

It was then that one of the younger guests, Xavi, butted in rather drunkenly and accused them all of myth-making.

Suddenly the tone of the gathering changed, and threatened to become not just political but dangerously so. 'The only reason we can't compete is because of Athletic's policy of recruiting only players with Basque blood in them. Athletic is the most xenophobic club in Spain!' It was the point at which the camaraderie began to disintegrate as Xavi found himself having to fend off accusations of belonging to dark forces from Madrid – a member of the centre-right Partido Popular, or worse still an unreconstructed fascist and a closet Real Madrid fan – all of which he virulently denied. Later I stumbled into the night, well fed, well drunk and yet sensitive to the fact that no one had once alluded to the British connection – a reminder that Spanish football, wherever it was played, had achieved some kind of unilateral independence given a further edge by local politics.

When it comes to Spanish football, I have been on a learning curve for a while now, and this was another lesson. An earlier visit to the region was in 2003 when I was following David Beckham, during his first season at Real Madrid. I was struck by the radicalism of the local fans when the team played away in Pamplona against Osasuna. During Pamplona's famous bullfighting festival, the football fans ran the bulls and mocked the conservative families that occupied the best seats. At Osasuna's El Sadar stadium they occupied the stands behind the north goal, waved Basque nationalist flags and chanted slogans in support of ETA, the Basque terrorist group, when not shouting abuse at Beckham and the other Real Madrid players. At one point a young ballboy threw a missile at Beckham while he was taking a corner. Beckham looked back and gestured like a teacher admonishing a wayward pupil. The gesture generated uproar among the local fans. They weren't going to take any lessons from Beckham, or any other *Ingles* for that matter.

Seven years later, in Bilbao, I sat in a library in the city's British-style gentleman's club delving into old newspapers. I discovered that Basque football's declaration of independence came one spring day in 1894 when a group of *Bilbainos* published an advertisement in a local newspaper challenging the team of *Los Ingleses* to a football match. *Los Ingleses* – not just Englishmen but Scots, Welsh and Irishmen too – won the toss and chose to play the first half with the sun behind them. They played a very physical game, felling their opponents on several occasions with heavy tackles or barges, which surprised and angered the *Bilbainos* and allowed *Los Ingleses* to secure a two-goal advantage by the time the half-time whistle blew at approximately 11 a.m.

At this point the *Bilbainos*' low spirits were lifted by the surprise delivery to their changing rooms of eleven exquisitely roasted chickens, a gift from their opponents. The match was delayed to allow the local team to enjoy their meal, just as *Los Ingleses* had planned. By the time play resumed, the sun was setting and it was once again facing the *Bilbainos*. Blinded by the light, pushed, bruised and somewhat indigested, the *Bilbainos* lost 0–6. Only belatedly did the *Bilbainos* realise the trickery of a team that boasted to be the teachers of fair play. The locals pledged there and then to build up a team that would never again suffer such humiliation, either on or off the field.

The year that game was played is mostly remembered by present-day *Bilbainos* as the day Sabino Arana, the Basque country's most influential ideologue, founded the Basque Nationalist Party (PNV). By the time he died nine years later, at the age of thirty-eight, the PNV had become a significant force that was to endure to this day. Arana left behind not only an ideology but a flag, an anthem and a name for a new-and-ancient nation – Euzkadi.

Arana started off proclaiming the party's goal to be total independence from Spain, but before he died he ended up apparently accepting that 'maximum autonomy' within the Spanish state was more desirable. Despite such ambiguities the spirit of nationalism that he engendered had its impact on local football from its very beginnings. In 1898, four years after the fateful chicken match, a group of Basque football enthusiasts were confident enough about their own abilities to form their own football club called Athletic Club. By then football had spread from the Basque Country across northern Spain to Catalonia and up from the south to the capital Madrid.

FC Barcelona team bus

5

Catalans

It was in the fishing port of Palamós on Catalonia's Costa Brava in 1889 that a local merchant, Gaspar Matas i Danés, who had studied in England, formed Palamós Foot-Ball Club. The Costa Brava, like much of Spain's coastline, has long been invaded and transformed by foreign tourists and property speculators. But the fish market and maritime museum are still there, dedicated to the generations of local men who risked their lives to keep local traditions going. Palamós is one of the few towns along the Costa Brava that has managed to preserve its identity amid the plundering of the rest of the coastline by mass tourism.

Palamós' football roots are nonetheless discreetly stated on a fading plaque, well off the tourist track. Its history is hidden out of sight down a poorly lit inner gallery of a small archaic English-style stadium built more than a century ago on its outskirts, one of the first such structures to be built on Spanish soil and which has endured to this day, like a long-abandoned church.

When I visited it, the place was not only unkempt but eerily silent. Despite repeated enquiries, I was told by a part-time volunteer secretary that no spokesman of the club was immediately available and would not be for several hours. She suggested there was not much they would enlighten me on anyway. She certainly had neither the time or inclination to help. A groundsman I found emerging from a rusty latrine seemed marginally more forthcoming. He took me on a quick tour of the decaying stadium, bemoaning the lack of funds and cuts in public spending that were hitting local government following the credit crunch and the collapse of the property market. He was an immigrant from the Ivory Coast. 'I like watching Barça but Didier Drogba has always been my hero.'

That a fellow Ivorian Drogba, the Chelsea star and captain of the Ivory Coast's national team, was marked out as his hero was hardly a surprise. Nor was the fact that he saw no contradiction in Barça being his favourite club. Another star fellow-countryman Yaya Touré had only recently joined his brother Kolo at Manchester City after making a success of his time in the Catalan capital. Anyway, the presence of FC Barcelona just up the coast had long put Palamós in the shadows.

For in the same year, 1889, that Palamós FC was formed, an occasion took place in Catalonia that was to prove altogether more providential. In a field in the neighbourhood called Bonavona in Barcelona, the capital city of the region and a major Catalan port, a group of players kicked a ball around, dressed for the first time in the red and blue colours of what later became one of the world's great sporting institutions.

If football had come only belatedly to this part of Spain it was because Catalans, regardless of class, were too caught up in local politics. There was a growing urban working class in Barcelona that had grown, as in Bilbao, from the region's early industrialisation, and a thriving business class that had profited from external commerce. But in the second half of the nineteenth century Catalonia, and Barcelona in particular, became embroiled in a seemingly endless cycle of repression and violence that left little time to watch, let alone learn, an innovative sport. As for the middle classes, while they enjoyed something of an economic boom in the last dozen years of the nineteenth century, their conservative society was threatened by escalating strikes and anarchist-inspired bombing campaigns.

Political and class divisions intensified following the final demise of the Spanish Empire with the loss of Cuba in 1898. This provoked a great deal of soul-searching among some of Spain's politicians and intellectuals as to why the one-time empire had ended up being brought to its knees by a group of Latin American insurrectionists, although no national consensus emerged around the diagnosis, still less any cure. In Catalonia it turned Catalanism – a belief that the region constituted a separate entity from the rest of Spain by virtue of its culture, tradition and economic development, demanding special treatment – from a minority creed into a vehicle for generalised protest.

In such a nationalist atmosphere it was perhaps nothing short of miraculous that the majority of FC Barcelona's first ever team were foreigners, notably Englishmen. The goalkeeper was called Brown, the club's first secretary Wild, and two key players, Arthur and Ernest Witty, brothers in arms. Their father had immigrated to Barcelona in the middle of the nineteenth century and set up a shipping business, acting as agents for all the British merchant vessels that sailed in and out of the port city. As schoolboys the Wittys had been educated at Merchant Taylors, an English private boarding school with a long-established tradition of intelligent sportsmanship or, as its legendary founder put it, 'training the body as well as the mind'.

In the spring of 1998, I went looking for Arthur Witty's oldest surviving descendant in an old people's care home near the seaside resort of Castelldefels, south of Barcelona. Frederick Witty was hard of hearing and suffering from a cancer which would kill him a few months later, but he had retained a good memory and was happy to share it.

Frederick seemed the epitome of a post-imperial Englishman abroad, with his tweed jacket and silk cravat, and heavily accented Spanish and Catalan. We were surrounded by geriatrics holding on to their existence with the help of pills and tubes and the humanity of the nursing staff. So he was glad when I wheeled him out into the garden under a warm spring Mediterranean sun. He showed me old team photographs of his father Arthur, a rather upright Colonel Blimp type with black hair and a heavy moustache, about five foot ten and strongly built. 'When he was at school in England my father played rugby as a forward. Then he came to Barcelona and played football as a fullback,' Frederick recalled. 'To play rugby in Spain in those days was impossible because none of the sports grounds were fully turfed, whereas with football you could learn quickly enough to kick a ball around on any surface.'

Only later did I think Frederick's comments might hold the key to offering another explanation as to why Spanish football had evolved the way it had. The Spanish landscape – its sheer geological variety and contrast – was one of the explanations of its political problems and economic underdevelopment. Spain has some regions where it rains like Ireland, and others that seem an extension of the Sahara. It has regions covered in mountains, and others covered in vast arid plains. It has fertile valleys and rivers that are dry for most of the year. One of the main still-unresolved challenges of Spain's evolution as a nation has been how to find ways of linking up its diverse regions not just by roads, rail and air but also constitutionally, in a way that shares out Spain's development as a country while respecting political and cultural autonomies with their own historic identities, like the Basque Country and Catalonia.

Of course, modern methods of irrigation and power generation along with one of the boldest road and railway building projects since the Second World War have helped to make Spain more accessible both without and within, have allowed most stadiums to be turfed, and helped more football fans travel. But the landscape has yet to be fully tamed and the playgrounds for the aspiring stars of the future remain varied.

But back to *El Ingles* Witty. We drank tea on the well-watered lawn of his nursing home, as the Mediterranean sun went down and his breathing became laboured. Frederick shared a few more insights about his father. 'He never did any specialised training – none of that stuff you see these days, with players having orders shouted at them by coaches acting like camp commandants. But he knew how to keep fit, and did so by going for long runs.

'He played a lot of football between games of tennis. His favourite family outing was to walk all the way to the top of the Tibidabo, Barcelona city's highest vantage point, and down again. In their styles, there was little to choose between him and the other early founders. They played with a combination of acceleration, toughness, ball control and goal-scoring potential.'

The Witty story came to be overshadowed in the mythology of FC Barcelona by the figure of Hans Gamper. He was the Swiss-born Barcelona businessman who helped assemble the

early FC Barcelona players and was the club's founding president. Gamper proved himself to be a man well in touch with
the social and political changes taking place in his adoptive
country. He quickly learned Catalan and supported Catalonia's
drive towards greater autonomy from Madrid. While the official history of FC Barcelona has it that the colours were
imported by Gamper from Switzerland, the Witty version is
that they were inspired by the maroon and blue of Arthur's old
school colours at Merchant Taylors. It seemed to me that Barça
may have opted in later years to accept the Gamper version –
with its prominence in neutral understated Switzerland – as a
way of liberating itself from its British colonial roots.

Francisco Giner de los Rios: 'Sport maketh the man'

6

Madridistas

The club that was destined to become Barça's eternal rival, Real Madrid (or Madrid FC as it was called originally when it was registered for the first time in 1902), also had its early personality shaped by Englishmen, with its first book of rules imported from Manchester. The white colours which have distinguished the club to this day were copied from those of the Corinthians, one of London's first amateur football clubs. Prior to the foundation of any football club in the capital, the first kick-arounds took place in a field near the old bullring, with participants using a room in a local bullfighting tavern as one of their meeting places. Spanish football from its early days, far from displacing bullfighting as a cultural and social phenomenon, coexisted with it. In time great players would join great *toreros* or *matadors* in the pantheon of popular mythology.

And yet even in pre-modern traditionalist Madrid, Spanish football owed much to its foreign roots. One of the first Madrid players was Arthur Johnson, a freethinking English businessman who shared his footballing skills and philosophy of life with a group of young Spanish disciples of Francisco Giner de los Rios, one of the most influential of Spain's intellectuals at the end of the nineteenth century.

De los Rios founded the Institución Libre de Enseñanza – the Free Institute of Learning – dedicated to the ideal of a non-official, non-dogmatic education that, freed from the shackles of those conservative forces like the Catholic Church and the military, would nurture a new generation of Spaniards capable of transforming post-imperial Spain from a failed to a modern state. De los Rios was a huge admirer of Anglo-Saxon (post-Reformation) civilisation and the Enlightenment. He encouraged the teaching of sport, alongside excursions in the countryside, as an essential element in the syllabus, first of his university and later the schools he developed, with mixed success, when the political extremes on the left and right took hold of Spanish politics in the early decades of the twentieth century. Nevertheless, De los Rios believed football, played according to its emerging set of rules, was a sport that would appeal across class lines and would in time come to overtake the popularity of bullfighting, which he considered a legacy of primitiveness and repression. To that extent he proved prophetic.

Real Madrid has kept a portrait of Johnson written by a Spanish friend of his. The writer contrasts Johnson's dedication and knowledge of the game with the chaos that characterised the play of some of the Spaniards in the first Madrid squad, not least the goalkeeper. According to the chronicler, Johnson 'not only knew more about the game than anybody else'; he was also *un Ingles muy simpatico* – a very friendly Englishman. In 1902, the year after Madrid FC's foundation, the 23-year-old Johnson was the veteran of a team whose average age was nineteen and whose youngest player, sixteen-year-old Pedro Parages, had learned the game in England. 'Johnson is the captain of the team – he distinguished himself with his tackling, agility and elegance of body. He plays in various positions, centre-half, centre-forward and goalkeeper.' The rest of the team was made up of a former player from Athletic Bilbao, seven other Spaniards – two of them born in Cuba and one in Guatemala – and a Frenchman by the name of Chalmandier who had also learned to play in England. Chalmandier played at right-half and distinguished himself by the great sense of self-confidence and elegance with which he played.

The first two administrators of Madrid FC, Juan and Carlos Padros, were born in Catalonia, a fact that sits awkwardly with the enduring rivalry between the two clubs. It is a curious paradox which serves as a reminder that beneath the myths created by the warring factions, or their apologists, the history of Spanish football, like the history of Spain, was never quite so easily delineated, but subject to complex shades.

Partisanship has inevitably meant that the Padros brothers have been used by some Catalans to embarrass *Madridistas* about their non-Castilian roots, as when the Barcelona sports tabloid *Mundo Deportivo* in December 1992 boldly headlined an article: 'A Catalan Founded (Real) Madrid!'

The fact that the newspaper could claim an exposé nine decades after the event was the consequence of the refusal of Real Madrid's official historians to even mention the fact of Catalans being among the club's founding fathers. And yet whatever the myths and obfuscations, the Padros brothers were first and foremost motivated by football not by politics, and there is little evidence that they shared any particular sympathy for Catalanism as a separate political and cultural movement to the rest of Spain.

The Padros brothers were young children when their parents moved to Madrid from Barcelona in 1876. Their father was a cloth merchant who spoke French as his second language and made frequent visits to the north of England to look at textiles. He was drawn to Madrid by the prospect of more business when the Spanish capital was poised on the edge of political reform that promised to make civil war and military coups a thing of the past. The Bourbon dynasty had been restored under King Alfonso XII – father of the future Alfonso XIII – and one of Spain's greatest statesmen, Antonio Cánovas del Castillo, had helped draw up a liberal constitution that he hoped would make Madrid the respected European capital of a country united under a constitutional monarchy.

It was Carlos, the elder of the Padros brothers, whose idea it was to set up a small office to run FC Madrid's early affairs in a back room of his father's textile shop. Carlos was crippled in one foot from birth so he grew up using an orthopaedic boot and could never play football himself. Nonetheless, he had picked up an enthusiasm for the game when accompanying his father on his visits to England and France. In 1902 he temporarily overcame his disability and managed to referee the final of the first tournament in Spanish football club history to coincide with the celebrations surrounding the coronation of King Alfonso XIII.

The Coronation Tournament provided a good guide to the emergent footballing geography of Spain. The latest Bourbon to assume the Spanish throne was only sixteen at a time when modern sport was becoming internationalised. The modern Olympic movement had been founded six years prior to the coronation. Within four years of it taking place, Spain's northern neighbour France had organised its first major cycling tour and sports car Grand Prix. The young King Alfonso, flushed with the energy of youth and as yet uncorrupted politically as he was destined to be, considered himself an open-minded forward-looking king who was happy to give the 'modern' game of football his blessing from the outset of his reign. The first championship, known as the Coronation Cup, was donated in his name by the mayor of Madrid, Alberto Aguilera. (The trophy was subsequently renamed the King's Cup, the Copa del Rey.) It was contested by five teams: two based in Catalonia, FC Barcelona and Espanyol; Athletic Bilbao, using the name of the Basque province from where the club emanated, Vizcaya; and Madrid FC and another team, New Football Club de Madrid, that had formed in the capital but would soon be absorbed by its rival and eventually named Real Madrid.

The matches were played in the capital's hippodrome, which was then in open ground where today's Spanish Ministry buildings are, near the modern Bernabéu stadium. The event drew an audience of 2,000 to 5,000 spectators, which was less than a quarter of the crowd that could fit into Madrid's main bullring. Nevertheless it was the first mass gathering of football fans on Spanish soil and was evidence of the sport's nascent popularity. Gamper's FC Barcelona beat Padros' Madrid 3–1 and then was beaten 1–2 by Vizcaya. All three teams played with English players but with a majority of Basque, Catalan and other Spanish players. The trophy was taken back to Bilbao where it has remained to this day in the offices of Athletic Bilbao, a club that went on to win four successive King's Cups and would remain central to the development of Spanish football in its early decades.

King Alfonso XIII – he put 'Real' into Spanish football

7

Growing Pains

While many English fans can justifiably claim tribal loyalties dating back to Victorian times, the first Spanish football enthusiasts at the end of the nineteenth and the early twentieth century were in a small privileged minority and to my knowledge my Spanish great-grandmother, resolved to seeing out her twilight years in the fading light of the island of Cuba, the Spanish Empire's last colonial outpost, was not one of them.

Yet the hopes and dreams of early Spanish football fans contrasted with the incoherence of Spanish society as a whole. At the turn of the century, this was evident in the survival of traditional structures and attitudes which clashed with those pushing for reform. Spain still lacked a fully functioning national railway system and other communications were generally poor. Large swathes of rural Spain remained semi-feudal, in the hands of local politically powerful land owners – caciques – with conditions of life among the peasant workforce comparable to the worst areas of Sicily and eastern Europe. Poverty was exacerbated by geology, with some regions beset by inadequate rainfall or poor soil or both. Many rural workers in parts of the south and Galicia in the north, for example, escaped from semi-starvation by emigrating to South America or moving to the cities. By contrast, financiers and large-scale industrial entrepreneurs came to dominate the economic and social life of the towns of Bilbao and Barcelona on Spain's northern coast, along with a growing and increasingly militant urban working class.

Meanwhile King Alfonso XIII in Madrid developed a taste for political intrigue, with an inflated belief in his capacity to ensure the stability and unity of the nation. He was ultimately incapable of conceiving a form of government other than a highly centralised one with the support of the military. Spanish politics was characterised by deep-rooted antagonisms between conservative and progressive politicians, the enduring influence of a reactionary military and Catholic Church, and separate nationalist aspirations in Catalonia and the Basque Country.

Separate societies evolving within a country and markedly different rates of change was the common experience of Europe under the impulse of industrialisation. Spain was distinguished by its tardiness, its sporadic incidence of development. At a more general level, unlike northern Europe, Spain lacked a well-rooted middle class, which eliminated a channel through which aristocratic taste could be distilled or primitive popular taste refined and diluted. Spain was a country where popular arts like flamenco, religious festivals and bullfighting had triumphed and endured.

It is this cultural, social and political context which explains the belated development of Spanish football into a mass sport in which both leading clubs and the national team came to be drawn into the political struggle between nation and regions. In spite of the attempts of Spanish reformers, the spread of football across class lines proved a protracted affair, its social inclusiveness made all the more complicated by the absence of a unified national consciousness.

The clubs that competed in Spain's early national tournaments could between them boast only relatively small numbers of supporters at a time when gates for big cup and league games in England were already regularly reaching the 20,000 mark. In 1901, the year before Spain staged its first club championship before a crowd of no more than 5,000, the English FA Cup final between Spurs and Sheffield United at Crystal Palace drew a crowd of over 110,000. Seven years later, long before anything resembling a Spanish national squad had been assembled, a Scotland–England match at Hampden Park drew over 120,000, the largest ever for an international.

Nevertheless, in the first decade of the twentieth century a growing number of cities and regions in Spain acquired a focus of civil identity around their football clubs. The early pioneers in Huelva, Madrid, Bilbao and Barcelona were followed by the foundation of clubs in Asturias (Sporting Gijón, 1905) and Galicia (Deportivo La Coruña, 1906). In Andalusia, Sevilla and Betis were formed within two years of each other (1905 and 1907 respectively).

An early anomaly in the geographical landscape was Atlético Madrid, founded in 1903 in the Spanish capital by a group of Basques as a subsidiary of Athletic Bilbao. Both clubs agreed not to compete with each other in tournaments and shared players, an arrangement that persisted until the early 1920s when Atlético became independent.

In Catalonia, Sociedad Española de Football was founded in 1900 by a group of aristocratic university students, who adopted the crest of Roger de Lauria, a medieval Sicilian-born warlord who served the Crown of Aragon in its defence of Catalonia from the marauding French. Within a year it had been renamed Club Español de Fútbol before it became Club Deportivo Español. All these titles were a conscious reaction to FC Barcelona's identity as a Catalan club which was nonetheless open to other Europeans. Español's founding statute declared: 'We create this club to compete with the foreigners of FC Barcelona.' By foreigners it meant not just FC Barcelona's English and Swiss founding fathers, but its emerging branding as *the* club of Catalonia, a nation with a discernible cultural and political claim that separated it from the rest of Spain. Español made much of its claim that it was the first Spanish club to be made up exclusively of Spanish players, which included those born in Catalonia, although by 1911 it had three Englishmen playing for it. Español drew its fan base from among Spanish civil servants, migrants and pro-monarchist right-wingers who were happy to have Catalonia remain subservient to a centralised Spanish state headquartered in Madrid.

In 1912 Español was one of the Spanish clubs who were granted royal patronage by King Alfonso XIII and thus entitled to add the word Real to their name, and put the crown on their colours. Others similarly ennobled in the Spanish sports world included Real Madrid, Real Sociedad, Real Club Celta de Vigo, Real Unión de Irún, and Real Club Deportivo Mallorca, as well as Real Betis. The King appears to have aimed to broaden his popularity by extending his patronage of the game across the regions.

It is perhaps worth noting here that Español's existence did not stop the creation of a Catalan football league in 1901 and a distinct Catalan Football Association in 1904, both long in advance of the Spanish league and the Spanish Football Association.

Alfonso XIII engaged with football fans more readily than any member of the English royal family at the time (it was only in 1914 that a British monarch appeared for the first time at the final of the FA Cup). But Spain being Spain, the case of Real Madrid and Español's royal appointments simply fuelled regional political antagonisms and bitter rivalries that would endure.

Spain's neutrality during the First World War meant that football faced no interruptions, and the popularity of the sport continued to grow after a group of small Basque businessmen and entrepreneurs funded the building and inauguration of Spain's first purpose-built football stadium, San Mamés in Bilbao, in 1913, ushering in an extended period during which Basque players dominated Spanish football. Until that point football remained too incipient for it to be officially adopted by the Spanish state as a national sport, even as the first moves were made north of the Pyrenees to regularise the game internationally.

Spain was one of seven countries that in 1904 attended an inaugural meeting in Paris of the Fédération Internationale de Football Association (FIFA). The Spanish delegate was from Madrid FC, whose claim to represent the whole of Spain was questionable. FIFA anyway was destined to spend its early years in formulating regulations, providing referees and deciding who could join and who play rather than organising any major international tournament.

For its part Spain had neither the money nor the organisation to attend the Olympics in London (1908) and Stockholm (1912). After that there was no major international sporting event during the First World War and both the IOA and FIFA went into cold storage. It was only at the first post-war Olympics in Antwerp in 1920 that Spain grasped for the first time an opportunity to test its football players in a major international tournament.

Rafael Moreno Aranzadi 'Pichichi' – a great Basque

8

Football with *Cojones*

The circumstances surrounding the Spanish squad's first major international test at the 1920 Olympic Games were far from ideal. The previous Olympics, due to take place in 1916 in Berlin, capital of the German Empire, were cancelled as a result of the outbreak of war. The 1920 Games were awarded to Antwerp to honour the people of that city after their suffering during the war. Participant countries struggled to come to terms with the spirit of sportsmanship after a conflict that had led to the death of nine million soldiers. A total of twenty-nine nations participated in the Antwerp Games. In breach of the Olympic spirit, Germany, Austria, Hungary, Bulgaria and Turkey were excluded, having been on the losing side in the war. Officially, they were not banned. But they were not invited either. Also absent was the new Russian Soviet Republic, a revolutionary power that the West deeply distrusted. Instead the dysfunctional Olympic family – using doves as a symbol of peace – embraced as new arrivals the newly created European states of Estonia and Czechoslovakia, and the emerging football nation, Spain.

War had ravaged most of Europe, so these first post-war Olympics were organised on a shoestring and poorly attended. Footballers, like the rest of the athletes, were housed in cramped conditions and slept on folding cots. And yet Spain had every reason to take the Games very seriously. Its presence in the Olympics signified an open door into an increasingly international sport. Thus of the fifty-eight Spanish sportsmen that went to compete, more than a third were footballers.

The most curious member of the squad was its coach Francisco Bru. Born in Madrid, Bru had played for FC Barcelona and Español before becoming one of the country's more eccentric referees in 1916, choosing to carry a pistol attached to a holster whenever he officiated a match. Asked by a player why he needed to carry a gun, Bru answered deadpan: 'I want tranquillity.' Thankfully he was never given cause to use it.

The squad was picked after a series of friendly matches across Spain between teams identified as 'probables' and 'possibles' by a triumvirate of officials who between them represented a consensual balance of power: one from Catalonia, one from the Basque Country, and one from Madrid. In early selection meetings, Basque officials argued successfully that the Olympic squad should be drawn mainly from the Basque Country for it was there that the most successful football was being played at club level at the time.

Among the players that went on the Olympic expedition in the end, thirteen were Basque born and played for clubs based in the Basque Country, four were born in Catalonia or played for FC Barcelona, while three others were from Galicia. Northern Spain dominated the selection. The absence of any players from Madrid or the main southern region of Andalusia may have partly reflected the then general superiority of teams further north. However, the selectors provided a further explanation. Unlike the north of Spain, football in Madrid and the south was still largely played on unturfed grounds. Because the Olympics were to be played on grass, this – it was judged – disqualified certain players from selection.

The average age of the squad was twenty-nine years old, evidence that selectors had opted generally for experience and enduring popularity rather than taking a risk on young talent that had yet to be really tested in competitive terms. The youngest player in the squad was FC Barcelona's eighteen-year-old José Samitier, on whom more later. Spanish club football was still some way from making its mark on the international scene, so expectations of Spanish success in the Olympics of 1920 were not high.

Spain began the tournament by beating Denmark 1–0 and was then beaten in the quarter-final by Belgium 1–3. But an unexpected opportunity came its way when the Belgium v Czechoslovakia final failed to secure a legitimate runner-up. The English referee of the final so upset the Czechs with his handling of the game that they walked off the pitch in the forty-third minute and refused to return. A pitch invasion – led, bizarrely, by Belgian soldiers – ended all hope of the match being restarted and the Czechs were eventually disqualified. So Spain found itself playing for a runner's-up medal, beating first Sweden 2–1, then Italy 2–0 and finally taking the silver when it beat the Netherlands 3–1.

That Spain achieved what it did in the end by a mixture of luck and default mattered little. Spain's achievement was legitimately governed by the rules at the time, under the so-called Bergvall system. This was named after Eric Bergvall, a pioneering Swedish journalist and Olympic sportsman (he played water polo) who wanted to give strong teams defeated in the earlier rounds a further chance to remain in the tournament and fight for second and third place. Thus a fair distribution of medals would be secured and with a minimum of matches, according to Bergvall. Besides the usual knockout method, teams defeated by the eventual winner could compete for second place and those defeated by the second place could continue to compete for third place.

Spain found the system made to measure. And by winning a 'silver' medal in its first major international tournament, Bru's squad achieved mythical proportions in the annals of Spanish football history. It was one of only two medals won by Spanish sporting teams in those Olympics but easily the most important. The football silver was widely celebrated back home, in contrast to the other silver – for polo – which barely penetrated the collective consciousness.

Football became established as the country's most popular sport and was on its way to generating a mass following on a par with bullfighting. And this was in part thanks to the legend that was built up around one goal in particular: José María Belauste's winning goal against Sweden which set Spain on course for its medal. It was one of those moments of football history forever embedded in the collective memory of a people thanks to the literary imagination of a participant. The writer with the power of the pen in this case was Manolo de Castro, a popular football journalist who wrote for a Spanish newspaper under the pseudonym *Handicap*.

De Castro wrote:

When play resumed after half-time, Spain seemed to rally behind a call to battle and launched an attack of such ferocity that within two minutes it had secured a free-kick just outside the penalty spot. Sabino was about to take the kick when José Maria (Belauste), in a predatory advanced position amidst the Swedes, with his back to the goal screams: 'Sabino, give me the ball and I'll wipe them out!' And that's what happened. Sabino kicked the ball upwards, a Swede tried to reach it but only to find Belauste head the ball with such strength that he and various Swedes tumbled together into the goal. It was a really herculean goal!

In time the goal – not subject to any action replay but at the mercy of every football pundit's imagination – became elaborated. Thus in a book of memoirs written ten years later by the Spanish goalkeeper Zamora, it was claimed that Belauste drove the ball into goal, balanced on his chest and with four Swedes clinging to his shirt. By then a mythology had already been born – that of *La Furia Española* or Spanish fury – a particularly muscular and aggressive style of football, blessed with nobility of intent and execution, over which the Basques at club level had already claimed a kind of copyright but which was absorbed into the broader national psyche.

Curiously the first recorded use of the phrase *La Furia* is not to be found in any Spanish media but in a Dutch newspaper that reported the day after Spain's victory by drawing an analogy with the fearsome tactics used by Spain's imperial soldiers when they had sacked and pillaged Antwerp in November 1576.

From the 1920 Olympics, a few members of the Spanish squad became legends. The first was the captain Belauste. The ninth child born into a family with Basque nationalist leanings, Belauste studied law at Deusto, the prestigious Jesuit University in Bilbao, founded, like the city's first football ground, on the banks of the River Nervión. Contemporary photographs of Belauste barely hint at his relatively comfortable upbringing. They show a gentle giant, bruised and battered by endless battles, sporting a bandaged knee, a broken nose, with heavily shadowed indented eyes, and large ears clasped back by a four-cornered white handkerchief, tightly bound to protect him from an incipient alopecia; the six foot three Belauste was fifteen stones of pure square-shaped muscle which had nobly endured countless injuries.

Belauste was by all accounts a down-to-earth guy who shunned stardom. His favourite hobby was practicing *palanka*, the traditional Basque rural pastime of throwing a metal bar, otherwise known as 'the miners' sport'. It was a game that tested an individual's physical resistance to the full. But it was on the football pitch that the Basque showed himself a worthy captain of the national squad, mobile and visionary enough to order play from midfield when not using his strength and height to create or deliver goals upfront. He began playing for Athletic Bilbao at the age of fifteen and retired in 1922, aged thirty-six, to pursue his career as a lawyer. It proved a turning point in his life, drawing him increasingly into Basque nationalist politics in a way that would overshadow all else, including his love of football.

Another famous Basque from that Olympic side was Rafael Moreno Aranzadi, known as 'Pichichi' – the 'little duck'. Together with Belauste he provided the key ingredients in making Athletic Bilbao one of Spain's leading clubs in the years 1911–21.

In the days before the creation of the Spanish league, Pichichi was Spanish football's first great goal-scorer. He scored 77 goals in 89 Copa del Rey matches and 200 goals in 170 matches in total, most of which came in the northern regional champion-ship. He played in six Copa del Rey finals, and was a major contributor to winning four of them. From a highly literate Basque family (his great-uncle was the internationally respected philosopher and author Miguel de Unamuno) Pichichi's intel-ligence as well as his skill on the field more than made up for his generally diminutive body. He was five feet in height and weighed just under eight stone. He too played with a handker-chief covering his head and tied. He said it was to better protect himself from a ball that in those days was stitched in panels, like a jigsaw. If you failed to avoid heading the ball at the lace bit you ran the risk of a cut or a headache. The handkerchief minimised the cuts.

Like many Basque players, Pichici developed a love of foot-ball as a young boy in a private school run by a Catholic religious order imbued with the discipline and sporting ethos of the British public school. This connection contrasts with the ideology of some of the early players in other parts of Spain who experimented with a lay education and saw football as liberation from traditional Spain, of which they saw the Catholic Church as playing an inseparable part.

However, the strong links Basque football has with Catholicism reflect the close links between Basque culture as a whole and the cult of St Ignatius of Loyola, the sixteenth-century Basque soldier who became a hermit and then founded the Jesuit order. Joséba Zulaika, a leading Basque academic, lays great emphasis on the religious formation of Basque nationalists, and in particular what he sees as the metamorphosis of religious vocation into an ideology predi-cated on commitment and action. Zulaika argues that this in turn has also had a decisive influence in reinforcing a Basque cultural tendency to see complex issues in antagonistic black-and-white terms.

Zulaika's subject of examination is Basque nationalism in its most extreme form, which is that of the Basque separatist group ETA, which was founded – he argues not coincidentally – on 31 July 1959, the feast day of St Ignatius. The saint may also have been partly responsible for laying the seeds of *La Furia* among the Basque players who have had such a formative influence on Spanish football.

But to return to Pichichi: his first games as an adolescent were played in the Campa de Los Ingleses, near the River Nervión. Legend has it that the nickname – a derivative of *pichon* or *puichin* and a term of affection usually accorded to small people – was first used on him in these early kick-arounds and that it stuck when he was later spotted by a club scout.

Pichichi joined Athletic in 1910 when the team was shedding some of its British roots and developing a Basque identity by restricting the recruitment of players to those of Basque stock. Here was born the notion of *La Cantera* – literarily translated as quarry, this draws on a mining term to describe the source of a player's heritage. In its early Bilbao version it applied, as it still does to a certain extent, to a cultural and racial pre-condition, although over the years the term has been used more widely to apply to youth academies across Spanish football.

Pichichi was Basque born and bred. His playing days in the first team of Athletic and Spain's national squad coincided with the club presidency of Alejandro de la Sota, a Basque nationalist politician and businessman whose more famous brother Ramon rented half his shipping fleet to the British in the First World War and was honoured with a knighthood.

A fitness fanatic, Pichichi used his pace and dribbling skills to get round the often brutal stratagems of Basque defenders much bigger and stronger than him, while proving himself a hugely effective striker of the ball. He managed to score a great many goals with his feet, and not a few with his head. Local journalists headlined him *El Rey Del Shoot*, the Strike King. One of his most faithful fans was his cousin Alfonso Moreno, a Jesuit priest and a football writer in his spare time. It was said at the time that if you were young and lived in the Basque country your best career paths lay in the Society of Jesus or with Athletic Bilbao. In fact both organisations locally shared recruits and philosophies to the point of being indistinguishable – they were both militant Catholics and fervently Basque. Of Pichichi the player, Fr Alfonso wrote:

My cousin 'Pichichi' is the best player in Athletic and the best player in Spain. He's a tremendous striker, with a low centre of gravity and very powerful, so that there isn't a goalkeeper capable of stopping him. But above all he dribbles better than anybody and goes from one end of the pitch to another with the ball stuck to his feet and without anyone taking it away from him, until he has scored his genius goal. He also has an extraordinary ability to head the ball, particularly in set play, off corner kicks. When things are going badly for the team, the crowd expects Pichichi to remedy the situation . . . The only criticism is that he sometimes plays like an individual and loses sight of the team. Nevertheless there are various English teams who would like to take him away from us even if Rafael has no thought of leaving Bilbao . . .

As Athletic's star player, Pichichi generated the kind of popular passions which until then had been mainly the preserve of top bullfighters. A certain element of self-belief mixed with vanity pushed him to continue playing long after he lost form, something for which the fans did not thank him. During his last three years at Athletic, which included playing as an international, Pichici was often jeered and criticised by the home crowd. The silver medal he obtained with the Spanish team was the swan song of a star player already in decline. He retired in 1921, the year after the Olympics, having scored his last goal in a match against West Ham United. He briefly embarked on a new career as a referee but found the profession lacking excitement. He was saved from growing old and bitter by an early death. After a meal of oysters, he was struck down by typhus and died in 1922, aged only twenty-nine. His last words were whispered to one of his former team-mates, Aquilino 'Chomin' Gomez Acedo: 'Chomin, mind you look after my wife and daughter,' he pleaded.

Pichichi's reputation grew after his death, and he achieved a certain immortality among his fellow Basques as a romantic hero thanks to the large mural-like paintings that were made of him by leading Basque painters. The most popular were created by the artist Aurelio Arteta, who idealised a Basque culture he believed was threatened by the advance of industrialisation. In perhaps the most famous and arguably most striking painting ever done of a footballer, Arteta painted an elongated Pichichi, darkly handsome and powerful in club colours, courting a beautiful young woman in a white shirt and similarly fashionable long skirt and shoes – modeled on his young wife Avelina – against the backdrop of a Basque rural landscape. Painted the year before Pichichi's retirement, Arteta called it *Idilio en los*

Camps ode Sport, 'An Idyll in the Sporting Fields'. Today the painting hangs in the president's office of Athletic's administrative headquarters, the magnificently decorated Ibaigane Palace, although copies – whether in poster or postcard form – remain best-sellers of Athletic's illustrated history.

The figure of Pichichi has another enduring symbol in a small bust of the player installed in the San Mamés stadium in 1926 and thereafter a place where teams visiting the stadium for the first time lay a bouquet of flowers. The bust was erected in memory of the player that scored the first ever goal in one of Spain's oldest-built stadiums (as distinct from the oldest surviving professional playing fields, which is El Molinon, the site of Sporting Gijón's stadium in Asturias) on 21 August 1913 in the inaugural match against Racing Irún.

Finally Pichichi was given a central place in La Liga thanks to the decision taken by the sports newspaper *Marca* in 1953 to introduce the Trofeo Pichichi, an annual award for Spain's top scorer, which has remained to this day. Ignored in the numerous books about Athletic published in the Basque country is any attempt at an explanation as to why *Marca*, a newspaper allied with Franco from its early days and supportive of Real Madrid, should have opted to celebrate a Basque player in such a high-profile manner. The reasons lie in the fact that Basque nationalists are not the only party guilty of playing highly charged political games in the Basque Country.

Spanish right-wing nationalists like Franco have traditionally been sympathetic to the idea that the Basque Country contains the seeds of 'true Spanishness', inseparable from Catholicism and Spain's history of empire, conquest and surviving against the odds in a hostile environment. The Basques fit into this world-view essentially as members of Spain's warrior class whose essential values, steeped in virility, are bravery, self-sacrifice, obedience to leaders and a sense of honour.

It is no coincidence that the Pichichi prize came into being when Athletic was enjoying a post-war resurgence in its fortunes after being temporarily purged of Basque nationalist sentiment by a right-wing presidency hand-picked by the regime. Franco was quite at ease with himself in celebrating Athletic as a Spanish football team of blood, guts and attitude. Indeed, it was his favourite Spanish football team, in the days before Real Madrid became great. As for Pichichi and the other prominent Basques who also played for Spain, they could be seen through the myopic prism of Francoism as true patriots in the tradition of those Basque soldiers who were prominent in the Christian reconquest of Islamic Iberia and the subsequent 'discovery' and conquest of Spanish America.

Two other personalities that featured in Spanish football's first major venture onto the international stage are worth mentioning here. They were close friends as well as FC Barcelona team-mates. The first was José Samitier, who travelled to the Olympics in Belgium only a year after being signed by the Catalan club, aged seventeen, on 31 May 1919.

Of Samitier, one can say that his alleged humble beginnings belied his early transformation into a star, on and off the pitch. The story of his early triumphant years as a player were eventually the subject of the first mass-circulation Spanish football biography. As the Uruguayan author Eduardo Galeano has written: 'Samitier was the team's ace player and his biography was on news-stands all over the city. His name was on the lips of cabaret *chanteuses*, bandied about on the stage and revered in sports columns where they praised the "Mediterranean style" invented by him.'

'Samitier, a striker with a devastating shot, stood out for his cleverness, his domination of the ball, his utter lack of respect for the rules of logic, and his Olympian scorn for the borders of space and time,' wrote Galeano. While he initially played in defence, there was no position off-limits to him, as he feinted and dribbled his way from one end of the field to the other, baffling his opponents, and often leaving his team-mates to a purely supporting role, shifting their own positions to accommodate his talent. *El Sami* was also blessed with an extraordinary ability to defy gravity, not least with his trademark kick while flying through the air – arms and legs splayed – which earned him the nickname 'the Lobster Man'.

I was fortunate that I was able to gain some insight into the man and the player from someone who had known *El Sami* in his early years and had lived long enough to tell me the tale before he died.

In 1997, I met *El Sami*'s longest-living admirer, the former Barça vice-president Nicolas Casaus. Aged eighty-four at the time, Casaus shared his memory of meeting Samitier in 1922, when the player had turned twenty and Casaus was nine years old. 'They'd organised a friendly between Barça and Igualada, and Samitier came to play. In those days you had to pay twenty-five cents to get into the stadium, but I couldn't afford it. So what the boys and I did was organise ourselves into porters. When the team bus arrived we ran along and offered our services. I had the good luck of picking up Samitier's suitcase. He thought I was a funny kid – fat and small as I was then – but he made me a member of the club there and then.' Those were the days when players could fuel a popular following without being millionaires.

It was the same with Ricardo Zamora, who perhaps more

than any other goalkeeper achieved the title of 'great' during the 1920 Olympics. He was 'the pearl' of the Spanish team in the opinion of one of Spain's most distinguished football writers Alfredo Relaño. It was during the Olympics that he was consecrated by the emerging critics of international sport as a superstar (*supedotado*), the destiny of his team quite literally in his hands. Zamora had made his debut as a major club player with Espanyol in 1917, aged sixteen, before moving to FC Barcelona after a row with one of his early bosses. In Belgium he was the youngest in the squad and among the least experienced, but his physique (he was tall and strong) and emerging talent as a player had already made Zamora a personality. He wore a broad tweed cloth cap in deference to the memory of the early English pioneers and a white polo-neck jumper for no other reason than that he believed he should be dressed as elegantly on the pitch as off it.

During the Olympics Zamora showed himself to be strong, courageous and skilful. He used his acute sense of anticipation and timing to block attacks, while his extraordinary vision of play had him launching counterattacks well beyond his own goal line, often leading the charge himself. He also used his height to good effect, winning cross balls or reaching up and out to deflect an attempted header at goal. No other goalkeeper had yet appeared in Spanish football with his talent, and after the Olympics his reputation grew in such a way that he came to be considered one of the great Spanish sportsmen of all time. In Spain, fans across the club divide nicknamed him *El Divino*, the Divine One. Of Zamora, the lyrical if not always precise South American Galeano has this to say: 'He sowed panic among strikers. If they looked his way they were lost: with Zamora in the goal, the net would shrink and the posts would lose themselves in the distance. For twenty years he was the best goalkeeper in the world.' And that despite a daily diet of three packs of cigarettes, an occasional cigar and a cognac or two.

On the Spanish team's return from the Olympics, Zamora's team-mates decided they would play a joke on him, stuffing his suitcase with contraband liquor and cigarettes without his knowledge. When the train reached the Pyrenean border, the French gendarmes discovered the load and arrested him. Zamora spent the night in a cell before the Spanish authorities convinced their French counterparts that one of the great stars of the Olympics was no criminal but the victim of a cruel hoax by unknown conspirators.

Once reunited, Zamora and the rest of Spanish squad received a heroes' welcome across the country. In time his name would be immortalised on the annual trophy given to the best Spanish goalkeeper. For Spanish football, the Olympics proved a point of arrival as well as departure. Spain had gained international recognition, and the stars that won that silver medal would forever be celebrated in the collective memory. But it would be many years before a national squad would again prove to be as collegiate or successful.

Fred Pentland – El Mister in the bowler hat

9

The Magic of Mr Pentland

Athletic Bilbao, the club that had contributed most players to the 1920 Olympic squad, was plunged into a management crisis during the 1921–22 season with the departure of its English coach Billy Barnes – but it proved short-lived.

The son of a London docker, Barnes had played as a seventeen-year-old with Thames Ironworks – the club that would later become West Ham United – before signing for Sheffield United and later playing for West Ham, Luton Town and Queen's Park Rangers. While his brother, the Labour MP Alfred Barnes, chose a life in politics, later becoming a minister in Clement Attlee's post-war government, Willy retired as a player in 1914, aged thirty-five, and sailed to Bilbao, initially to escape the Great War and pursue a career as a coach.

In England, as in much of Europe, war brought professional football to an effective halt, symbolised by the fact that Britain's pioneering Football Association had its London headquarters requisitioned by the War Office. Football players across the continent were among the first to volunteer and then increasingly to be conscripted because of their youth and physical fitness.

By contrast, Spain, while still without a professional league, kept its young men away from the trenches, having declared its neutrality in the war. Football continued as a growing popular entertainment, and Spain became a land of opportunity for any retired former player turned coach. Englishmen, because of their historical connections as the harbingers of the game in Spain, were in pole position to offer themselves up for hiring.

Athletic was pursuing its policy of Basque-only players, but of all Spain's clubs, it remained the most anglophile. Its main financial backers – the family-owned de la Sota industrial and shipping conglomerate – supported the Allies, with whom they continued to have business dealings throughout the war. Barnes was the latest in a line of imported English coaches.

Barnes took the club to victory in the King's Cup over his first two seasons, after which he returned to Britain and briefly signed up for military service. He returned to Bilbao in August 1920 for a further short stint. Soon after his arrival, he told a local journalist: 'Basque football has progressed a lot since I was last here. When I first came it was a patient, slow game of short passing – elegant to watch but totally unpractical, Scots style. I introduced at Athletic a fast game with long passing, taking the ball from wing to wing, and fast players in the centre capable of scoring goals. Today I find most clubs have a tendency to play this way whereas Athletic seems to have lost its way.'

Barnes stayed on for another season at the end of which Athletic once again won the King's Cup, beating Atlético Madrid 4–1 at San Mamés in 1921. His departure provoked a tortuous search for a suitable replacement. Advertisements placed in the *Daily Mail* and *Sporting Life* drew hundreds of enthusiastic but unsuitable applications from demobbed British aficionados. The success of one applicant, who went by the name of 'Mr Burton', proved short-lived. He had inhaled so much mustard gas in the trenches that he lasted two months in his new job before his lungs collapsed. For a short period the club struggled under a temporary emergency management committee of limited organisational ability made up of two ex-players – Juan Arzuaga and Luis Iceta – and the captain German Echevarria. Then another Englishman, by the name of Fred Pentland, came to the club's rescue.

Pentland was born in Wolverhampton in 1883. He played for Blackburn Rovers, Brentford, Middlesbrough, Halifax and Stoke and won five caps for England. After retiring as a player, Pentland travelled to Berlin in 1914 and took charge of the German Olympic football team. Within months, the First World War broke out, and he was interned in a civilian detention camp at Ruhleben. Famously, Pentland helped to organise hundreds of prisoners – some of them professional players – into teams to play an informal league championship. After the war he coached the French national team before moving across the Pyrenees to Spain and taking on the job of coach at Santander's Racing.

Since its foundation in 1913, Racing had developed a reputation as one of Spain's better teams, with a proven record of attacking football. Several of its young players 'graduated' to bigger clubs like Real Madrid. The strategy and tactics of the team improved still further with the arrival of Pentland. He was an advocate of the short-passing game, focused on technique and ball skills he had learned at Blackburn. Pentland dissuaded his players from copying the long ball and rough tactics Spaniards associated with *Los Ingleses* while encouraging them to pursue the courage and determination on the field which had earned the Spanish national squad its first major victory on the world stage at the 1920 Olympics.

In Bilbao, Pentland took on the airs of the archetypal English gentleman, smoking cigars and wearing a bowler hat – on and off the field – for which he earned the nickname *El Bombin* or 'The Man in the Bowler Hat'. One of Pentland's first initiatives at Athletic was to implement a new dress code. Photographs of that time show a somewhat stern mustachioed figure in a dark suit with an impeccably folded pocket hand-kerchief. He taught his players how to tie their bootlaces correctly – 'get the simple things right and the rest will follow' was among his favourite mantras. He was not a man who took himself too seriously so that even in his sternest poses there was a hint of an ironic smile beneath his moustache and unyielding stare. He was happy to tell his players early on that they could celebrate a famous victory by collectively stamping on his hat as he had a good stock he could replenish it from. The fact that he got through several hats was an enduring testimony to his success at the club.

Pentland became the most successful manager ever to sit on the bench at San Mamés, taking Athletic in two spells at the club to five cup wins and two league championships, and in the process becoming the first manager in the history of Spanish football to win a La Liga and Cup double. His 'records' include taking Athletic to a 12–1 win over FC Barcelona in 1931, the worst defeat ever suffered by the Catalan team.

Two years earlier Pentland helped coach the Spanish national squad to its first significant international achievement since it had won its medal in the 1920 Olympics – and it was in a game against England. His appointment followed a spell at Atlético

Madrid whom he had guided to victory in the Campeonato del Centro, central Spain's regional championship, a rare achievement for the historically underperforming 'other' Madrid team. Pentland had a unique insight into the game, gathered from his personal experience of both British and Spanish football, and was adept at picking teams that could combine virility with style and speed.

The Spanish national team that played England on 15 May 1929 drew over half of its squad from Real Madrid. There was a dominating presence of Basque-born players who had moved to the Spanish capital or continued to play for regional clubs like Real Sociedad and Osasuna. The backbone of the team was formed of players that were destined to distinguish themselves in one of Real Madrid's most successful periods in the early 1930s. They included Basque-born Jacinto Quincoces – a champion pelota pala player – who with Ciriaco formed one of the most skilled and toughest defences in Real Madrid's history, helping the club secure two successive league championships in 1932 and 1933, and then winning two Spanish Cups (as the King's cup was known in the years of the Second Republic) after finishing runners-up in the league.

The international fixture, played at Atlético Madrid's Metropolitano stadium, was held in the same year that Barcelona hosted FIFA's historic meeting at which member countries agreed on the staging of the first ever World Cup. Spain was being taken seriously as a footballing nation.

With tickets sold out two days previously, some 45,000 fans gathered to watch a match that, although a 'friendly', also had national pride at stake. England went into the match on the back of a 4–1 win over France and a 5–1 victory over Belgium, but with true form under scrutiny following a number of questionable refereeing decisions. 'The Englishmen played none too well. They lacked speed and will have to play better if they are to beat Spain, who a month ago beat France by eight goals to one,' reported the *Daily Sketch and Graphic*. Significantly, one of England's star players, the Middlesbrough forward George Camsell, had been injured in the match.

Nevertheless, this was the 167th international match England had played since 1872. Spain by contrast was playing only its 32nd game since its first major foreign engagement in 1920. Only a year earlier it had suffered a humiliating 1–7 defeat at the hands of Italy in the Amsterdam Olympics. In the preceding 24 matches against non-British teams, England had won 23 and drawn one, scoring a total of 121 goals and conceding only 27. All the major European national teams had been crushed by the seemingly invincible English squad: Austria (three times), Hungary (three times), Bohemia (once), Belgium (seven times), France (six times), Sweden (twice) and Luxembourg (once).

It was hardly surprising that Spain's chances of success were poorly rated by the British media. Their perception of Spanish players was that, while capable of passing the ball around neatly enough, they lacked the drive and ruthlessness of Anglo-Saxons in front of goal. Spain was viewed by the British media, somewhat patronisingly, as a football nation whose star was rising and with the potential of being the best continental side, but not up to the standards maintained by the English.

Early on, the match seemed to prove the pundits right with England gaining a clear superiority of two goals within the first twenty minutes. The first had Leicester City's outside right Hugh Adcock beating several Spaniards before finishing off with a fine cross which Joe Carter of West Bromwich Albion delivered on. A similar movement from both players led to the second goal within a few minutes. Then, just when a lesser team might have collapsed, Spain rallied in what the home media would later portray as a heroic fightback, worthy of the best fighting spirit of *La Furia*. Real Madrid's Gaspar Rubio headed their first before his club team-mate Jaime Lazcano scored with what the *Times* correspondent conceded was a 'brilliant shot'. The two teams were level by half-time.

In a match that enraptured the stadium and was conveyed live nationally across Spain on radio for the first time, both teams returned to the second half determined to do battle. According to the *Times*, England rallied first after their goal-keeper Ted Hufton had thwarted a Spanish attack and the forwards swept down 'in fine style' leaving it to Joe Bradford to put them ahead. 'With the game drawing to a close England looked like good winners,' *Sporting Life* reported. Then Spain drew level with a goal on the 79th minute by Lazcano, followed by a fourth by the only amateur in the squad, Severino Goiburu, eight minutes before the final whistle.

'I never thought I would live to see the day when eleven Spanish players humbled the might – more or less – of English soccer,' wrote the correspondent of the *Daily Express* days after the game, although they, along with most English papers, had not bothered to cover it on a major scale.

As football writer Jonathan Wilson has noted in his forensic historical analysis of the match, the under-reporting by the English was perhaps one of its most striking aspects from a modern perspective given the historic ties and animosity between the two nations. As Wilson notes, 'Among the stories deemed more important than England's first defeat to foreign opposition were the presentation of a grandmother clock to Wally Hammond, Tottenham's 2–0 victory over the Army on a tour of Malta, Portsmouth signing William Hill from Scunthorpe United and the fact that the final of the British Women's Open gold was to be contested between Miss Joyce Wethered and Miss Glenna Collett.'

At international level, Spain's national team revived some of the glory of the early Olympic days. Its 4–3 victory on 15 May 1929, was the first time the English team had ever lost a match outside a Home Championship. As far as the Spaniards were concerned the man in the bowler hat had come up trumps.

However, any hopes that Spain might have had of replacing England's hegemony in international football proved premature. When the two sides met again at Highbury in 1931, Spain was thrashed 7–1. Prior to the game the Spanish had picked up some more impressive victories over Italy, Yugoslavia and Portugal, with just one defeat to Czechoslovakia. But as the Austrian Willy Meisl, one of the leading sports journalists at that time, wrote: 'What the English could not know was the incredible inferiority complex under which these early Continental sides laboured when they stepped on to a British football field. For them it was sacred soil. They were so over-awed they hardly dared put a foot down. If they were hit by an early goal, let alone by a couple, their strained nerves were shattered and they were beaten before they had a chance to get going.'

And that is exactly what happened. Only four minutes into the game, Spain already found themselves two down, with goals from Portsmouth's Jack Smith and Everton's Tommy Johnson (formerly of Manchester City) and from then on it was all downhill, or almost. After conceding the seventh goal, Spain got a small consolation: Athletic's Gorostiza, the Basque-born outside-left, nicknamed *la bala roja* because of his red hair and fiery shooting, hit a powerful strike which the England goalkeeper Hibbs could not stop.

The Spaniards struggled to control their dribbling and passing play in the muddy turf conditions and were overwhelmed by the physicality of the English players. England's defenders were content to pump the ball forward for the strikers to chase. The ease of the victory restored the myth of England's superiority and created a perception among English fans that the earlier defeat of 1929 was an aberration, caused by the Spanish heat, the poverty of the Spanish soil, and the absence of England's best players. Nevertheless, in Spain's former colonies new ideas were being embraced that would in time provide renewed life to Spanish football.

José Leandro Andrade – Captain of Uruguay
and Olympic gold medallist, 1924

10

The South American Connection

The shortcomings of Athletic, one of Spain's most successful football clubs, when faced with foreign competition in the first decades of the twentieth century and the emergence, by contrast, of a new footballing power outside Spain was only too evident during a South American tour by a group of Basque players in the European summer of 1921. The players, many of them Spanish internationals, set off from Lisbon on 27 June. They included Belauste, the Olympic goal-scorer who had become a national legend. Travelling by ship, the team arrived just over two weeks later, to be received like heroes by a large and enthusiastic Spanish (mainly Basque) immigrant community in the port of Buenos Aires.

Their first match was against a selection of players from the Argentine capital. Most came from the working-class neighbourhood of Barracas where Alfredo Di Stéfano was born five years later. The visitors were overwhelmed by the superior style and skill of their hosts. The Argentines put on an extraordinary display of *tiki-taka* football – control, possession, quick short movements of the ball.

In Argentina, football had escaped from the manicured pitches of the rich and discovered new roots in the slums, on barren earth and against makeshift walls. It delivered a new language which connected the local underclass with the poor immigrants who arrived from southern Europe, northern Spain, Italy and the Middle East. As the South American novelist Eduardo Galeano has written: 'A home-grown way of playing football, like the home-grown way of dancing, came to be born. Dancers drew filigrees on a single floor tile, and football players created their own language in that tiny space where they chose to retain and possess the ball rather than kick it, as if their feet were hands braiding the leather . . . On the feet of the first *Creole* virtuosos *el toque,* the touch, was born: the ball was strummed as it were a guitar, a source of music.'

The Basque team lost 0–4. They recovered some of their honour in the following matches played in the cities of Rosario in Argentina, Montevideo in Uruguay and Sao Paolo in Brazil but this did not turn into the triumphant tour they had expected. The final tally was two victories, one draw and five defeats.

While Spanish club football had mixed fortunes when faced with the emerging power of South America, Spain's national squad simply found itself humiliated. The squad returned from the 1924 Olympics – effectively a world championship – empty-handed, with Uruguay taking the gold. It was Uruguay that was set to place South America firmly on the map of world football when its team swept down on the Paris Olympics and crushed all opponents.

Other South American countries, Germany and the United Kingdom were absent from the Olympics and yet football confirmed itself as one of the world's most popular sports with thousands of spectators watching twenty-five matches over a two-week period. Uruguay beat Switzerland 3–0 after demolishing Yugoslavia, the United States, France and Holland. A French writer, Gabriel Hanot, reported on the arrival of an exciting new footballing nation: 'The principal quality of the victors was a marvelous virtuosity in receiving the ball, controlling it and using it. They have such a complete technique that they also have the necessary leisure to note the position of partners and team-mates. They do not stand still waiting for a pass. They are on the move, away from markers, to make it easy for team-mates . . .'

Hanot went on to compare the Uruguayans with the early English pioneers that had such an influence on Spanish football: 'The English are excellent at geometry and remarkable surveyors . . . They play a tight game with vigour and some inflexibility.' By contrast, the Uruguayans 'are supple disciples of the spirit of fitness rather than geometry. They have pushed towards perfection the art of the feint and swerve and the dodge, but they know also how to play directly and quickly. They are not all ball jugglers . . . They create a beautiful football, elegant but at the same time varied, rapid, powerful and effective.' Hanot's conclusion left little room to doubt that a revolution on no small scale was sweeping through international football. 'These fine athletes are to the English professionals as Arab thoroughbreds are to farm horses.'

In a press conference attended mainly by French journalists, the Uruguayan captain José Leandro Andrade said that his players had trained chasing chickens on the ground.

The early influence of Latin Americans on Spanish football had a magical quality to it, verging on the fantastical. The skills involved were real enough, however, and foreshadowed some of the great figures of Spanish club football, from Di Stéfano to Maradona and Ronaldo, and later Lionel Messi.

Andrade himself was an emblemic figure with the *La Celeste Olimpica* as the Uruguayan team came to be known. He was also the first black player to earn respect at international level, despite his off-pitch extravagances. When the Paris tournament was over Andrade stayed on for a while in the French capital, enjoying a bohemian lifestyle and becoming a popular figure of the night-life cabaret scene – dressed in a top hat, striped jacket, silk scarf, bright yellow gloves and a cane with a silver handle.

Four years later he won his second Olympic gold medal, when Uruguay faced off a strong challenge from Argentina in the final, and in 1930 again was instrumental in the Uruguayan team's success, this time conquering the first ever World Cup to be organised by FIFA. Thirteen countries took part in the tournament hosted by the twice Olympic champions, only four of them from Europe: Belgium, Romania, Yugoslavia and France. In common with other countries that absented themselves, Spain argued that taking its team across the Atlantic in the midst of a growing recession was something the country could not afford, a poor excuse given that Uruguay agreed to cover all the costs including travel.

In reality Spain was struggling to come to terms with the humiliating fact that its former Latin American colonies were producing as good if not better football – the old colonial master was in danger of reverting to pupil status. The 'Black Marvel' Andrade was not the only player to dazzle fans with his exquisite plays. Another of the cast of South American legends was Ramón Unzaga, the inventor of the bicycle kick or *chilena* in tribute to his nationality, which was first used on Spanish soil by a fellow national David Arellano during a tour of the country by the Chilean team *Colo-Colo* in 1927.

By then the growing superiority of Latin American players showed in their ability to bring down to earth some of the great myths of Spanish club and international football history. For example, in a home match played between Uruguay's Peñarol and Español of Barcelona, the 36-year-old veteran Uruguayan striker José Piendibene managed to completely outfox the great goalkeeper Zamora with a typical display of masterful ball control. Galeano takes us through the moves:

The play came from behind. Anselmo slipped around two adversaries, sent the ball across to Suffiati and then took off expecting a pass back. But Piendibene asked for it. He caught the pass, eluded Urquizu and closed in on the goal. Zamora saw that Piendibene was shooting for the right corner and he leapt to block it. The ball hadn't moved. She was asleep on his foot: Piendibene tossed her softly to the left side of the empty net. Zamora managed to jump back, a cat's leap, and grazed the ball with his fingertips when it was already too late.

People still talk about that goal in Uruguay although the suggestion that Piendibene was given a new house as a prize for beating the greatest footballer in the world proved false. He was given a gold medal instead. After the Basque squad and Español, other teams like Barça and Real Madrid toured the Southern Cone. The experience for a while raised the standard of play in the nascent Spanish league which was formed in 1926. However, the promise of Spanish football as epitomised by Spain's victory over England three years later floundered amid the growing political instability in the run-up to the country's civil war.

Josep Sunyol – Catalan politician and FC Barcelona president.
He was executed by Franco forces in 1936

11

Gathering Storms

When in the early 1920s the dust had temporarily settled on the cataclysms of war, revolution, hyper-inflation and austerity, there was in all these societies a profound need and desire for hedonism and escape, for pleasure and for play, from the fabulously rich to the appalling poor. Football was one of these pleasures.'

David Goldblatt, *The Ball is Round*

Spain was not immune to the transformation of the political and social landscape that impacted on most of Europe as a result of the First World War. If the development of her football still lagged behind that of several other countries on both sides of the Atlantic, it was because her development as a country too seemed out of step, out on a limb, and seemingly permanently in crisis.

Between 1921 and 1922, the emerging giants of Spanish club football, FC Barcelona and Real Madrid, each inaugurated new stadiums. Of the two, FC Barcelona's Les Corts, built a few blocks away from Barça's current stadium the Camp Nou, had the bigger capacity, with 20,000 seats and a covered stand for a further 1,500 spectators. Real Madrid's Chamartin stadium, constructed on the very site where the Santiago Bernabéu stadium stands today, had a capacity of only 15,000.

While there can be little doubt that attendance records generally for Spanish football matches had been increasing up to and during the First World War, the growth was still of a lower order of magnitude to that of England during the early twentieth century, or of the emerging nation states in Central Europe. For example in 1922, the crowds of that year for the most popular game – that between Austria and Hungary – had swollen in just four years from 15,000 to 65,000.

The following year the young Spanish prince Don Gonzalo marked the inauguration of Real Madrid's stadium by kicking the ball of honour and in a boyish voice crying out, '*Hala, Madrid!*' – 'Let's go, Madrid!' The phrase would be adopted as the club's official rallying cry, and echoed by generations of fans to this day. Just four months later on 13 September 1923 Captain General Miguel Primo de Rivera staged a bloodless military coup and shut down parliament, claiming that party politics had become corrupt, and the monarchy ineffectual, while making a token gesture to the aristocracy by leaving Alfonso XIII as a symbolic king without power.

Prompted into action in part by the politicians' mishandling of a protracted Spanish colonial war in Morocco, Primo de Rivera was an emotional Spanish patriot of the old school, believing that Spaniards should be Catholic and united. He considered atheism, including all its manifestations such as Marxism, to be a mark of the devil. His greatest enemies were

Spaniards who called themselves anything but Spaniards and toyed with the idea of becoming more separate from Madrid, by pursuing their own devolved government and speaking their own language.

Among Spain's most powerful regions, it was Catalonia that was posing the greatest threat in the eyes of the dictator, with its nationalist movement becoming increasingly radicalised and lurching to the left. A clash between the new military government and Catalonia's potent sporting symbol FC Barcelona seemed inevitable, and so it proved.

The date of 14 June 1925 came to be remembered in the collective memory of Catalan nationalism and many Barça fans as a day of infamy. The occasion was a fundraising match FC Barcelona had organised for the Orfeo Catala, a choral society set up to carry on the work of the father figure of Catalan music Josep Anselm Clavé. At half-time, the crowd whistled as a band of English marines from a visiting Royal Navy vessel played the first notes of the Spanish national anthem. When the marines abruptly stopped and then struck up again, playing the English national anthem, the crowd broke into spontaneous applause. The demonstration had been fuelled by Primo de Rivera days earlier banning the public use of the Catalan language and closing down local government offices. Now the Madrid government moved in with a vengeance with Barcelona's newly appointed Civil Governor Joaquin Milans Del Bosch fining the Barça directors and imposing a six-month ban on Barcelona's activities as a club and as a team.

A majority of Spaniards were immensely relieved when the increasingly ineffectual Primo de Rivera resigned and left Spain in January 1930. But the dictatorship had also alienated popular support for a king who had passively acquiesced in the authoritarian regime. King Alfonso XIII was forced to abdicate and go into exile when Spain's new Republican government was proclaimed by a group of liberal intellectuals.

Newsreel film of those heady days shows thousands of Spaniards taking to the streets of Madrid and Barcelona following the proclamation on 14 April 1931. Suddenly, after centuries of political instability fuelled by dynastic struggles and military interventions, there seemed to be the possibility of a truly democratic Spain. It proved a pipe dream as a succession of increasingly radicalised short-lived left- and right-wing elected civilian governments struggled with the reality of Spain's continuing economic and political underdevelopment: vast disparities between rich and poor, particularly in the countryside; unresolved tensions between centralists and the regions, as Catalan and Basque nationalists pressed for increasing autonomy from Madrid; bitter quarrels among groups of democrats about how far left, anticlerical, and decentralised the new Republic should be; and all against the enduring presence of two traditionally powerful institutions – the military and the Catholic Church – that saw their privileges under threat.

In Barcelona, politics and football became an increasingly volatile mix. In 1928, as the Primo de Rivera regime was entering its death throes, a young radical lawyer called Josep Sunyol became a member of FC Barcelona's governing board and president of the Federation of Associated Catalan Football Clubs.

Sunyol used his newspaper *La Rambla* – which split its coverage between sport and non-sport items – to appeal to a new social order where football and politics formed an essential part of a new democratic society. While the perspective of football through the prism of a reformist political agenda seemed to mirror the enlightened ideals of the early founders of Real

Madrid, Sunyol's politics were firmly rooted in Catalonia, with FC Barcelona as a role model. In an early manifesto, Sunyol explained what he meant by his slogan 'Sport and Citizenship'. He wrote: 'To speak of sport is to speak of race, enthusiasm, and the optimistic struggle of youth. To speak of citizenship is to speak of the Catalan civilisation, liberalism, democracy, and spiritual endeavour.'

As a lawyer and a journalist, Sunyol tried to present himself as first and foremost a Catalan patriot rather than a party dogmatist, and a true football fan. In July 1935, he was elected FC Barcelona's president. In his acceptance speech he declared that he would endeavour not to let politics get in the way of his work for the club. But for all his love of sport, Sunyol was primarily a politician, and regarded the football of FC Barcelona as a means to an end rather than an end in itself. Four years earlier, in the summer of 1931 after the proclamation of the Second Republic, he had been elected as a deputy to the new parliament in Madrid as a representative of Esquerra Republicana de Catalunya, a new pro-independence party.

In October 1933, in reaction to the emergence of a conservative government in Madrid, Sunyol's party was among those who backed the unilateral proclamation of a Catalan government – a 'Catalan state within the federal republic of Spain'. The initiative was blocked by Madrid only to be revived and enacted after a Popular Front coalition of socialists and communists was swept to power in February 1936, when Sunyol and other Catalan radical nationalists once again took centre stage.

For all the political effervescence, this was not a period of sporting success for FC Barcelona under Sunyol's presidency, and the club failed to win either the new league championship or the Spanish Cup in the 1930s.

By contrast Real Madrid on 6 May 1934 ended a seventeen-year drought in the Spanish Cup, beating Valencia 2–1 in the final and ending Athletic Bilbao's run of success in the tournament. The final against Valencia was played in Barcelona. When the Madrid team arrived back at the Spanish capital's Atocha station they were greeted with a rendering of the *Himno de Riego*, the new national anthem of the Republican government after the demise of the Primo de Rivera dictatorship and the abdication and exile of King Alfonso XIII. The club had dropped 'Royal' from its title in deference to the political situation.

Two seasons later on 22 June 1936, Madrid played FC Barcelona in their first ever Spanish Cup final clash. The game was played in Valencia's Mestalla stadium. Madrid was leading 2–1 when Zamora threw himself full-stretch towards the left-hand goalpost and blocked a last-ditch attempt at an equaliser by the Catalan striker Escolà. Within minutes the game was over and Zamora, *El Divino*, was raised on the shoulders of his joyous fans. The team received an even more ecstatic welcome when they returned by train to the Spanish capital, as Madrid fans once again converged on Atocha station.

By then, however, no amount of celebration could hide the fact that Spain was on the verge of disintegration, the incompatible politics of left and right lurching out of control towards civil war in a context of increasing violence. A day after the Madrid–Barcelona match, General Francisco Franco, then the Captain General of the Canary Islands, wrote to the Spanish Prime Minister Casares Quiroga warning of growing military unrest. Franco had yet fully to throw his hat into the ring with the plotters of military officers and right-wing civilians but it was just a matter of time before he did. The conspirators, concerned about the violent anti-clericalism and the growing militancy of industrial and agricultural workers, and what they saw as the breakdown of order, were plotting a coup to stop the country lurching further towards socialism. On 18 July the military uprising began and the country's history of failure, division and frustration gave birth to its ultimate despair, the Spanish Civil War.

Republican troops – Madrid stadium

12

Football against the Enemy (1)

On 19 July 1936, the day after the military uprising had been initiated in the south, local fans in the northern Galician city of Corunna turned up in their thousands to watch a match in the Riazor stadium between the local team Deportivo and their regional rival Celta. A match-day report in the local newspaper *Voz de Galicia* commented: 'In these times in which emotions are stirred in all sorts of different ways, a football match is a welcome event because, while it might seem paradoxical, it can act as a sedative to our shattered nerves.'

Initial support for the military uprising varied from region to region. Thus while Madrid and much of Catalonia resisted the coup, other parts of Spain like Andalusia fell to the insurgents. Galicia was one of the areas where the initial coup was successful and it remained in Nationalist (Franco's army) hands throughout the Civil War. While there were no pitched battles, the calm in Galicia proved elusive. As in the rest of the country, Galicians – many of them no doubt football fans – were soon killing each other for reasons that ranged from personal vendettas to ideological beliefs.

As the Civil War deepened and the military rebels captured increasing amounts of territory, the political map of Spain became like an abstract patchwork with football mirroring the new reality of tactical alliances and severed ties.

In Galicia, in deference perhaps to Franco's own Galician roots, further matches were organised between locally based clubs once the region had been taken over by rebel forces in the early days of the conflict. The next major match between the old rivals Deportivo and Celta was played before thousands of pro-Franco fans in Vigo as a testimonial to General Millán Astray, the controversial founder of the Spanish Foreign Legion. An extreme right-wing fanatic, Millán Astray had lost his left arm and right eye in a previous military campaign in Morocco, earning him the title *glorioso mutilado* (glorious amputee). His most popular war cry was *Viva la Muerte* – 'Long Live Death'. Millán Astray was a grotesque caricature of the Quixotic myth of heroic non-compromise, the personification of violence, cruelty and fanatical obsession with death which hangs over much of Spanish history.

For a while, football in some parts of Spain proved a social palliative, one of the few public acts of the Civil War where the participants treated each other with respect. Other teams that took part in the Galician championship while the Civil War raged elsewhere included Lugo, Racing de Ferrol (the club of Franco's birthplace), and the Pontevedra club Eiriña. Isolated games were also played in parts of Andalusia where Seville and other towns fell early on to the military insurgents, and in the Levante region where a Mediterranean championship involving Valencia, FC Barcelona, and Espanyol (the club's name had been Catalanised under a new pro-Republic administration) was played under the control of the loyal government forces. Elsewhere in Spain's regions, Navarre and Aragon sided early on with the military uprising so that local teams Osasuna and Zaragoza reorganised themselves under the auspices of the Francoist authorities.

But the perception that the world of Spanish football could continue much as before proved delusional, as events in the capital were to show. By the end of November 1936, the initial military uprising in Madrid had been thwarted and the capital city had settled into a long siege. For its own safety, the Republican government moved its headquarters to Valencia, leaving Madrid in the hands of communist and anarchist militias with the support of the International Brigades of non-Spanish volunteers, many of them from the UK. Days were punctuated with the sound of air-raid warnings and the revolutionary propaganda that spewed out from loudspeakers in squares and the main avenues. At night and at daybreak came the sinister sound of isolated bursts of machine-gun and rifle fire as Francoist suspects were rounded up and shot.

Since its foundation in 1902, Madrid (whether Real or simply FC) had survived the various changes of regime, adapting to political developments and managing to continue to grow as one of the country's most popular sporting institutions. But now the club faced a major challenge to its organisation and sense of identity, with its members, players and officials dragged unwittingly into the bloodiest civilian strife the capital had ever experienced. The moderate president of the club, Rafael Sánchez Guerra, was unceremoniously sacked by a workers' committee headed by two Soviet-style commissars. Later there would be further political intervention in the club's affairs by a communist army officer Lieutenant Colonel Antonio Ortega, who took his orders from the Soviet secret police.

Thus Madrid (its royal status having been ditched under the Republic as had that of other clubs), which over the years had increased its popularity across the social divide, was monopolised by a bunch of revolutionaries. One of their first acts was to order a review of the club's membership lists to identify political enemies. Sport in the besieged capital, to the extent that it could be played at all, became a crude propaganda vehicle. Chamartin, the Madrid stadium, was used for parades by militias and Soviet-style mass exhibitions by the youth of the newly created 'Spanish Battalion of Sport', which aimed to project an air of revolutionary discipline and health. In the final stages of the siege of Madrid, the stadium's benches and fences were torn up and burned for fuel, bricks and other building materials pilfered, and the turf turned into a rough collectivised vegetable plot to help feed an increasingly starving population.

But by then any concept of a national football league had been lost in the fog of war. FC Barcelona, for example, rejected a request from Madrid FC and Atlético Madrid that they be allowed to compete in the Catalan championship in areas of Spain that remained in Republican hands. Barça officials argued that the involvement of clubs from central Spain would undermine the traditional 'Catalan' spirit of the competition. The Catalan championship went ahead nevertheless in the first year of the Civil War with six 'Catalan' teams instead of the usual twenty: FC Barcelona, Espanyol, Girona, Jupiter, Badalona and Sabadell. It proved short-lived however.

Catalonia resisted the military uprising for much of the Civil

War. Nonetheless these were turbulent and unpredictable times, not least in the Catalan capital Barcelona where the chaotic and violent revolutionary atmosphere was being documented by the English volunteer soldier and author George Orwell for his masterly work, *Homage to Catalonia*. Orwell would write of his time in Barcelona:

> During all those weeks that I spent there, there was a peculiar evil feeling in the air – an atmosphere of suspicion, fear, uncertainty and veiled hatred . . . At the Red Cross aid centre on the corner of the *Placa de Catalunya* the police had amused themselves by smashing most of the windows . . . Down at the bottom of the *Ramblas* near the quay, I came across a queer sight: a row of militiamen, still ragged and muddy from the front, sprawling exhaustedly on the chairs placed there for the boot blacks.

For a while FC Barcelona endured as best it could, given the circumstances. A reduced number of local members kept coming to the stadium and occasional games were played by conscripts on leave. But the club, in the hands of another 'workers committee', was drawn into the increasingly radicalised politics of the city. By the spring of 1937, politically moderate FC Barcelona officials and those players that had not been conscripted were looking for a way of escape. It came in the form of an invitation from a Mexican benefactor, basketball-player-turned-businessman, Manuel Soriano. He invited FC Barcelona to travel to Mexico and play a series of matches with leading local teams. The deal was that he would pay Barça US$15,000 in cash with an upfront payment of US$8,000 deposited in the loyally pro-Republican Spanish consulate in

Mexico City. He would also cover the cost of travel and all other expenses.

FC Barcelona's coach at the time was Patrick O'Connell. A former captain of Ireland, O'Connell had had a distinguished career, beginning in Belfast before playing in England for Sheffield Wednesday and Manchester United. His Spanish football career started in 1922 when he replaced Fred Pentland as coach of Racing Santander. The Irishman impressed the club's owners by building on Pentland's methods, encouraging the native skills of dribbling with the ball, while training his defenders in the long up-field passing and crosses that he had learned as a young player in Ireland and Britain. He also placed great emphasis on fitness, discipline and teamwork. This represented a cultural shift for many Spaniards, on and off the pitch.

The seven years O'Connell spent at Racing were formative ones for the club. O'Connell's own experience as a defender proved hugely valuable when during the 1926–27 season a new offside rule was introduced. He trained his defenders in moving forward so as to catch the other side's attacking forward and leave him offside when he gathered the ball from a pass. His main achievement, however, was in establishing Racing's rightful claim to be treated as an important football club by its loftier rivals. Thanks to O'Connell, Racing was able to successfully challenge an attempt by a small group of clubs led by FC Barcelona, Real Madrid and Athletic Bilbao to restrict the access of smaller clubs to the new Spanish league. The so-called 'minimalists' wanted the Primera Liga to be composed only of them and three Basque clubs, Real Sociedad, Arenas and Real Unión de Irún. The 'maximalist lists' made up of all the other smaller Spanish clubs organised a parallel championship which Racing won. A subsequent compromise agreement led to the creation of an expanded Primera Liga in which Racing was among those allowed to play.

Having secured Racing's place in top Spanish football, O'Connell spent two seasons as manager of Real Oviedo in Asturias, helping to mould the newly created club into a competitive sporting institution. O'Connell then spent a further three seasons at Betis where he became a popular figure with the Andalusians and developed a love of flamenco.

O'Connell, or Don Patricio as he was now popularly called, had become accustomed to his expatriate status, and was seemingly content to maintain a distant if dutiful relationship with the family he had left in England, sending them regular bank transfers drawn from the income he earned as manager. He spent these turbulent years in regions of Spain with a strong tradition of industrial and rural militancy that surfaced in the run-up to the Spanish Civil War. His Irish background had left him better prepared than most expatriates for the volatile atmosphere of Spanish politics and he fitted in well with a club that was proud of its populist roots.

Under O'Connell, Betis achieved considerable success on the field. After becoming the first Andalusian club to qualify for the Primera Liga, Betis went on to win the championship on 28 April 1935 with a crushing 5–0 victory over Racing. The night before the game, which was played in Santander, O'Connell visited the Racing squad at a hotel where they were staying. Racing was way down in the league table and had no chance of winning the championship, regardless of the outcome of the game. By contrast, Betis was at the top of the table but had to win if it was not to be overtaken and lose the championship to its main rival that season, (Real) Madrid.

O'Connell shared a drink or two with his former club

colleagues and then suggested that they might do him a favour: 'You've got nothing to play for tomorrow. You won't kill your-selves to beat us, will you?' he asked. The answer from one of the leading players was unequivocal: 'I'm sorry, *mister*, but Madrid wants us to win. Our president, José María Cossio, is a Madrid fan himself and is offering us 1,000 pesetas per player if we win.'

It was perhaps just as well that O'Connell left the matter to rest there. To have pursued the conversation with an offer of a counter bonus (or bribe) would, if found out, have risked taint-ing his reputation and possibly curtailing his career. Instead he went on to become manager of FC Barcelona. The timing of his arrival in the Catalan capital suggests that behind O'Connell's ambition to manage one of Europe's leading teams lay the politics of a man not prepared to remain indifferent to the Spanish Civil War. For O'Connell took up his new job after Catalonia had emerged as one of the regions in Spain where there was a significant proportion of the population determined to defend the Spanish Republic from the right-wing plotters and their friends in the military.

O'Connell arrived in Barcelona in the summer of 1935, days after the football club had elected as its president the radical Catalan nationalist Josep Sunyol. Nevertheless, rather than stick it out in revolutionary Barcelona, O'Connell happily volunteered to go on FC Barcelona's 1937 tour of Mexico. The team was composed of players that had played with mixed success in the pre-war Spanish championship under the tute-lage of the Hungarian goalkeeper-turned-coach Franz Platko. They included some of the club's legends such as Balmanya, Escolà, Ventolrà and Zabalo, an Anglo-Catalan born in South Shields, England, who had played for Spain at the 1934 World

Cup. The team's physio was Angel Mur. I caught up with Mur, the only surviving member of the squad, many years later. I was fortunate in finding him a lucid and amusing interviewee, with a good memory.

Mur recalled how he had been working as a gardener at the club's Les Corts stadium when *El Mister* (O'Connell) told him that he was looking for a replacement for the masseur who had just quit. When Mur said that he only knew about looking after the turf of football pitches, O'Connell reassured him that he would quickly learn something about the human body. 'And that's how I ended up going to Mexico with a suit I was given by one player, and a suitcase I was given by another player,' Mur told me. 'I bought myself a couple of books on the anatomy of the human body and got to learn something about the vulnerable parts . . .'

In Mexico City, the team was given a warm official reception by the authorities and local media. But on their first night in the capital, the politics of the Civil War came back to haunt them. Arriving for dinner at a Spanish dining club, they saw the monarchist flag used by Franco's forces flying over the entrance. Then some of the players found themselves barracked by a group of Spanish businessmen who criticised them for being anti-Francoist.

FC Barcelona went on to play six matches against local opposition, of which it won four. One local newspaper report in *El Universo* reported that the team did not play the best football in Spain (such an accolade was left at the time for the Basques) but that the tour itself had left a 'good taste' because the players had 'behaved like true gentlemen'. After Mexico, the expedition moved north of the Rio Grande and had an unbeaten run of four matches in New York against teams that ranged from a US 'selection' to others put together separately by the Hispanic, Jewish and Irish communities. By the end of September 1937 Barça had run out of places to escape to, and Rosendo Calvet, the club secretary, gathered everyone to a crisis meeting.

The 'tourists' were offered a stark choice: they could return to Barcelona and face whatever uncertain outcome awaited them, or they could stay away from Spain, effectively as exiles. Of the sixteen players, seven chose to follow Calvet, O'Connell, Mur and the team doctor back home, while nine decided to stay in Mexico – they included Ventolrà who had fallen in love with the niece of the Mexican President, Làzaro Càrdenas. When the rump of the team returned, FC Barcelona struggled to stay afloat as Calvet had taken $US12,000 clear profit from the tour and transferred it to an account in Paris. On 8 January 1939, a Barça reserve team played the last football game in Spanish territory held by the Republic against a minor local team called Martinenc, and won 3–1. Eighteen days later, Franco's army entered the city of Barcelona, the pavements and balconies lining the city's main artery the Diagonal filled with cheering supporters. On 27 March Franco took Madrid, the last major city held by Republican forces.

Basque Refugee Children at the North Stoneham Camp
in Eastleigh, Southampton, May 1937

13

Football against the Enemy (2)

On 22 May 1937, the Spanish Civil War had another two years to run when nearly four thousand refugee children accompanied by teachers and priests arrived in the port of Southampton on board the SS *Habana* after crossing the Bay of Biscay from northern Spain.

The ship had left a day earlier with its human cargo – the biggest single influx ever of child refugees into Britain – from Bilbao, as the Basque port faced conquest and occupation by the besieging forces loyal to General Francisco Franco.

The children had been evacuated to escape the horrors of the conflict. Amid much political controversy back at home, Britain had waived its policy of non-intervention and agreed to escort Basque refugee ships to a safe haven.

Conditions aboard the SS *Habana* were cramped and depressing, exacerbating the children's feelings of distress at being separated from their families and sent off to a foreign land and an uncertain future. As the ship tossed and turned in the rough seas, children cried in the night, calling out for their mothers and fathers. Among them were fourteen-year-old Raimundo Lezama and his brother Luis from Bilbao's industrial suburb of Barakaldo, the sons of a ship worker who had been detained in the Republican-held port of Sagunto and would spend much of the Civil War in prison.

While Mrs Lezama was left caring for her only remaining child, a young baby girl, the two boys were thrown into an extraordinary new environment on arrival on English soil. Waiting for them were hundreds of volunteers and government officials with a relief operation that in its generosity exemplified the deep popular emotions stirred in Britain by the Spanish Civil War. Tumultuous scenes greeted the *Habana* as it berthed in Southampton dock. The next day, the local newspaper the *Echo* headlined with the words 'Basque children cheerfully taking to camp life' and commented on 'the excitement of feeding the multitude' in the temporary relief camps set up nearby.

Hundreds of sympathisers converged on the town from around the UK, bearing gifts and food. A Salvation Army band played, a BBC crew filmed, and all amid bunting left over from the coronation of King George VI that had taken place less than a fortnight before and had been deliberately left hanging to give the occasion a festive air. Later one of the children would recall: 'When we entered the bay of Southampton we thought we had entered a wonderland. Every little house lining the bay had its own pretty garden, well-tended, and all decorated to celebrate the coronation. Everything was bunting, flags, music playing, and people waving their handkerchiefs at us . . .'

It was not quite so idyllic. Fearful that they might be bearers of typhoid or some other potentially deadly infectious disease from the war zone, the Home Office insisted that each child be meticulously examined by health officers and disinfected in public baths. The camp where the children were initially taken and housed in tents soon turned into a muddy quagmire after two violent thunderstorms. Inexperienced volunteer aid workers struggled to communicate with children who spoke only in Spanish and in some cases Basque. And yet the adults tried to keep the young amused with excursions, film shows and a representation of Shakespeare's *A Midsummer Night's Dream*.

But Southampton's North Stoneham facility was only ever envisaged as a transit camp and by September 1937 the Lezama brothers along with the other children had been dispersed to private homes and government-run residences.

Raimundo Lezama, separated from his brother, stayed in Southampton. He was given shelter, food and rudimentary English lessons in a hostel run by nuns called Nazareth House, about half a mile away from The Dell, the stadium of Southampton FC. Raimundo was fed well by the nuns, and subjected to a relatively benign regime that included music, and outdoor activities, which consisted mainly of football. While still a teenager he was scouted by Southampton FC, progressing from schoolboy ranks to the club's 'B' team and making his first-team debut as a goalkeeper on 1 June 1940, nine months after the outbreak of the Second World War. A few months later, and after a brief period working as a driver for the RAF, Raimundo was reunited with his brother and both returned to Spain, where Franco had emerged victorious in the Civil War a year earlier.

In March 1937, at about the time the Lezama brothers boarded the *Habana*, local politicians redefined Athletic Bilbao as the matrix of a national team representing the Basque Country called

El Euskadi. The cause of the new national team had as one of its most fervent supporters and organisers José Antonio Aguirre, the first *lehendakari* or president of Euskadi (the Basque lands of Spain not including Navarre) during the Spanish Civil War. Aguirre in his youth had himself played for Athletic. Although he never made his mark as a player, Aguirre had developed a politician's instinct. He had a keen sense of the club's popular cultural roots and of the growing propaganda value of football as it developed into an international mass sport.

Aguirre's Basque government was formed at a time when most of the region it claimed to represent was already occupied by the military rebels' troops, except for the region of Vizcaya with Bilbao at its heart. After setting about creating a Basque army to fight for the Republic's survival, Aguirre hit on the idea of having a football squad from the region go on a foreign tour to raise funds and international support for his cause. At the end of March 1937, with the Civil War reaching new levels of brutality on both sides, and at a time when the national football league was no longer functioning, a group of players responded to Aguirre's call to arms by presenting themselves for training and selection at Bilbao's San Mamés stadium. There were some key reinforcements, among them two Basque-born leading Spanish internationals, the brothers Luis and Pedro Regueiro, who had spent the years leading up to the Spanish Civil War playing for FC Madrid, and Isidro Lángara from Real Oviedo in Asturias. While playing at the Asturian club, Lángara became a three-times winner of the Pichichi trophy, awarded to the top scorer in the Spanish league. The striker became the figurehead of the celebrated *delanteros electricos* (electric forwards) whose youthful talent and speed with the ball steamrollered opponents.

Other Basque players that travelled from various regions of Spain for the historic gathering in San Mamés included Enrique Larrinaga from Racing Santander and two of the best Spanish defenders of the 1930s. One was Pedro Areso, an FC Barcelona player formerly of Betis, whose ability to disrupt even the best-planned attack from the opposing side earned him the nickname *El Stop*. The other was Serafin Aedo, who played alongside Areso at Betis during the 1934–35 season when the Sevillian team won the Spanish Liga for the first and only time in its history. Aedo was hoping to follow his friend Areso and pursue his professional career at FC Barcelona when the outbreak of civil war frustrated his plans after playing only one friendly with the Catalan club.

As part of the Basque diaspora, the bulk of the volunteers were Athletic players who had played in the Spanish national squad during the Republic: Gorostiza, Blasco, Iraragorri, Cilaurren, Muguerza, Echevarria, Zubieta, Aguirrezabala. The players had also been involved in the trophy-hunting of one of the strongest and most successful clubs in pre-war Spanish football. This was the Athletic that between 1930 and 1935 marked up the extraordinary record of two Pichichis (twice won by Gorostiza), a Zamora prize for the best goalie (Blasco), the biggest thrashing in the history of the Spanish league (a 12–1 victory over FC Barcelona in 1931), two Spanish Cups and four league championships.

The squad was coached over a period of nearly a month at San Mamés – and prior to the start of the extended siege of Bilbao – by a veteran Athletic centre-forward of the early 1920s, Manuel Lopez Llamosos, nicknamed Travieso (Artful Dodger) for his mischievous wit, cunning and restless unpredictability. Travieso took good care of the players, including supervising the tailoring of the team colours. However, for reasons that remain a mystery, he decided not to join them the day they set off on their foreign tour with a squad of eighteen.

His place as coach was taken by Pedro Vallana, a former Spanish international who had played for Arenas Club de Getxo before becoming a referee. He was accompanied by Athletic's massagist Periko Birichinaga, a sympathetic local journalist Melchor Alegria, and two officials, Ricardo Irazabal, vice-president of the Spanish Football Federation under the Republic, and former Athletic president Manuel de la Sota, a member of one of Bilbao's richest industrial dynasties.

The squad was captained by Luis Regueiro. Such was the propaganda value of the former (Real) Madrid player and Spanish international that pro-Franco military rebels spun a story that he had disappeared after being executed by forces loyal to the Republican government. Regueiro's sympathies were clearly with the Basque cause. He recalled many years later: 'With Franco's revolt under way it was no longer possible to play football (in Spain). There was however a huge need to bring home to the rest of the world that we Basques were different to what some wanted to make us out to be. It was this idea that inspired us both in and outside the stadiums we played in abroad, winning games on the pitches, and generating sympathy and friends beyond them.'

Not every player was equally enthusiastic about the tour. Some hoped that, like the Civil War, it would prove short-lived. Both turned out to be protracted, fuelling divisions that were exacerbated as the war turned in Franco's favour. One of the players, Zubieta, recalled years later: 'We became nomads with our football as our only arm . . . We had embarked on a new life, without knowing where we were heading, and I think that when we crossed the frontier into France, our hope was that we would return soon.'

The squad arrived in Paris in the spring and, after being greeted by local representatives of the Basque government, laid a wreath wrapped in the Basque national colours at the Tomb of the Unknown Soldier. In their first match, against the French Racing Club on 24 April 1937 in the Parc des Princes stadium, they won 3–0, with Lángara scoring a hat-trick. Celebrations over the victory proved short-lived as news came in over French radio of the bombing by the pro-Franco Luftwaffe of the Basque town Guernica on 26 April. While the bombing and the ensuing mass fatalities among the civilian population became an important propaganda tool for the Republican government, it raised concerns among the players for the safety of the families they had left behind, while also making them think more deeply about where their true political loyalties lay as Franco moved to extend his control across the Basque country.

From Paris, the tour continued through Czechoslovakia and Poland before reaching Russia, where the squad stayed for two and half months. Authorised accounts of the tour were written later by individual players, most of which were published during the censorship of the Franco years when the cause of Basque nationalism became mythified by exiles. They focus on the footballing success of El Euskadi with a majority of matches won against national as well as local club teams and the occasional defeats blamed on a lack of that 'fair play' the Basques had learned from the English. Thus of the 4–2 defeat against a Czech team in Prague, Lángara recalled: 'It was an outright robbery. They beat us on penalties. The referee, who seemed to be nervous because of an accident he had suffered just before the game, whistled penalties against us to calm his nerves. And whenever our goalkeeper Blasco blocked the ball, he insisted that the penalty had to be taken again, claiming unjustly that Blasco had moved.'

In Moscow, the squad was not short of photo-opportunities as when they were filmed visiting a school and residence where Basque children who had been evacuated were being cared for. But the propaganda seemed to serve Stalin's Russia rather more than the cause of the Basque Country. Another player, Zubieta, recalled: 'Playing football, drinking vodka, and staying in the hotel was how we spent our time in that faraway and strange land and we had no contact with anything other than the world of sport.' The games played in Moscow drew large crowds of loyal Communist Party officials and members in a display of international solidarity as news reached the squad that the city of Bilbao had fallen to Franco's troops. In Moscow the Basque football team's local minders appear to have ensured that the visitors be screened from local political realities, not least Stalin's terrible political repression that was then reaching a particularly brutal point. 1937 may still be remembered by Basque nationalists as the year of the heroic expedition abroad of El Euskadi – a noble high point in the history of Spanish football – but this was also the most tragic and fateful year in the history of the Soviet Union. 1937 was the year when Stalin extended his 'terror' with the aim of physically annihilating the substantial socialist opposition to his bureaucratic and repressive rule.

Nevertheless, such awkward coincidences were ignored when memoirs of the tour were published after Franco's death. Thus the journalist who accompanied the players, Melchor Alegria, recalled in 1987: 'Moscow was a huge success. All the games were played in a magnificent atmosphere, which was also very moving as it showed the understanding that the Russian people had for the suffering of the Basque nation. What proved particularly gratifying was when we were in Leningrad and were asked to stay in Russia at the request of the trade unions and other organisations.'

Such a rose-tinted view of the tour was not shared by everyone in the football community. The growing influence within football's nascent international body FIFA of officials sympathetic to the Franco cause meant that some national football federations like Argentina's tried to make life complicated for the Basque squad, cancelling some planned games. When El Euskadi eventually returned to Paris some of the players were secretly contacted by Francoist emissaries telling them they were embarked on a lost cause and urging them to defect.

Only a very small minority of the squad broke ranks but they were of sufficient standing to prove helpful propaganda tools for Franco during the final two years of the Civil War. The first to quit and sign up to the Franco cause was Athletic's legendary Gorostiza whose lightning speed as a left-wing forward earned him the nickname *Bala Roja* or Red Bullet. He was followed by another Athletic star player and international, the midfielder Echevarria, and by the massagist Birichinaga. Days later, on a windy autumnal day in October 1937, what remained of the squad boarded a transatlantic French liner *Ile de France* in Le Havre and sailed via Cuba to Mexico, where during the 1938–39 season El Euskadi were allowed to compete in the local national competition, ending runners-up in the league table.

Soon afterwards, when the Civil War ended in Spain with Franco's victory, El Euskadi was disbanded, with each player receiving a payment of 10,000 pesetas. A year earlier their coach Vallana had left the tour in controversial circumstances. Before departing, he secretly negotiated a payoff equivalent to a two-month salary when his players had not yet been paid a cent. The incident did nothing to enhance a reputation damaged years earlier when in the 1924 Paris Olympics Vallana scored a disastrous own goal in a match against Italy which ended with Spain's early exit from the competition. Rather than return to Franco's Spain, Vallana chose to live as an exile in Uruguay where he worked as a sports journalist after retiring from football.

The majority of the team chose to spend the rest of their playing years in other countries in Latin America, thus contributing unwittingly to the football cross-fertilisation between Spain and its former colonies that has continued to this day. In Argentina, Zubieta, Lángara, Iraragorri and Emilin signed with San Lorenzo de Almagro, while Blasco, Cilaurren, Areso and Aedo joined *River Plate*. Others were signed up by the Mexican clubs Asturias and – irony of ironies – España. Luis Regueiro and Aguirrezabala retired but settled respectively in Mexico and Buenos Aires. While some of these players like Iraragorri returned quietly to Spain after the Franco regime had long been established, the myth of the defiant squad with a strong sense of its separate cultural and political identity endured.

As Manuel de la Sota, one of the financial backers of El Euskadi wrote in a prologue to a book on the team published after Franco had died: 'Bad luck had united us, but that luck turned out to be one of the most fortunate in my life. For thanks to it I came to know examples of our race who as well as being artists of a sport which they taught foreigners to play, were also standard bearers of the dignity of a small people whose name was Euzkadi.'

Months before Luis Regueiro played his first games abroad with the Basque national team, another former Real Madrid player, Santiago Bernabéu, whose name would in time grace one of the great stadiums of world football, had enlisted in the Franco forces. While Regueiro's Republican sympathies had left him unharmed after the initial military uprising was frustrated in the Spanish capital, Bernabéu's right-wing leanings had put him immediately at risk. He was saved from a Republican firing squad thanks to the intercession on his behalf of another Madrid supporter and friend, the socialist Spanish ambassador in Paris, Álvaro de Albornoz. Thanks to the diplomat, Bernabéu was granted asylum by the French Embassy in Madrid before being smuggled across the Pyrenees. He returned a few months later, in 1937, crossing into Spain from France at Irún and enlisting straight away with the Franco forces that had taken the Basque town.

Bernabéu's arrival in Irún, in the midst of the Civil War, was like a chronicle foretold. For it was here during the early 1920s when playing as a young Madrid player that Bernabéu had famously suggested to his team-mates in a game against Real Unión de Irún that they should celebrate each goal they scored with the cry 'Viva España', a phrase which the Franco forces later adopted as one of their rallying phrases. With the passage of time it was reinvented as a popular chant by Real Madrid fans, and came to have wider use whenever the Spanish national team played.

There is an old photograph of a still relatively young if already somewhat corpulent Bernabéu, as a corporal in the Franco army, dressed in military cloak and fatigues and smoking his pipe. He is strolling along the streets of the Basque seaside resort of San Sebastián looking somewhat content with life. And he was. The original photograph was taken after Bernabéu had earned his first military medal for contributing to the rout of the pro-Republican units in the Pyrenean town of Bielsa on 6 June 1938. A few months later, just before Christmas the first 'national' sports newspaper to be published under Franco's rule hit the streets of San Sebastián and other towns 'liberated' by the military rebels. It was called *Marca* (meaning brand or mark) in deference to the neo-fascist worship of totemic symbols. The tabloid newspaper, published initially as a weekly and later as a daily, served two interrelated purposes: to act as the official organ of the Franco authorities on sports matters, and to turn the mass following of football that had been developing since the 1920s from the left to the right of the political spectrum. While adopting from the outset a clearly identifiable propagandist tone, it came to mirror the profound changes in the organisation and politics of Spanish football that deepened as the Civil War reached its end and paved the way for a dictatorship.

Marca's first front page appeared heavily influenced by the racist obsessions of Nazi Germany, which from the outset of the Civil War had helped arm the insurgents and provided further military assistance. It had a photograph of a blonde girl making the fascist salute in tribute to 'all the Spanish sportsmen and women'. In fact the Civil War had meant that individual football players were no longer respected by either side for their skills, but supported or condemned depending on what side of the political divide they were perceived to sit. This would inflict long-term damage on the evolution of Spanish football, although Bernabéu himself would reap a good harvest from Franco's victory because of his enduring loyalty to the Generalissimo. During his billeting in San Sebastián, Bernabéu was profiled in

Marca as an iconic figure. The article paid homage to him as a man who in the 1920s had given Real Madrid some 'great days of glory' as a player before serving as a director, and then resigning in order to devote himself to 'The (anti-communist) Cause'. *Marca* dramatised Bernabéu's departure from Madrid, describing his 'escape from the ferocious persecution of the red hordes' and noting that while he had sought asylum 'in an embassy' (no mention of the French or the Spanish socialist ambassador who had saved his neck), his deliverance into safe hands came only after a series of further dramatic twists in the story of his heroic bid for freedom. The alleged dramas included taking cover as a patient in a general hospital, and hiding in a chicken run, before escaping through a trap door.

The newspaper profile included some memorable quotes from Bernabéu. In one he defined what he saw as the essence of sport in the New Spain that would emerge with Franco victorious: 'The spectacle of a few sweaty youths must disappear and give way to a youth that is healthy in body and spirit under the direction of specialist trainers.' The article concluded with a final fawning tribute to its subject, noting that it was not just the character of players that was destined to change in the New Spain, but also the fans of Real Madrid, many of whom had supported the Republican government. 'If we can count among them (the fans) people like our interviewee, the club's resurgence will be rapid,' the article's author stated.

The writer was none other than *El Divino* himself, Ricardo Zamora, the one-time goalkeeper of FC Barcelona who had transferred to Real Madrid before making one of the most spectacular saves in the history of Spanish football. The fate of clubs, players and fans was sealed as much by where organisations or individuals happened to be as by an ideological preference, with conflicting loyalties resolved by death or the threat of it. At the outbreak of civil war, Zamora was confronted by an anarchist militiaman, brandishing a knife and condemning him as a right-wing extremist for contributing occasionally to the conservative Catholic newspaper *Ya*. Zamora, so he related later, had little doubt that his assailant was bent on killing him. But to his surprise the militiaman suddenly dropped the knife and embraced him after identifying himself as a Madrid FC fan. During the ensuing dialogue over the relative merits of Spanish clubs and their star players, the militiaman praised Zamora for all the great saves he had made and for helping his club become champions.

While the two men parted company the best of friends, Zamora was arrested days later and imprisoned without trial in Madrid's Modelo jail. While he was there, a military broadcast from the Andalusian capital of Seville, which had been occupied by forces loyal to Franco, reported that the 'nation's goalkeeper' was among dozens of well-known personalities who had been executed by the 'reds'. The rumour was initially taken seriously enough for Masses to be organised in Zamora's memory in the town that had fallen to the Catholic rebels. But it was pure invention, part of the propaganda war.

In the Modelo prison Zamora was periodically paraded by his captors in front of visiting officials as if he were a prize possession. To be called out from your cell in those days was to confront the real prospect that you were on your way to a firing squad. Zamora later recalled his legs would physically tremble every time he was summoned. However, he was able to survive mentally and physically thanks to the occasional football matches jailers and their prisoners played with each other in the Modelo's main yard. Zamora was eventually released after an international campaign was mounted on his behalf from France, and he took refuge in the Argentine embassy in Madrid where arrangements were made to transport him, his wife and young son out of Spain. By then Zamora had decided that his best interests lay in remaining unrecognised by the public, at least until he was safely across the Pyrenees. So one day, once his escape plan had been hatched, he emerged from the embassy wearing dark glasses and having grown a beard. The disguise did not fool the militiaman who was on sentry duty. 'Hey, Zamora, *hombre*, what you doing with the beard?' The interrogator turned out to be another FC Madrid fan so that safe passage was assured.

Zamora made his way to temporary exile via the ports of Valencia and Marseille, to Paris. While in the French capital, Zamora gave an interview to the newspaper *Paris Soir* in which he described himself as a 'one hundred per cent Spaniard'. While carefully avoiding expressing on what side his patriotic sympathies lay, Zamora said he believed he deserved to be better treated by some of his compatriots rather than to be made to fear for his life. He then journeyed to Nice where he played for a time with his old friend Pepe Samitier, *El Sami*, the other star footballer who had transferred from FC Barcelona to Real Madrid before the Civil War. *El Sami*'s escape from the 'reds' also entered the mythology of the conflict thanks to the newly created sports paper *Marca*. It gave full coverage to Samitier's narrow escape from arrest, his days in hiding and his eventual arrival on French territory 'with two suits, a lot of hunger, and exhausted'.

There were other stories of escape and survival. For example, the star international Jacinto Quincoces served in the pro-Francoist Navarra Brigades and returned to his old club Real

Madrid after the Civil War. Paulino Alcántara, the FC Barcelona star of the 1920s who retired from football to become a doctor, was on a death list for his alleged right-wing sympathies but managed to escape Republican-held Catalonia the day after the military uprising, across to France, before eventually returning to a life of retirement under Franco's rule following a brief and uneventful spell as coach of Spain's national team in 1951.

Not everyone, by any means, had such luck. Nearly one million Spaniards died in the Civil War. They included football officials and players who were executed or shot in battle – mostly not because they had worn the colours of any particular club but because they were associated with the enemy side. The victims came from clubs across the divided landscape. They included Gonzalo Aguirre and Valero Rivera, former vice-president and treasurer respectively of Real Madrid; Damien Cabellas, secretary of Espanyol; José German and Sr Vinas, two former presidents of Sabadell; Ángel Arocha, the Spanish international and FC Barcelona player; Ramon 'Monchin' Triana y del Arroyo, who played for Atlético and Real Madrid. Other 'disappeared' players included Oviedo's Gonzalo Diaz Cale, Deportivo La Coruña's Barreras, and Hércules FC's Manuel Suárez de Begoña, a former player and coach. In addition at least four club locations suffered major damage: Real Madrid's Chamartin stadium, Betis's Heliopolis stadium and administrative offices, Oviedo's stadium, and FC Barcelona's social club and archive.

Few personal stories in the history of Spanish football sum up the tragedy of the Spanish Civil War as that of Josep Sunyol, elected member of the Catalan Parliament and president of FC Barcelona. His last act as club president was on 30 July 1936, a few days after the outbreak of the Civil War, when he presided over an emergency meeting of FC Barcelona's management board. He then drove south to Madrid and up into the nearby Guadarrama hills. He was visiting some Catalan militias who were defending the Spanish capital from the military insurgents when he lost his way and drove into hostile territory. Sunyol was detained and shot on 6 August and his body was thrown into an unmarked grave.

Although his body was never found, Sunyol was posthumously prosecuted for 'political crimes' on 28 September 1939 by the Francoist state that had emerged victorious from the Civil War. Two months later an official report condemned Sunyol the politician and president of FC Barcelona for being anti-Spanish.

Franco and his wife Doña Carmen at the Bernabéu stadium

14

Franco Rules

Among the thousands of Republicans summarily executed after the surrender of the Spanish capital to Franco's forces was Lieutenant Colonel Ortega, the former head of security who had for a while taken over the running of Madrid FC as a Soviet-style workers federation.

The new regime moved rapidly to take control of all football institutions across the country. A super sports ministry with overarching power over the Spanish Football Federation was staffed mainly by right-wing Falangists. Its chief was General José Moscardó, one of Franco's most loyal officers. Major sporting events, including football competitions, resonated to the sound of the old Civil War rallying cries, '*Arriba España*' and '*Viva Franco*'. The fact that both were echoed in the same breath showed the extent to which the old battle cries of Spain's imperial warriors evoking one nation and its patron warrior Santiago (St James, mythified as anti-Muslim warrior as well as apostle of Christ) had been subsumed into the public discourse of the Franco dictatorship. Spaniards were expected to put the

Civil War behind them while absorbing a war ethic in which military values transcended the level of mere personal valour and were placed at the service of the Francoist state.

Athletic Bilbao was ordered to drop its traditional English title and stick to the Spanish Atlético. The regime resurrected the phrase *furia Española* or Spanish fury as its favourite sporting mantra. Franco held up Basque footballers as examples of how the game should be played, while stripping the Basque nation, along with Catalonia, of its rights and freedoms. He dusted off the image of the ideal Spaniard and of traditional Spain and transferred it to the football stadium, there to share company with Don Quixote, in the spirit of non-compromise. No matter that in time such inflexibility might tilt against Quixote's self-interest and against reality. His hopeless failure could be forgotten beside the nobility of purpose. Thus the quintessential virtues of the Spanish footballer were destined to be bravery, honour and pride in his endeavour to conquer the enemy.

The myth of a deluded Castilian knight had been walking across much of Spanish history, leaving behind him a trail of stereotypes and conditioning an entire aesthetic of the Spaniard. But it was given fresh stimulus by the Spanish right-wing militarism that was fuelled by the Spanish Civil War.

It was in the town of Salamanca, turned by Franco from one of Spain's great centres of academic learning into his military headquarters, that a new hybrid football emerged from the trenches. For it was there in 1937 that a young non-commissioned officer called Francisco González picked the best football players among his soldiers and, during their periods of rest from military duties, trained them as a team called Aviación Nacional or National Air Force. It competed in an embryonic

'Copa del Generalissimo' with teams from other towns occupied by Franco forces such as Zaragoza and Real Sociedad of San Sebastián.

Aviación played in blue shorts and trousers, the same colours as the Spanish Falange. It included German, Vazquez and Campos – young recruits from the Canaries who had learned the ball skills associated with Latin Americans – and some veterans of the old Atlético Madrid team, such as Mesa, Gomez, and Machin, who played a more aggressive game with some flair. A coherent style of play was not a priority. What mattered was the spirit.

The old Atlético had been relegated to the Second Division prior to the military uprising, and was lumbered with a debt estimated at one million pesetas. Eight of Atlético's players were killed while fighting in the subsequent Civil War. Once the conflict was over, Atlético was forced into a merger with the nascent Aviación. The new club, called Club Athletic de Aviación, was officially launched in October 1939. It was initially deeply unpopular with Atlético's traditional fans. Atlético had originally been founded by three Basques and grown up in the working-class outskirts of the capital near the River Manzanares. The appearance of Aviación came to symbolise the control which the emerging Franco regime wished to exert over football. The merger was forced through by the newly appointed high command of the Spanish Football Federation as a pre-condition for Aviación's registration as a First Division club.

The merged club agreed to play in Atlético's colours – red and white stripes, and blue shorts – as a token concession to tradition. But its senior management was composed of military men and civilian officials who had fought for Franco. They had firm views about football's political usefulness and how the game should be played by Spaniards. In 1947 the club reverted to the old name of Atlético Madrid and in subsequent years developed a reputation as the capital's 'bad lands', less establishment than Real Madrid and less rich.

In *Una Historia de Fabula* (A Book of Fables) the Spanish journalist and Atlético fan Carlos Merino Benito imagines the impact the hardline and dogmatic Francoist mentality had on the ethos of a club that had always taken pride in its creativity and unpredictability. In one episode, loosely based on oral history passed through generations of fans, an unnamed Francoist officer barks instructions at Ricardo Zamora, the legendary goalkeeper who was appointed the new club's coach in its first full post-war season, 1939–40. 'I'm telling you no, Ricardo, I don't want to hear your excuses or justifications – your team is not playing well, and you know it. What's lacking in this team, Richard, is *cojones,* a lot of *cojones* . . . the team has to run more and throw everything at the opposition. Zamora, stop trying to please so much . . . a coach needs to have a bit of spunk, impose discipline, use the whip now and again,' shouts the officer.

This was football played as if it were another battle of the Civil War, blood and *cojones* and fury, with no room or time for discussion or debate, let alone finessing technique and individual skill as part of a harmonious whole. It says something nevertheless about the quality of some of the players and the personality of Zamora himself, that Atlético Aviación went on to win the first two seasons of the post-war Spanish league. Then Zamora was unceremoniously sacked after several military officers linked to the club complained, falsely, that he had not been as loyal to the Franco forces as he should have been

during the Civil War. But such was *El Divino*'s popular standing that Zamora soon returned to the fold of Spanish football
as coach of the national team. It proved the biggest challenge of
his career.

Spain had not played in the 1938 World Cup, immersed as
it was in its Civil War, but the Franco regime was anxious to see
the national squad make up for lost time and gain a veneer of
diplomatic acceptance. So while the outbreak of the Second
World War effectively disrupted international football and the
cooperation of FIFA member states, Spain's football authorities organised a series of friendly matches. With the exception
of a game played against neutral Switzerland in Valencia, all the
national squad matches were played against representatives run
by extreme-right dictatorships or their collaborators: Portugal,
Vichy France, Nazi Germany, and Mussolini's Italy.

After beating a team of French Nazi collaborators, in Seville
on 12 April 1942 Spain played against the Third Reich's
Germany in Berlin's Olympic stadium in front of a crowd of
over 80,000. The match was widely reported by the Spanish
print media and broadcast live over Spanish radio. The Spanish
news agency EFE reported: 'On the occasion of this sporting act,
we recall the great friendship and solidarity that exists between
Germans and Spaniards, who today fight united in Russia with
the aim of annihilating criminal bolshevism.' Such solidarity
contrasted with the reception the German team received when it
played in the 1938 World Cup prior to the outbreak of the
Second World War. When Switzerland played Germany in the
opening match in Paris's Parc des Princes, French football fans
jeered the Nazi salute and pelted the German players with bottles,
eggs and tomatoes throughout the match.

In Berlin, most of the stadium, over 60,000 of the seats, for the Germany–Spain game were taken up by Germans. Of these 14,000 were reserved for the German Army, 6,000 for school-children and Nazi Youth, and another 5,000 for uniformed Nazi officials and their guests from the Spanish Falange. The remaining tickets were taken up by Spaniards working for Nazi Germany. They included wounded and resting soldiers from the Division Azul – Blue Division – the volunteer military force Franco had sent to the Eastern Front to fight alongside the Germans against the Russians.

The Spanish players who lined up before the start of the game alongside their German counterparts and joined in the Nazi salute symbolised the extent to which they had become political pawns on terms dictated from on high. They were acting under the orders of new manager Eduardo Teus, the former Real Madrid goalkeeper turned sports journalist with strong right-wing political views. Teus had been tasked by the Franco regime with the specific mission of 'reconstructing *La Furia*' – the football of *cojones* first mythologised during the 1920s Olympics which, encouraged by the Spanish military, would become part of the national football culture during the long years of the Franco regime.

Teus, in consultation with sports minister General Moscardó and other military officers, had selected a team of loyal patriots. The players were expected to show the dedication of crack units storming the enemy trenches. The coach was Ricardo Zamora, his reputation as a national icon restored after his brief banish-ment from football's front line. Zamora led the team in chants of 'Franco, Franco and Franco' and fascist salutes before the opening whistle.

The Spanish squad included several players from the newly created Athletic Aviación (German, Gabilongo, Campos and

Arencibia), Real Madrid's Jesús 'Chus' Fernández, Martorell and Teruel from Español (now renamed in Castilian), a couple of survivors from the Basque team that had toured South America (Juan Ramon and Gorostiza), and Epifanio Fernández Berrido 'Emilin', whose club Oviedo had had its stadium destroyed by anti-Franco forces during the Civil War.

One of the veteran Spanish internationals was the striker Campanal, a leading scorer in the Spanish league. Campanal was part of the legendary Stuka forwards in the Sevilla team named after the lethal ground-attack aircraft which made its combat debut in 1936 as part of the Luftwaffe's Condor Legion's intervention in the Spanish Civil War. With its infamous *Jericho-Trompete* (wailing siren), the Stuka became the propaganda symbol of Nazi air power and the blitzkrieg victories of 1939–42. Sevilla in the 1940–41 season ended in fifth place after pulverising FC Barcelona 11–1, the biggest win in the history of the club in the Primera division. Campanal scored five goals.

The Spanish Stuka was little in evidence in Berlin. Instead the Germans took an early lead within twelve minutes with a goal by Decker, before the visitors scored ten minutes from the end after a strange free-kick call by the referee, suggesting that the match may have been fixed beforehand. Certainly, the final score line – a 1–1 draw – suited both sides politically and diplomatically.

'Spanish football, dexterously ruled by the Falange, will give many days of glory to the (Spanish) Empire which now is reborn under the mandate of Generalissimo Franco, the Spaniard's immortal *fuehrer*,' declared a statement from the Third Reich's sports organisation the Nationalsozialistischer Reichsbund für Leibesübungen (NSRL). The Spanish media was no less enthusiastic, with the Barcelona-based *El Mundo Deportivo* declaring: 'The Spanish team has provoked a demonstration of affection that breaks through the strict boundaries of sport and enters the realm of mutual respect and passion.'

Before the week was out, the Spanish squad played against Italy in the San Siro, in Milan. The match, refereed by a German, was watched by another massive crowd, this time made up of pro-Mussolini Italian football fans and Blackshirts. Italian football was still basking in the glory years of the 1930s when it won two World Cups in succession (1934 and 1938) and a gold in the Olympics of 1936. As in Hitler's Germany and Franco's Spain, football in Mussolini's Italy was used to shape public opinion, inculcate mythical nationalist values and develop the country's standing in the international arena. The Spanish team was outclassed by the Italians and beaten 4–0. The defeat prompted recriminations against the squad when it returned home, with the media accusing it of not having fought bravely enough to defend the country's reputation.

At club level, Atlético Aviación regained some national honour when it beat a visiting side from the Italian Air Force at Christmas 1942 6–2. The game was played in the Metropolitan stadium, which had been rebuilt after suffering major damage during the Civil War. Its design and construction under military management was held up as an example of Franco's urban regeneration, rising, like Real Madrid's Santiago Bernabéu stadium, from the ruins of war.

Elsewhere in Spain, the renamed Atlético de Bilbao had regrouped and was posing the biggest challenge to the supremacy of the new pretenders in Madrid. The club had reformed with a new pro-Francoist administration itself and the rump of the Basque diaspora. Among the players who had returned voluntarily to Franco's Spain rather than join their colleagues in exile was Lezama, who as a young teenage Civil War refugee had started playing for Southampton as a goalkeeper.

In 1940 Lezama joined the Second Division Arenas Club de Getxo. A year later he signed for Atlético de Bilbao and made his La Liga debut on 27 September 1942 in a 5–0 win over Real Betis. After initially struggling to reassert itself after the Civil War, Athletic recovered some of its former glory, thanks to a team that included three emerging young internationals Telmo Zarra, José Luis Panizo, and Agustin Gainza.

Athletic won the league championship, three points ahead of Sevilla, and the Copa del Generalissimo when it defeated Real Madrid in the final. The club and its supporters marked both occasions with huge celebrations on the streets of Bilbao that seemed to be free of any political overtones. Whatever outpouring there was of Basque pride, it was suppressed, since the use of Basque political activity, language and flags was banned by the regime.

When the partying was over, the players were taken by club officials to Bilbao's University of Deusto to there undertake a discreet spiritual retreat at the hands of a Jesuit priest. The relationship between the club and the Jesuits – whose founder Ignatius, one of the Spanish Church's great saints, was born in the Basque country – was destined to strengthen throughout the Franco years, helping to deepen the mystique of Athletic's Basque cultural roots while offering it a measure of protection from the officially Catholic regime. Although at one point ETA tried to claim St Ignatius as their icon, the Jesuits were never as intimately involved with the terrorist organisation as some priests were, and often spoke out publicly against violence.

* * *

The Basque Country's strong religious identity is deeply embedded in its mountainous landscape as is Athletic's training ground and youth academy outside Bilbao, named Lezama in memory of the Basque refugee boy who returned to the fold. From the great spine of the Pyrenees to the multiple ribs of the Cantabrian Cordillera, the Basque Country is dotted with shrines, small chapels and churches, with the most famous sanctuary the Virgin of Aranzazu in Guipuzcoa, to whom St Ignatius made his vow of chastity over 500 years ago.

The post-war period saw the virtual beatification of another Basque legend: Zarraonandia, better known simply as Zarra. As the French journalist Enrique Terrachet has written in his history of Athletic: 'To talk of Zarra is to write another history exclusively dedicated to him. Zarra's popularity, even among those who were not football fans, and among his own colleagues, was extraordinary. Zarra was the symbol of *La Furia*, of courage, of pride, of heart.'

It is interesting here that Terrachet introduced the word heart, thus humanising as well as softening the definition of *La Furia* in a way that frees it from the rhetorical clutches of Spanish fascism. The spirited centre-forward became a prolific goal-scorer in his fifteen seasons at the club, winning the Pichichi trophy in six of them, a record unbeaten to this day. He scored more league goals (252) than any other player in Spanish football history, and an additional 81 cup goals. He also shared the record for most goals scored in a season: 38 in 1950–51.

Tall for a Spaniard of his generation at 5 feet 11 inches, strongly built like many of his fellow Basques, Zarra was a powerful and versatile striker, with a devastating left foot and equal ability to win balls in the air. But he was loved by Athletic fans as much for his personality as for his sporting talent. He always volunteered to play, even when badly injured, and led by example in his civility towards opponents, often offering a conciliatory handshake or stopping play whenever he felled an opponent.

Beneath his tough exterior lay a sensitive human being, as when he cried with a sense of injustice after being sent off for the only time in his career. It happened during a hard-fought final of the Copa del Generalissimo against Valencia at the Montjuic stadium in Barcelona. The referee accused Zarra of hitting back after being kicked in the mouth by Valencia's defender Alvaro, at the time one of La Liga's hard men with a reputation for ugly tactics. Zarra himself claimed that Alvaro had come into him hard with the intention of eliminating him from the match, but in the process had injured himself. 'At that point, when Alvaro was on the ground, Gainza came along and told me, 'Telmo, go ahead and stamp on his headband, so I feigned a stamp,' Zarra later recalled.

After his expulsion, Zarra sobbed uncontrollably in the changing room while the two teams continued head to head at 2–2 until in extra-time Irionda struck home Athletic's winner off a deflected shot by Gainza. During the ensuing celebrations in Bilbao's main square, fans demanded Zarra step out on the mayoral palace's balcony alone, not just once but twice, so they could honour him. Such was Zarra's popularity that in the following season fans were happy to adopt a moving ritual at San Mamés, on his suggestion. This was the use of specially trained messenger doves to signal to the patients of the nearby sanatorium of Santa Marina whenever Athletic scored goals.

Sadly such gestures contrasted with the vindictiveness and repression that characterised the Francoist regime. In 1942, Franco travelled to Barcelona to celebrate the third anniversary of his military victory. Three thousand doves were released in his honour as thousands of soldiers and Falangists marched along the city's main avenue. Franco wished to be seen as Spain's beloved leader who had not only won his nation's war but also secured the peace. For all this show of public self-confidence, Spain was a country politically divided within itself and football provided an escape valve for suppressed emotions.

A year later, the Francoist image of national unity was badly dented during two volatile games that Real Madrid and FC Barcelona played against each other during the semi-finals of the Spanish Cup, renamed La Copa Del Generalissimo. The first leg was played in Barcelona's Les Corts stadium with the home crowd spending most of the game booing and whistling the visitors and the referee, between huge celebrations every time Barça scored. Real Madrid were beaten 3–0.

In a post-match report in *Ya*, one of the main national newspapers, a former Real Madrid player Eduardo Teus accused the Catalans of a deliberate conspiracy against the state. Further inflammatory statements were made in the Madrid media and free whistles handed out to Real Madrid fans in the run-up to the second leg. Then, minutes before the game was due to start, the FC Barcelona players received an unexpected visit in the changing room from the Count of Mayalde, Franco's Director of State Security, who warned, 'Do not forget that some of you are playing only because of the generosity of the regime in forgiving you your lack of patriotism.'

His comment was interpreted by the players as a veiled threat against at least three of them who had left the country during the Civil War and who, despite returning to Franco's Spain, were suspected of being secretly opposed to his regime. They included Escola, dubbed *El Rojo* (the communist one) by right-wing Francoists. The Barça player was forced out of the first leg on a stretcher after being kicked in the stomach by a Real Madrid player.

The second leg went ahead with FC Barcelona this time finding itself at the receiving end of verbal abuse from the home crowd. Physio Angel Mur's memory of the event remained photographic many years later when I caught up with him in the Camp Nou changing room. He was long retired but still working for the club as a volunteer. He told me: 'The night before the game we had to change our hotel, and even then we didn't leave it all evening because we thought we would be lynched. Then when the game started our goalkeeper was so petrified of being hit by missiles that he spent most of the game as far forward from his goal as possible, allowing the Madrid players to get near our goal from all directions. Not so far from where we were sitting, there was a man dressed in military uniform who kept on screaming throughout the match, "Kill these red Catalans, kill these Catalan dogs." At one point I interrupted him and said, "Look, I may not have been born in Catalonia, but I feel I belong to it, and I will go on working there because it is different from the rest of Spain." The officer shouted, "You separatist son of a bitch!" and told me I was under arrest for sedition. It was at that point that the Marquis of Mesa de Asta, the president of Barça that Franco had appointed, intervened, telling the officer to leave me alone. The Marquis was a distinguished aristocrat and a close friend of General Moscardó, the sports minister. But the officer did not recognise him. "Who do you think you are?" the officer asked angrily. Then the Marquis showed his identity card and told the officer to accompany him.'

FC Barcelona lost the match 11–1. The journalist Eduardo

Teus described the result as the 'most resounding victory in the history of Real Madrid'. But another observer of the event provided a different version of the match, after using his pro-Franco political credentials to evade the censor's pen. He was Catalan-born Juan Antonio Samaranch. The future president of the International Olympic Committee, a keen roller hockey player as a young boy, had been conscripted as an eighteen-year-old medical orderly by the Republic during the Spanish Civil War, escaped to France, and then returned to nationalist Spain under Franco and enrolled in the Falange.

Samaranch covered the game as a sports writer with the conservative *La Prensa* newspaper. In his article he condemned the violent atmosphere surrounding the match, and concluded that the intimidation of FC Barcelona was not only unprecedented in the history of Spanish football but had made it impossible for there to be a fair game. Samaranch accused the referee of playing to the crowd when early on in the first half he sent off one of Barça's key players, Benito. The decision proved a turning point in the match. From that moment the ten Barcelona players faced an avalanche of goals and seemed either unable or unwilling to put up much resistance. Samaranch wrote:

Perhaps if the final result had been 4–0, it would have been possible to blame this or that player. But a ten-goal difference is too incredible for there not to be an alternative explanation. If Barça had played really badly, the result would have been different. But it was not a question of playing badly or well. Barça simply ended up by not playing at all. Individual players were fearful of making even the most innocent of tackles because of the crowd reaction and therefore hardly touched their opponents . . .

It was frankly sad having to watch the spectacle of a Barcelona team forcefully reduced to impotence by the coercion of the crowd . . . I won't deny there was some merit in Real Madrid's playing. Its midfield was marvellous, and the team as a whole dominated the match, but on reflection, one has to admit that it's not difficult to look great if you haven't got anyone playing against you. A children's team would probably have had more of an impact than Barcelona did in this match.

Samaranch's report drew such an outraged reaction from Real Madrid and its supporters that it cost him his job on the newspaper. A privileged and successful career still awaited Samaranch as a sports minister, deputy of parliament and, after Franco's death, the chairman of Catalonia's biggest savings bank La Caixa. He reached the pinnacle of his career as the IOC's top man, responsible for the Olympic community's first major TV and sponsorship deals and bringing the Russians in from the cold. Among Catalan football fans Samaranch would be remembered, somewhat generously given his political affiliations, as a true sportsman.

Ramallets – 'The cat of Maracana.'

15

World Cup 1950

In 1946, the United Nations imposed sanctions on Spain while both the US and the UK withdrew their ambassadors from Madrid in protest at the authoritarian nature of the Franco regime and its past ambiguous relationship with Nazi Germany. Ernest Davies, Parliamentary Undersecretary of State for Foreign Affairs in the post-war Labour Government, insisted that Britain would abide by the 1946 UN embargo resolution because the Franco regime remained 'repugnant'.

In response Franco rallied his countrymen around him, exploiting their rather skewed sense of patriotism, and turning to his own advantage the nation's sense of injustice. An indignant Franco attributed British hostility to Masonic plots and communists in the British Labour movement who had fought against him in the International Brigades during the Spanish Civil War.

Within four years, FIFA staged football's World Cup, the first to be held since 1938 because of the Second World War and its aftermath. Spain was not among the favourites – England and hosts Brazil were – but its presence in the high-profile sports tournament had a strong political dimension to it. It presented the Spanish national squad with an opportunity to come in from the cold of their country's diplomatic isolation.

Spain's pool match with England generated excitement in both countries, although it was the Franco regime that approached it in propaganda terms, determined to be seen to hit back at its diplomatic detractor, and to stir up nationalist feelings over Spain's historic claim over Gibraltar. The recovery of the British colony, long considered by Spanish nationalists a part of Spain in foreign hands, was an ambition long cherished by Franco, who always liked to emulate the great warrior conquering heroes of Spanish history. Just as the Catholic Kings had expelled the Moors, he wanted to expel the Brits from Gibraltar – or at least defeat them on a football pitch.

The government-controlled Spanish media had little difficulty in stirring up anti-British feeling among home football fans, portraying Spain as a courageous underdog against an English squad that was among the favourites to win with players like Wright and Ramsey, Finney and Mortensen, Mannion and Matthews.

England and Spain won their opening games, against Chile (2–0) and the United States (3–1) respectively. But then, in a surprise result, England lost to the US 0–1, while Spain beat Chile 2–0. The Spaniards thus faced the English with an unbeaten record in the competition so far and needing only a draw to enter the final stages. Despite their shock defeat to the US, England were in confident mode. Reports had reached the English camp that the Spanish backs played square and were therefore vulnerable to the through pass and the speed of Matthews and Finney on the wings. The English were further encouraged by the decision of the Spanish coach to gamble on Ramallets, one of their reserve goalkeepers, a rising star in FC Barcelona but as yet untested on the international stage.

But the Spaniards were up for a fight. FC Barcelona and Athletic Bilbao provided the majority of players in a squad that was not short of spirit or talent either. Apart from Zarra and his club colleagues Gainza, Panizo and Nando, Spain counted on the Barça stars Basora and Cesar and Real Madrid's Luis Molowny, who had been picked for his quick precision passing, skilful ball control and lightning attacking football. Molowny was born in the Canary Islands, a part of Spain that had always considered itself geographically and in spirit between the old continent of Europe and the new continent of Latin America. If the Spanish media came close to seeing the match as some kind for revenge for the Armada, Guillermo Eizaguirre, the Spanish manager, seemed well suited for the job – not so much because of any special talent as coach but because he was a loyal Francoist. Eizaguirre had been something of a legend in his own time, dubbed the 'flying angel' during his heyday as goal-keeper with Sevilla in the run-up to the Civil War when the Andalusian club became Spanish Cup champions. Eizaguirre then volunteered to fight for Franco and ended up serving as a captain in the fanatical Spanish Legion, receiving a medal for bravery in the field of battle.

Spanish media coverage of the game was heavily biased in keeping with the political circumstances, not least the national radio coverage to which thousands of Spaniards tuned in. The only Spanish live radio commentator was Matias Prats. Utterly loyal to the Franco regime, Prats' portentous turn of phrase and excitable tone made him a hugely popular figure among listeners and a useful propaganda arm of the regime. Fourteen minutes into the game Milburn headed Finney's centre past the Spanish goalkeeper Ramallets but the goal was disallowed by the Italian referee Signor Galeati. Newsreel photographs show a Spanish defender playing Milburn onside. Prats described it as 'clearly offside'. But with the second goal there was no dispute. Three minutes into the second half, Ramallets stepped well off his goal line and launched a counterattack, throwing the ball to Gonzalo. After an interchange of passes the ball was intercepted by Wright but went loose and fell at the feet of Gabriel Alonso, who found Gainza. His header was met by Zarra, who volleyed it home with his right foot. It was the only goal of the game.

Prats' extended '*Goooool*' went on for the best part of a minute and enthralled thousands of Spanish listeners. As Prats later recalled, 'Zarra put the goal in the net, and I put the goal in the mind of all Spaniards.' Thanks to Prats, it became another of those mythical goals in Spanish football. The Armada had prevailed after all. With that goal, Franco's Spain had not just defied England, but had reasserted its imperial honour. As the author Vázquez Montalbán would later recall with his characteristic sharp sense of irony: 'Thanks to Prats, the land of Bread and Bulls became the land of Bread and Football – that GOOL is the origin of "We Count on You" (the slogan used by the Franco regime to unify Spanish youth through the practice of sport), of the development of tourism, of Massiel's triumph in the Eurovision Song Contest . . . and of the Seventh Development Plan.' In other words, Franco felt he had found his national squad worth showcasing, a priceless support at home and abroad. At home it would give Spaniards a new sense of pride. Abroad, it was a ticket towards diplomatic recognition, or so he thought.

In his post-match comment, the president of the Spanish Football Federation Armando Muñoz Calero – a veteran of Franco's Blue Division that had fought alongside the Nazis against the Russians on the Eastern Front – told Prats, 'We have defeated the Perfidious Albion,' a remark that infuriated the British Foreign Office and unsettled FIFA, but delighted Franco and his supporters. In deference to FIFA and the influence within it which the English FA exerted in those days, Calero later, somewhat disingenuously, claimed that he had actually used the adjective 'blond' instead of 'perfidious'. However it was his early remarks that had set the jingoistic and triumphalist tone of the Spanish media, and sharpened the sword of Spanish diplomacy. 'England defeated!' screamed the headline in *Marca*. It reported: 'Zarra scored the goal of the most glorious Spanish victory . . . we have taught a sublime lesson to the alleged masters . . . a splendid demonstration to the whole world that the traditional Hispanic virtues of passion, aggression, fury, virility and impetuosity have been completely recovered in the "New Spain" born out of that bloody conflict – the Civil War.'

The Spanish coverage included an invented quote from the English team manager Walter Winterbottom predicting that Spain would go on to win the World Cup. As things turned out, in the round-robin final format Spain first drew against Uruguay, on 13 July 1950 was swamped 1–6 by Brazil, and then 1–3 by Sweden. The Spanish team failed to qualify for four of the next six World Cups, and performed badly in the two that it did contest. Spain had to wait sixty years before winning the tournament.

Nevertheless, the year 1950 represents a before and after in the history of modern Spain and her football. By that year the worst of the post-Civil War repression was over and what had been consolidated was an authoritarian, conservative Catholic regime with Franco at its apex. Tarred with the fascist brush and linked to Hitler's Germany and Mussolini's Italy, Franco's Spain was initially cold-shouldered by the international community in the wake of the Second World War. This isolation allowed Franco to stoke up an exaggerated feeling of nationalism based on a traditional view of a single Spanish identity, the myth that Spain was a nation inhabited by a population which felt itself to be Spanish and shared a similar loyalty to a single political centre, the capital Madrid.

A sustained anti-Spain campaign might have threatened Franco's survival early on in his regime. But instead Spain became a player in the Cold War between the West and the Soviet Union, its uncompromising anti-communism supported by the US. The post-war UN embargo was lifted in the year of the 1950 World Cup and three years later Spain agreed to the setting up of US military bases on Spanish territory in return for substantial economic aid. Meanwhile the Spanish coastline, which until then had been characterised in the main by a succession of little fishing villages and untenanted coves and beaches, experienced the arrival of the first charter flights filled with tourists, what in time would turn into a mass invasion of foreigners less interested in the country's politics than they were in a cheap holiday under the sun.

The Franco regime lasted for much longer than anyone foresaw, and from the 1950s onwards, as the economic situation improved, gradually grew somewhat more liberal. Thus while the country as a whole remained culturally hamstrung, Spanish football did indeed begin to act as a bridge to the outside world. The performance of the Spanish team in Brazil in 1950 was judged of sufficient significance to transform Spain from a post-war diplomatic outcast into a full member of the international football community. Spain was voted for the first time onto the executive committee of FIFA with the support of South American countries.

Of that 1950 squad, Zarra was one of two players that gained a very special place in the hearts of Spanish football fans. The other was Ramallets. He had been nicknamed the 'Cat of Maracana' for it was in Rio's stadium that he showed his agility in the air and his intelligent distribution of the ball. He was also strong and brave, and played without gloves. Spain may well never have won their mythical victory were it not for his defiant defence of his goal line. But for that 'offside' goal the English found him unbeatable. Ramallets' achievement was all the more remarkable given that he was neither the first- nor second-choice goalkeeper but the third, so that he entered the tournament belatedly, and by default rather than choice.

I caught up with Ramallets many years later. It was the autumn of 2010, a few weeks after the World Cup. I had thought that Ramallets, like so many veterans, would choose the safe territory of club offices (in his case FC Barcelona's) for the interview. But instead he asked that I visit him at home. This was no palatial residence in a leafy neighbourhood of Barcelona, but a small stone cottage in Mediona, a village in the rolling wine county of the Alt Penedès.

Ramallets belonged to the last generation of Spanish footballers that weren't able to enrich themselves through their profession. On retiring he had embraced the austerity of a hermit. 'Ask at the old pensioners' bar and they will give you the final directions to where I live,' a rather croaky old man's voice had told me over the phone.

His tiny house was along a narrow street beyond which you could see the open country and then the foothills of the Pyrenees. Ramallets himself, at eighty-six, had a face weathered by the years, his skin as wrinkled as a ploughed field. But he still stood tall with only a slight suggestion of a stoop. What struck me most, apart from his simplicity, was his mental alertness and just how big were his hands and strong his handshake. Time had been kind to his gifted assets. We sat by an open hearth surrounded by photographs and newspaper cuttings donated by friends of his days as a player, when he inherited Zamora's title as the best goalkeeper in Spain and became a source of inspiration for other great number ones from Iribar and Zubizaretta to Reina, Valdés and Casillas.

We began talking about goalkeeping, that most undervalued of positions in sport but which in Spain has produced some of its most loved and respected footballers, from *El Divino* Zamora to La Roja's Iker Casillas, with other legends along the way, as if this country, so torn throughout its history by violence and betrayal, had a need of good reliable saviours.

'Zamora is a legend from whom all the others follow. He was a man who personified, like no other, the solitary figure of the goalkeeper in all its potential for greatness: a strong personality, who saw the imperative of limiting failure. The goalkeeper depends on his team-mates. But only he can win or lose a match and that's what makes him such a key figure.'

Perhaps it is true, as Peter Chapman argued in his book *The Goalkeeper's History of Britain*, that football around the world has waged war against the goalie – from the early days when a striker could bundle a keeper across the goal line and score to the more contemporary indignities of the back-pass rule – and it's a universal truth that the best of us is to be found in our struggles to 'keep a clean sheet'.

But just as Chapman goes on to suggest that Britain's character as an island nation finds its sporting embodiment in the shape and stance of the man between the uprights, may I also venture a similarly whimsical premise to explain Spanish goalkeeping. And that is that the Spanish goalie – and I am talking in particular about one that has risen to play in the national squad – has inevitably been caught up in the enduring figure of Don Quixote. He thus personifies those high ideals which were supposed to make Spain great, a bastion against the enemy as well as an excuse for failure.

The goalkeeper would carry the destiny of the Spanish squad on his shoulders long after Franco died in 1975. Nine years after his death Spain reached the final of the European Championship against France where the Spanish captain, Real Sociedad's Luis Arconada, famously smothered a free-kick by Michel Platini under his chest in a diving save, only to fumble the ball, which slid off under his body and rolled into the net. The blunder was blamed for Spain's eventual defeat in a competition it thought it could win.

Rather than ponder on such demons, Ramallets recalled the 1950 World Cup and *that* game with the English. 'The tournament wasn't easy for us. I guess we were not as fit as we should have been, and it was very hot. We ended up in fourth place. But we beat England who were one of the favourites and who played a fast and attacking style of football. The English refused to give up after we scored and kept coming at me forcing me to make saves or clear the ball even after they'd run into my net. They had a great team. I know they had Matthews but the player I remember most of all was Finney, who played on the left wing and was really fast.'

That English 'goal'? 'It was clearly offside. The fact is I saw it and lifted my arm to appeal even before the referee blew his whistle.'

Born into a poor family, Ramallets was just twelve when the Spanish Civil War broke out. He spent most of it in Barcelona digging earth to help build bomb shelters. For someone who had suffered Franco's bombs, what was it like playing for his national team? 'We were all good friends and felt pretty separate from politics. I'd get on well with the Basques but also with the Real Madrid players and those from other clubs. If you were selected you just became part of a team, you felt part of it. We all felt equal,' he said.

I asked whether the mood changed once they crossed the frontier. 'Wherever we went, we had Spanish immigrants or exiles giving us a good reception – I think it was because they felt true Spaniards. They would ask us, when is the regime going to change? This was what concerned them, more than the football we played. They wanted to know how and when they could return.'

So what happened to Spanish football over those years of dictatorship?

Ramallets paused, briefly closed his eyes and then said, 'I think the Civil War produced a gap in the development of our football . . . Many players were killed and it took many years to reorganise the national game. I think football in Spain began to become something from 1950 onwards. I think we learned from the foreigners who came in. I think it was these foreigners who marked a before and afterwards in the history of Spanish football.'

Francisco Seygas surrounded by family in the port of
Buenos Aires – an early Argentine import

16

The Boys from Almagro

The neighbourhood of Almagro in Buenos Aires, west of the centre of the city, boasts a colourful history of enterprising Basque and Italian immigrant workshops, street brawls and tangos: 'Neighbourhood of my soul, where I spent my youth and spent nights of love,' the great tango singer Gardel would sing in the 1930s.

Almagro is west of the centre of Buenos Aires, a city where I worked and lived for several years, in pursuit of the Argentine football legend Diego Maradona. Long before Maradona – otherwise known as the Hand of God – came to play for FC Barcelona in the early 1980s, Buenos Aires, thanks to Almagro, earned a place in the history of Spanish football because of the lesson a neighbourhood team gave when they toured Spain in the winter of 1946–47.

The lesson is a chronicle foretold in the development of Spanish football from the mythological beginnings of *La Furia* so beloved of the Franco regime over many years to the refinement of *La Roja* – the national squad that won Spain's first ever World Cup at the start of the second decade of the new millennium.

This story has its beginnings in the early 1900s, when a street gang based in Almagro would invite gangs from other neighbourhoods to play street football by painting walls with the legend *Los Forzosos de Almagro desafían* (Almagro's strongmen dare you). Almagro was then criss-crossed by tramway and bus lines so playing football was a risky business. When one day a young boy was run over by a tramway car, a local Catholic priest, Father Lorenzo Massa, took charge and hosted football games in the backyard of his parish church in the Avenida de Mexico. It was there that the first organised teams of San Lorenzo de Almagro came into being, becoming with the passage of time one of Buenos Aires' top clubs, along with Boca Juniors, Independiente, River Plate, and Racing. San Lorenzo recruited from the immigrant Basques, with their tradition of tough, physical football, and from a mixture of Italians, Spaniards and mixed-Indian bloods drawn from the provinces, players known as *los gauchos*, like the wild lawless cowboys that roamed the extensive pampas.

The Basques, with their seemingly unquenchable physical reserves and uncomplicated, aggressive play – tough tackling, then heading, crossing and occasional long balls – drew some of their inspiration from the English. But the back streets of Buenos Aires and the dry state of the turf that came to characterise Argentine football stadiums contributed to a productive melting pot of styles, with an emerging native culture putting a greater emphasis on individual trickery and dexterity.

Such football had its precursor in the 1920s when neighbouring Uruguay won two Olympic football gold medals in succession, an achievement the writer Eduardo Galeano (a

Uruguayan) has described as The Second Discovery of America. 'The English . . . had perfected the long pass and the high ball, but these disinherited children from far-off America didn't walk in their father's footsteps. They chose to invent a game of close passes directly to the foot, with lightning changes of rhythm and high-speed dribbling,' wrote Galeano.

South American footballers were destined to have an important influence on the evolution of Spanish football. An early pioneer, if unsung hero, was Francisco Seijas, one of the rising stars of Argentine football who signed for Celta Vigo in 1930. I stumbled on his story by chance some years ago, when I visited for the first time what would become one of my favourite eating places in London – an Argentine meat restaurant called El Gaucho. It was owned and run by Luis, a retired dancer who in his youth had shown off his tango skills in Hollywood and Las Vegas before marrying a very beautiful Chilean woman, a dancer like himself. One night Luis showed me two fading photographs. The first showed him dressed as a *gaucho* when he worked with a circus troupe. The other showed someone remarkably similar to him but dressed in a suit and a fedora hat, surrounded by adoring women on the quayside of some old port.

'That's my dad Francisco when he was about to board the ship for Spain – the first professional Argentine football player to leave for a European club,' Luis told me proudly. An enduring friendship was sealed there and then with El Gaucho becoming an unofficial watering hole for Maradona fanatics like myself.

'Back then Francisco Seijas would not have dreamed of the kind of fame that Maradona achieved and other Argentines since, like Messi. For him it was an adventure, a challenge, but without the celebrity, or the money,' his son told me.

The Galician club Francisco chose to play for was one of the late arrivals on the Spanish football scene having been founded in 1923. Despite inaugurating the impressive Balaidos stadium in 1928 in anticipation of a more professional era, Celta was struggling to make its mark in Spain's Second Division. Within weeks of his arrival, Seijas had established himself as the club's leading goal-scorer, after scoring four goals in his debut against Athletic Bilbao. To compensate for his short height, Seijas had a low centre of gravity which gave him near-perfect ball control and an ability to glide past defenders. He was not the first nor last Argentine to have such qualities, but he can uniquely claim to have helped Celta on its way to promotion.

The migration of players like Seijas to La Liga slowed during the 1930s. Argentine football belatedly became professionalised while Spain was thrown into economic and political turmoil. As David Goldblatt has written: 'Cut off from the carnage, freed from the imperatives of war and survival, Argentinean football could create a distinct blend of instrumentalism, art and entertainment,' with the Argentine media articulating a 'working mythology of a unique national playing style'.

This rich alchemy of styles was what San Lorenzo de Almagro brought with them when they toured Portugal and Spain in 1946–47. The team had just won the Argentine league title, thereby breaking the River Plate hegemony of the legendary *La Máquina* (the Machine). This was the name given to the relentless and well-oiled attacking football exemplified by River Plate's legendary forward quintet – Muñoz, Moreno, Pedernera, Labruna and Lousteau. After dethroning River Plate, the Iberian tour was a high mark in San Lorenzo's history. San Lorenzo arrived at Madrid's newly enlarged Barajas airport four days before Christmas 1946 in an Iberia DC4, after refuelling in the Canary Islands. First to walk down the steps to the tarmac was Bilbao-born Ángel Zubieta, who had stayed in Argentina after touring with the Basque squad during the Spanish Civil War. Zubieta was greeted by his mother and sister. The emotional reunion between the returning one-time Spanish international, now playing for the Argentine champions, and two seemingly happy Basque citizens of Franco's Spain served its political purpose in the regime's favour.

In the following weeks local football fans, encouraged by the extensive coverage provided by the Spanish football media, marvelled at the play of the Argentine visitors. What they saw was the best of the attacking football made famous by *La Máquina* and now made part of an intricate display of quick short passes and turns, skilful flicks and lobs, and magical goals. The team came to be known as *El Ciclon* (the Cyclone) because of the speed and artistry with which it mesmerised and ran circles round most opponents. 'What occurred between 21 December and the end of January 1947 seemed unreal and inexpressible,' commented the Spanish newspaper *El Pais* in a tribute published on the fiftieth anniversary of the tour. 'The daily press and the magazines doubled their normal football coverage. San Lorenzo, despite playing with the cold, snow, and intense rainfall of that winter, caused a sensation.'

In their first game in Madrid's Metropolitano stadium, with most of their players still recovering from an exhausting transatlantic flight, San Lorenzo beat hosts Atlético Aviación 4–1. Two days later the Argentine club played in the same stadium and lost by the same margin to Real Madrid. On the eve of the match, San Lorenzo's captain, the Basque Zubieta, was overheard telling a friend that he hoped his team would double their scorecard against the winners that season of the Copa del Generallisimo. 'Beating Real Madrid will be the real marker for the whole tour because they are well known in Argentina and are today Spanish champions,' Zubieta said. The boast prompted the Madrid captain Ipiña, another Basque, to rally his players. At a meeting on the eve of the match he told them: 'I am prepared to bust a gut tomorrow, and I expect the same from all of you. What on no account must we do is fight with the same arms as them.'

Ipiña proposed quite simply that the team focus on closing down San Lorenzo's game and beating them on the counterattack. The strategy would include man-to-man marking and a solid midfield being able to count on the speed on and off the ball of Molowny and Belmar, strong defenders who could also be lethal in attack. And so it proved. The trickery and patient build-up play of the visitors was smothered by the stoic defence of the Spanish champions. San Lorenzo's passing game was typically fluent, but all too often played in front of the Real players rather than in behind them.

On the few occasions the Argentines had a sight of the opposing goal, the attacking player was crowded out. Real were quick on the break, with Pruden scoring two goals and Belmar a third by half-time after lightning counterattacks down both sides and lethal finishing. It was a fiercely fought encounter for a friendly. Ipiña was carried off injured after a bruising tackle before Alsúa struck home the winning fourth goal. But although Real Madrid would make much of its victory, the match barely dented San Lorenzo's reputation.

For the rest of the tour the visitors proved unbeatable, with three players in particular – Farro, Potoni and Martino, the so-called *trio de oro* (golden trio) – playing hugely entertaining football. Potoni was offered a contract with FC Barcelona but turned it down, while Martino ended up playing for Juventus.

San Lorenzo beat FC Barcelona and drew with three other Spanish clubs: Athletic Bilbao, Valencia and Sevilla. Of the three, the match that made the biggest impact on local fans was played at Bilbao's San Mamés, where the popularity of San Lorenzo's captain Zubieta had endured while that of Athletic's Panizo had always been questioned. While Zubieta's Basque workmanship and team spirit was held up as an example, Panizo found himself criticised by Athletic fans for playing with the ball too much. But when the crowd watched the San Lorenzo players show off their ball control and passing skills, word went round San Mamés with a newly discovered sense of admiration: 'But they all play like Panizo!'

It was however against the Spanish national squad that San Lorenzo pulled off its most assertive victory, winning by 13–5 over two games. As Jaume Olive, the coach of FC Barcelona's youth team, put it many years later: 'There was a before and after in Spanish football which was delineated by the San Lorenzo visit. The Argentine champions left a deep imprint . . . an elaborate football of short passes, of triangulation, in contrast to the more direct football of a Spain where to talk about tactics was regarded as heresy. The Argentines believed in making the best use of the ball and strategy – against these Spaniards could only respond with *La Furia*, and improvisation.'

Alfredo Di Stéfano – Real Madrid and European Cup star

17

Di Stéfano

The Argentine club's tour laid the seeds for one of the most exciting periods of Spanish football club history, with Real Madrid in particular showing greater respect for foreign imports than its triumphalist tones on beating San Lorenzo had suggested.

Among those who had watched Real Madrid's victory over San Lorenzo in that winter of 1946 was Santiago Bernabéu, the Spanish club's first post-war president, and one of the great figures of international football. Bernabéu, as well as being a former player and a hugely enthusiastic football fan, was a man of ambition and vision, if not opportunism, who managed to harness his allegiance to the Franco regime so as to benefit his club. In 1943, Bernabéu took advantage of Spain's neutrality in the Second World War to draft plans for a new stadium as part of Madrid's post-Civil War urban regeneration. Bernabéu had little trouble in convincing Franco and his ministers that the stadium – planned as one of the largest in the world – once populated with star players would draw to it

Spaniards of diverse social backgrounds and act as a bridge to the outside world.

Bernabéu saw his opportunity to seize on South American skills at the end of March 1952 when as part of its fiftieth anniversary celebrations Real Madrid played against the Colombian team Millonarios in their new stadium along Madrid's Castellana avenue. Of the players that appeared that day, one in particular, Alfredo Di Stéfano, caught Bernabéu's eye because of his evident versatility and skill as well as strength on and off the ball. Although billed as a centre-forward, Di Stéfano showed an extraordinary work ethos, one moment tracking back into defence, the next leading a fast counteroffensive, and striking with disarming accuracy. 'This guy smells of good football,' Bernabéu remarked after watching him play.

Di Stéfano, the son of working-class Italian immigrants, was born in Argentina, a country that, like Spain, had learned how to play football from the British but had developed a style of its own, fast, magical and mischievous. His first home was just a few yards away from the Boca Juniors stadium, in the port of Buenos Aires, where Argentine football's earliest teachers, the English sailors and merchants, had made their mark. He learned to play street football with the school kids of his *barrio* while his father earned enough money as a foreman in the local market to buy some land. It was against walls and on hard surfaces, whether on the dusty pavements or on dry grass, that Di Stéfano discovered his talent in dribbling and passing while developing his skills as a sharpshooter with his left and right foot.

Di Stéfano grew up amid the *potreros* – the small yards and fields of the sprawling metropolis of Buenos Aires – where large groups of kids would often find themselves fighting for the ball with adult men. It was there that he learned to use his individual instincts while fighting for his team. One of the first teams he played for in the *barrio* were called Unidos y Venceremos (United and we will Win). It was with them that he learned to fight not just to defend, but also to play to win. He made his reputation playing for River Plate during the late 1940s when Argentine club football enjoyed one of its golden periods, as *La Nuestra* – 'ours', meaning our (Argentinean) style of play – came into its own.

Di Stéfano in his memoirs recognised what he and many others owed to the early pioneers. He wrote: 'We should pay tribute to the English, who went all over the world with their railways, but also with their football . . . They went to America, to Asia, to Africa . . . In Spain, in Huelva, Rio Tinto they were also the first to introduce football . . . thanks to them, we have become a (footballing) family.' But while *La Nuestra* owed its beginnings to the British Empire, it forged its identity in the social context of post-colonial South America. The football came to claim a style of its own, creative and surprising, with players turning into magicians. Their range of tricks included bicycle kicks and scissor kicks, incredible flicks and back-heels, individual juggling and the collective painting of elaborate tapestries with quick, perfectly controlled passes.

Such football was both elegant and mischievous, it mesmerised and brought smiles out on people's faces, as much ballet as circus, as the players dribbled and passed the ball between each other, each move an attempt to up the entertainment, each goal a surprise. While playing at River Plate Di Stéfano's trainer and inspiration was Carlos Peucelle, who in his days as a player was nicknamed *Barullo* ('Mayhem') because of his tendency to play all over the pitch in no defined role other than as a constant threat or bulwark. Of Di Stéfano himself, perhaps the most evocative portrait has been written by Galeano, who said of his days at Real Madrid in *Football in Sun and Shadow*:

> The entire playing field fitted inside his shoes. From his feet the pitch sprouted and grew . . . he ran and reran the field from net to net. He would change flanks and change rhythm with the ball from a lazy trot to an unstoppable cyclone; without the ball he evaded his marker to gain open space, seeking air whenever a play got choked off . . . He never stood still. Holding his head high, he could see the entire pitch and cross it at a gallop to prise open the defence and launch the attack. He was there at the beginning, during, and at the end of every scoring play, and he scored goals of all colours . . .

Di Stéfano signed with Real Madrid on 15 September 1953 after protracted negotiations, made all the more controversial by thwarted counter-bids from FC Barcelona, which the Catalans blamed on dirty dealings in Madrid aided by the Franco government. What is beyond doubt is Bernabéu's ambition to make Di Stéfano the central actor in Real Madrid's transformation into one of the world's great clubs. Three months before the Argentine's arrival, Bernabéu signed Paco Gento, a young winger from Santander, one of several players who would blossom thanks to Di Stéfano's inspiration and support.

Gento was lacklustre and came close to being dropped from the team in his first season with the *merengues* ('the meringues' as Real Madrid were affectionately nicknamed by the popular Francoist radio commentator Matias Prats, for no other reason than he saw the resemblance between their white colours and one of his favourite desserts). But he survived thanks to Di Stéfano who argued, quite rightly as time would prove, that Gento was a winger with extraordinary pace but who needed to improve tactically, something which could only happen by playing alongside more experienced players like himself.

Undoubtedly Gento grew as a player thanks not just to Di Stéfano but to the array of (mainly foreign) talent that Bernabéu brought into the team. It was thanks to Di Stéfano's advice that Bernabéu enlisted José Héctor Rial, the Argentine inside-left, who had also played in Colombia. Di Stéfano wanted someone who could help him build up an attack from midfield with a series of quick one-two passes. But Rial also contributed to the team by connecting with Gento, a traditional winger, with his long passes, thus widening the team's attacking options. Rial helped improve Gento's timing and control while making full use of his speed to tear into defences. Gento soon earned the nickname *Supersonico*. Rial was joined at Real Madrid by other foreign stars – the Uruguayan José Santamaria, the Frenchman Raymond Kopa, and, last but by no means least, the Hungarian Ferenc Puskás.

'People say of those days that it was football played by five or six attackers and defended by the rest, but that's an outrageous misrepresentation,' Di Stéfano told the Spanish journalist Orfeo Suárez on the eve of the 2010 World Cup, 'What we had were wings that moved up the pitch, and forwards that tracked back in defence. It was a collective effort. I was taught that football is all about touch and mobility.'

Not everyone had the genius of Di Stéfano. He was ahead of his time. Of all the stars of Real Madrid's Golden Age, it was unquestionably that of Di Stéfano that shone the brightest. For without him there would have been stars but no firmament. Di

Stéfano's greatness lay in his ability to combine his individual skill with his talent for organisation. Miguel Muñoz, his first captain at Real Madrid, once said that with Di Stéfano on your side it felt like having two players in every position. Di Stéfano was responsible for casting a whole club in his image in a way that impacted on the development of Spanish football as a whole. He created a mythology around Real Madrid's invincibility that others struggled to emulate, and that unwittingly came to contrast with and highlight the underachievement of Spain's national squad and his inability to inspire it to greatness.

Ladislao Kubala – the genial Hungarian

18

Kubala and Other Hungarians

Real Madrid's glory years of the 1950s were the product of its hands-on president Santiago Bernabéu's policy of having his managers periodically renovate the team with new stars, even though Di Stéfano remained the central figure throughout this period.

Among the other star foreigners, Puskás had already earned a special place in history as a member of the Magic Magyars, communist Hungary's national team that had dominated European football in the early 1950s, crushing the English 6–3 at Wembley on 25 November 1953 with a superb display of innovative passing and tactical sophistication. Hungary, captained by Puskás, was the first national squad to break with the fifth forward of conventional football formations, withdrawing the centre-forward into a midfield which had already been depleted by one player playing deeper. Meanwhile the role of the two remaining midfield players was primarily organisational and attacking, supporting interplay and passing among the forwards. This was called 4–2–4.

During his time playing for Hungary, Puskás was dubbed the 'Galloping Major' because of his army rank. As the journalist Brian Glanville recalled, he was 'the star of stars, a squat little Budapest urchin-figure, plastered hair parted down the middle, with superb control, supreme energy, and above all a left-foot shot which was unrivalled in the world, dangerous from a distance up to thirty-five yards'. At Real Madrid, where he arrived aged thirty-one in 1958, Puskás won enormous affection and respect for all these qualities, despite the paunch that never left him in all his playing days.

One of my favourite Puskás tales involves *la barriguita* (little stomach), as it was diplomatically referred to. One day Antonio Calderon, one of the club directors under Santiago Bernabéu, called in the then trainer Camiglia to inform him that the club had signed Puskás. 'Is that so? Well, what are we going to do with that stomach of his?' asked Camiglia, making it clear that he was not best pleased. Calderon answered, 'That stomach is your responsibility to get rid of.' Hours later Puskás trained with the team for the first time. Then Calderon asked Di Stéfano what he thought of his new team-mate. Di Stéfano replied, 'He controls the ball better with the left leg than I do with my hand.' No one ever raised questions about Puskás's *barriguita* ever again and he came to be known instead as *Cañoncito* (the little cannon).

During his time at Real Madrid, Puskás scored twenty or more goals in each of his first six seasons in the Spanish league, and won the Pichichi four times. When he retired, aged forty, he had secured a place in the history books as one of the most prolific scorers in football history, with 514 goals in 529 matches in the Hungarian and Spanish leagues.

The golden years during which Real Madrid conquered

Europe was also a period when FC Barcelona refused to let up as the country's other major club, aping Santiago Bernabéu's grand architectural ambition and moving into its own huge stadium – the Camp Nou.

The expansion was principally aimed at accommodating the impact of Ladislav Kubala on the club's fortunes. Kubala arrived at FC Barcelona after an epic escape from his native Hungary where he had played for three clubs – Ferencváros, Slovan Bratislava and Vasas of Budapest. Football and politics had restarted in Hungary in 1946 following the end of the Second World War in the shadow of the Soviet armed forces. By 1948, as the division of Europe was being finalised, the Communist Party edged their conservative and social democrat coalition partners out of power and began to tighten its grip on all aspects of society, including football. On 25 January 1949, Kubala fled from communism to the West, initially to a US military zone in Austria and then to Italy, where he played for a while with a local team called Pro Patria in the town of Busto Arsizio.

The communist authorities denounced Kubala as a delinquent and a fraudster. He had in fact done a bunk while the ink was still wet on a contract he had signed with and been paid for by Vasas, for whom he had only played for a short while. The Hungarian Football Federation issued a formal extradition request on account of alleged financial crimes, his leaving the country without authorisation, and his failure to do military service. While the extradition request was ignored by the West, Hungary's growing influence as an emerging post-war football nation within FIFA secured him a one-year international ban.

Kubala once again packed his bags, this time moving with his young wife to a refugee camp in Italy under US military administration. There he met up with some fellow Hungarians who had similarly fled their country and formed a football team called Hungria. That summer he travelled to Spain on what was to prove the most defining journey of his football career.

I caught up with Kubala many years later in Barcelona. It was in late May 1998 and Kubala was playing in a veterans match on a small pitch near the Camp Nou, under a blazing midday sun. My first glimpse of him was that of an old man in shorts, bare-chested and holding a T-shirt like an emblem in one hand. Kubala seemed to be working harder than all the others, and suffering too, his bow-legs barely carrying his weight. And yet at one point this geriatric hero managed to conjure some energy from a mysterious inner reserve and dribble from his back line the length of the pitch before delivering a perfectly angled shot into the goal.

I struggled to understand this motivation so late in life and Laszi (Kubala) gave me an explanation of sorts later when I interviewed him in the veterans' office. No sooner had we begun talking than he lifted his suit trousers to the knees to reveal a close-up of scarred skin. 'Look at this . . . that's seven operations – and still things aren't quite the way they should be . . . The older one gets, the more problems, but I go on playing because I don't want the other "granddads" knowing about it, because if they found out they would give me nothing but trouble. So they don't know anything and that means we are all happier when we play together,' he said, speaking Spanish rapidly with the clipped accent of an Eastern European.

'My team was called Hungria because we were four or five Hungarians playing in it,' he went on, 'but there were also Czechs, two or three Croatians, a few Russians . . . they'd all escaped from communism . . . We travelled to Madrid to play in a friendly with the Spanish squad that was getting ready to play in the 1950 World Cup. Pepe Samitier, who was the Barça coach, was in the stadium and he watched me play. Afterwards he came up and said, "Why don't you come with us to Barcelona?" and I told him, "I would love to but FIFA does not allow me to play as a professional and I've left my country without authorisation." Then he said, "Don't worry, we'll fix it."'

Samitier's endeavours to draw Kubala away from the clutches of Real Madrid, who had expressed an interest, were helped by the Hungarian's extraordinary capacity for hard drinking. According to a well-sourced account I heard from Enrique Llaudet, a senior official of FC Barcelona at the time, *El Sami*'s seduction of Kubala verged on the farcical. It certainly endures as one of the most extraordinary transfer stories in Spanish football history. 'Kubala came to Spain thinking he was going to be signed by Real Madrid, but because he was half-pissed he didn't really know whether he was coming or going. If Kubala had one weakness it was that he drank too much – whisky, wine, whatever he got his hands on. Well, as things turned out there was real confusion on the train that took him from Madrid to Barcelona, with Kubala at one point turning to Samitier and saying, "Hey, we are going towards Madrid, aren't we?" and Samitier saying, "Sure we are," then Kubala insisting, "But the sign says Barcelona," which is when *El Sami* said, "Don't you worry. We are going to the club now." And that is how he brought us Kubala.'

As things turned out, Kubala struck a hard bargain when he signed with FC Barcelona. When he sat down to negotiate, Kubala took out a copy of a draft contract Real Madrid had prepared and insisted he wanted something similar or more.

The contract he signed with FC Barcelona made him the highest-paid player yet in the history of the club. Although Kubala spent the next nine months without playing a league game because of the FIFA ban, by the end of the 1950–51 season he had earned close to three quarters of a million pesetas for playing in just thirteen games. Next to him the best-paid member of the Barça squad was the team's new Czech coach Daučík, Kubala's father-in-law, whose hiring formed part of the deal *El Sami* had helped negotiate.

The ban on Kubala playing professional football was lifted by FIFA in April 1951. Subsequently Kubala was given Spanish nationality, his status fast-streamed through Spanish bureaucracy thanks to friendships Samitier had with members of the Madrid political establishment, and the personal intervention of the Francoist president of the Spanish Football Federation, Muñoz Calero. That they found sympathetic ears at the highest level of the regime was hardly surprising. Kubala's story of escape from Communist repression and delivery into the friendly hands of Spain perfectly suited Franco's efforts to exploit the developing Cold War to break out of his diplomatic isolation. Kubala's life story was given its crudest treatment in propaganda terms in a filmed dramatisation, called *The Stars Search for Peace*, which became a box office hit in Spain.

While unwittingly used for a while as a political pawn, Kubala's contribution to lifting the quality of Spanish football during the 1950s cannot be doubted. He brought to FC Barcelona a combination of skills and strength that Spanish clubs had until then rarely seen in one player. Kubala was quick on and off the ball, demonstrated extraordinary control when dribbling, and showed a good vision of the game, knowing when to pass. He was also a consummate goal-scorer, devastatingly accurate with both feet and a master with the dead ball, with his curling ball often defying even the best-constructed walls. To Kubala, his great rival Di Stéfano would pay a generous posthumous tribute when the Hungarian died in May 2002. 'Kubala was one of the best there has ever been. His game was pure, crystalline, a real joy for the fans,' said Di Stéfano. 'He was potent, technical, fast, and a great goal-scorer.'

In truth, little separated the sheer quality and creativity of both men. Together they provided so many examples of sheer brilliance that others in more modern times, from Maradona and Ronaldo to Zidane and Messi, would emulate. Many football fans would retain an enduring memory of a game Spain played against Belgium in 1957, when Di Stéfano dived full-length, before scoring with a back-heel from the air off a cross-kick from Miguel. Di Stéfano had a habit of scoring goals like that. Any open net, it appeared, was an invitation for a goal and much of the time he executed it ruthlessly.

Spanish football fans were given a tantalising glimpse of what might have been on 26 January 1955 when the two men played alongside each other wearing the FC Barcelona colours in a charity match and delivered an extraordinary exhibition of football skill and imagination, beating Italy's Bologna 6–1 with their combined goal-scoring power.

'The trick with Alfredo,' Kubala told me, 'was that you had to give him complete freedom of movement and a colleague who knew how to back him up. We would take turns going forward, but always supporting each other. We were constantly changing positions. This meant that we were always with the ball, and always creating problems for our adversaries, particularly when they tried to mark us. Alfredo and I were always two against one, and that made the game easier.'

So what was Di Stéfano's defining gift? 'He had speed, technique and a great vision. He also knew how to sacrifice himself for the good of the team.'

I guess football stars, like any competing artists, get nicer about each other with old age – it is their way of reconciling themselves with life. Certainly Di Stéfano and Kubala were kinder to each other as old men than as young players – they never really got on – and the two played a great many more games against each other than they did as team-mates. Circumstances beyond their control meant these players came to be embroiled in the history of enmity between Spain's two biggest rival clubs.

Perhaps what gave Di Stéfano the edge in football was his portentous presence on and off the field, in contrast to Kubala's somewhat Rabelaisian 'eat, drink, and be merry' way of living. What is certainly true is that personality, politics and fate conspired against both players forming an enduring partnership either at club or international level.

Neither Di Stéfano nor Kubala's help was sufficient to enable Spain to qualify for the World Cup in Sweden in 1958. Curiously it was a tournament where another of Bernabéu's foreign stars, the Frenchman Raymond Kopa, seemed to flourish in his national squad. At Real Madrid, he had been banished to the wing, not his natural position, in order to accommodate Di Stéfano's domineering presence. But with France, he flourished anew as an attacking midfielder, in control of the orchestra just as Di Stéfano was at Real Madrid. Kopa scored more goals per game for the national team than he did for his Spanish club.

It was Di Stéfano's ego and Kubala's indiscipline together that in the end excluded them from any enduring presence in the national squad once each player had taken on Spanish nationality. Some Spanish commentators criticised Kubala early on for playing rough, using his elbows too often, and having a tendency to monopolise the game. But his colleagues and the huge following of fans that he generated saw only the best in Kubala – a hard worker, who sweated the shirt with every game, and inspired the whole team with his unique talent and incurable, if naïve, generosity. Bernabéu used to say that Kubala had a hole in the palm of his hand where he kept the money he wanted to give to the people he thought needed it.

Despite being one of Spain's best-paid players, he shared with others as much as he spent on himself, supporting less fortunate Eastern European refugees and famously telling the police that he hoped the 200,000 pesetas stolen from his car once had helped a person in need.

'There are a lot of stories about Kubala . . . some were true but others were pure invention . . . I think he was a great player but also a normal guy who liked to have fun, particularly after really big matches when we thought the whole world was our play area . . . like when we won a match against Real Madrid – that was well worth celebrating,' recalled Ramallets, the Barça goalkeeper and Spanish international.

Kubala's inspiration helped Barça win the Spanish Cup on 27 May 1951, beating Real Sociedad 3–0. In the 1951–52 season that followed, Barça went on to win the Spanish double, and the Copa Latina (contested by the Spanish, Italian, French and Portuguese champions), together with two summer tournaments, the Martino Rosso and Eva Duarte tournaments. In one of several memorable performances in La Liga Kubala scored seven goals in a 9–1 victory over Sporting Gijón. The 'season of the five cups' marked FC Barcelona's transformation into a major international club. It was a time when the team not only played great football, but also showed that it had survived the Franco regime's repression to take its place in the emerging Spanish society as one of the country's most respected football institutions.

Many years later, when a democratic Catalonia was rediscovering its political and cultural identity after the death of Franco, one of Spain's most talented musicians, Joan Manuel Serrat, wrote a song of tribute to Kubala, and his colleagues Basora, Cesar, Moreno, and Machon who made up the front five. A passionate Barça fan, Serrat felt as close to Kubala in spirit as the Argentinean tango singer Carlos Gardel had to Pepe Samitier. As Serrat sang, 'For me there was no one like Kubala . . . I was happy to play with him, carry his portrait in my wallet'. Born four years after the end of the Spanish Civil War, in Poble Sec, a poor suburb of Barcelona, the son of an immigrant from the South, Serrat grew up among the shortages and diplomatic isolationism of the post-war years when Kubala's days of glory brought many afternoons of joy to football fans in Barcelona and beyond.

This was a time when live radio commentaries became increasing popular, football results were posted up in bars, and when TV, although as expensive as a first house, began to be bought for the sake of watching a big match. In 1959, there were 5,000 registered TV owners in Barcelona. Another 6,000 were sold in that year in the days leading up to live coverage of a Barça–Real Madrid match.

No other players contributed as much to Spanish club football's transformation during these years as Di Stéfano and Kubala. But it was a different story when it came to the national squad, where the players did themselves and the team no favours and where management proved so conflictive as to nullify any positive contribution they might have otherwise made.

Helenio Herrera – the Magician

19

Herrera, the Magician

In a period of twelve years, between the World Cup of 1950 and the World Cup of 1962, Spain's national squad appointed sixteen coach/managers, none of whom had the talent, organisation or vision to draw on the best from club football and transform it into a competitive squad capable of winning titles. Perhaps the one that did, Helenio Herrera, who served as Spain's national coach between 1959 and 1962, proved too arrogant a personality and too divisive in his tactics to ensure a truly national enterprise. While individual clubs enriched the game they played with foreign imports and the lessons they learned from a variety of talented coaches, Spain as a football nation would only grasp belatedly the foreign tricks and spells with which it had been briefly dazzled during the tour of San Lorenzo de Almagro. Of Herrera's many claims to fame, few can be as negative as the fact that he alienated both Alfredo Di Stéfano and Ladislav Kubala, two of of the greatest figures in the history of Spanish football.

Herrera was a nomad who, at his best, brought a magician's

touch along with a strong personality to the profession of football manager/coach. He was born in Argentina to Spanish immigrants – his father was an exiled anarchist. When he was aged four he immigrated with his parents to Casablanca where he adopted French citizenship. Herrera would later claim that he learned what he needed to know about football – his school of life as he called it – as a boy growing up in North Africa, mixing and playing with Arabs, Jews, French and Spaniards.

During his two-year stint at FC Barcelona (1958–60), he used his powers of psychology to motivate a team that all too often seemed overladen with its own self-conscious sense of history, and an underlying inferiority complex with respect to its rival Real Madrid. The way Barça emerged from one of its periodic doldrums and flourished under Herrera was so quick that it provoked conspiracy theories in Madrid of trickery, secret rituals, even illicit drugs, although much of the negative media coverage was fuelled by the coach's unashamed mercantilism. Nonetheless, he won the respect of his players, with the exception of the ageing Kubala, who he judged surplus to requirements.

As Fusté, one of the younger Barça players (and future Spanish international) at the time, recalled, 'Herrera was football's psychologist . . . he was very good at motivating his players . . . he would convince them they were better than the opponent . . . He got me into play when I was seventeen . . . I looked up to much older players like Kubala and Evaristo and Ramallets as if they were gods. Herrera knew how to make the best use of the resources at his command.'

Herrera brought Spanish and Italian club football into the modern era of coaches stamping a style and worldview on their players, in the process becoming the first manager to collect credit for his team's performance. Up to that time managers were more marginal, with the exception perhaps of the pre-war examples – eccentric Englishmen like Athletic's Mr Pentland or fearless Irishmen like FC Barcelona's Patrick O'Connell. During the 1950s teams were better known for their players than their managers, such as Di Stéfano's Real Madrid. And yet Catalans remember the Herrera era while Inter FC during the 1960s is still referred to as Herrera's Inter.

He came to be popularly known as 'The Magician' on account of his innovative psychological motivating skills, which some of today's most successful coaches like Pep Guardiola and José Mourinho were destined to emulate. His pep talks would be punctuated with phrases like 'He who doesn't give it all doesn't give anything.' Herrera was disdainful of other managers in Spain for their failure to engage with players and to bring about a real change in their attitude. His pre-match warm-ups, like his training sessions, were intense affairs, his press conferences usually controversial, as were his pre-match preparations. After providing his players with a cup of tea made up of spices and herbs only he knew the true identity of, Herrera would gather his players around him in a circle. Then, throwing the ball at each in turn, he would scream a question, looking each player directly in the eyes. 'What do you think of the match? How are we going to play? Why are we going to win?' he would demand. The questions gathered in speed and intensity as he went round the circle. Then, as a collective frenzy appeared to reach its climax, the circle would split and the players sprint before returning into the fold, at which point the team would shout, 'We are going to win.'

Herrera encouraged superstition, which he believed complemented the traditional Virgin cults to which most Spanish clubs were linked because of the Catholicism of a majority of players and fans. He found a susceptible target of his own tricks in the case of the Galician-born Luis Suárez, the attacking midfielder nicknamed *El Arquitecto* (The Architect) for his visionary passing and explosive goal-scoring ability. Galicia has never boasted as many football stars as other major regions of Spain. After Suárez, only Real Madrid's Amancio would lay claim to enduring fame and they both chose at an early stage in their careers to move to bigger non-Galician clubs. Other Spaniards say that the Gallegos lack the strength of Basques, the imagination of Catalans, the courage of Castilians and the mischievous artfulness of Andalusians. So the popular football joke goes: 'An Andalusian kicks the ball out of play and smiles. The Gallego takes twenty minutes to recover it.'

But Suárez was different. He was not only a fine and creative inside-forward, the first Spanish-born player to be voted European Footballer of the Year in 1960 – he was also deeply superstitious. Thus while looking on Suárez as Di Stéfano's 'legitimate heir', Herrera played on his star player's belief that a glass of wine, accidently spilled during a pre-match meal, augured well for his goal-scoring chances. When Suárez wasn't looking Herrera would give his wine glass a good tap and exclaim in a loud voice, 'What a pity we've ruined the table-cloth!' Suárez would then immediately run up, dip his finger in the spilled wine, and then with it touch first his forehead, then the tip of his shoe.

Despite his tricks, Herrera had a genuine knowledge of the game and how it could best be played to entertain and secure victory. He experimented with some innovative attacking foot-ball, using full-backs as wing-backs defensively supported by the libero or centre-half stopper to launch faster counterattacks and turn some of the easier matches into goal sprees. But he also knew how to close down opponents by having the sweeper stay behind the defence, with the rest of the team marking man-to-man and counterattacking on the break. Herrera claimed that his tactics were slightly different to the *catenaccio* (or cult of defence) that came to be identified with Italian teams with a reputation for negative play. He himself liked to use, among his options, a system whereby the centre-backs in front of the sweeper were markers, while the full-backs had to be able to run with the ball and attack.

Herrera was full of praise for two foreign signings by Barça, the Hungarian Kocsis, the 'Golden Head' who also had a sure touch and strength of foot, and Czibor, fast on and off the ball and similarly skilled in goal-scoring. While Czibor liked to describe himself as the 'engineer among the workers', Herrera insisted on collective team effort. A competitive spirit, strength and speed, and good technique were what constituted a winning formula. In an era of foreign imports, arguably Herrera's greatest contribution to the health of the Spanish league was in following the example of Athletic Bilbao and encouraging Barça's youth system, which produced players like Olivella, Gensana, Gracia, Verges and Tejada. 'We owe them many of our victories,' he said. 'They played not just with class but with an absolute dedication to the club colours.'

When some three years before he died in 1997, Herrera was visited at his Venice *palazzo* by the author Simon Kuper, and was asked to talk about his time in Spain, Herrera explained that he played his 'tricky foreigners in attack' – Kocsis, Villaverde, Czibor and so on – while basing his defence on home-grown talent, whom he referred to as 'my big Catalans' – Ramallets, Olivella, Rodro, Gracia, Segarra, Gensana. 'To the

Catalans, I talked "Colours of Catalonia, play for your nation", and to the foreigners I talked "money" . . .'

Herrera moved from FC Barcelona to Milan's Internazionale in 1960, where he continued to also coach the Spanish squad. As things turned out it was Galician-born Luis Suárez, neither a Catalan nor a foreigner, who ended up following in Herrera's footsteps in the same year, for 250 million Italian lire in the world's most expensive transfer deal.

Herrera's football career involved him coaching six Spanish clubs and his spell as a coach of Spain, which was to last from 1959 to 1962. He was in this post when, in May 1960, Franco's personal intervention forced Spain's withdrawal from its quarter-final matches against the Soviet Union in the first-ever European Nations Cup. The ties had been preceded by growing optimism in the Spanish camp after convincing victories in earlier qualifying matches against Poland and Yugoslavia and similar impressive victories in two friendlies – 3–1 against Italy at the Camp Nou, and 3–0 against England at the Bernabéu – all under the management of Herrera. He had taken charge of the Spanish squad in 1959 and from the outset counted on such talent as the Real Madrid stars Di Stéfano, Gento, Del Sol, Barça's Luis Suárez, Ramallets and Segarra, and Joaquín Peiró and 'Chus' Pereda, the attacking midfielders then playing for Atlético Madrid and Sevilla respectively.

Herrera convinced his men they would beat the Russians and go on to secure the title. And yet Franco squashed whatever dreams this fusion of the best of Spanish club football may have had of European football glory by not allowing the squad to play on Soviet territory, and insisting that both legs be played in neutral countries – a request that Moscow declined. Franco was partly influenced by consideration for Spanish veterans of the Blue Division who had fought and suffered with the Germans on the Eastern Front, some of who were reportedly still detained in Soviet concentration camps. But he later claimed that what ultimately led to his decision were the detailed police reports he received warning that the Soviet media were predicting huge support not just in Moscow but also at the Bernabéu for the Russian team.

Franco smelled a communist conspiracy: a Soviet-led propaganda exercise aimed at exposing the Spanish regime's unpopularity among exiles from the Civil War and surviving supporters of the Republic. This, combined with a Russian request that the Soviet anthem be played and the Soviet flag be flown in the Real Madrid stadium, proved altogether too much for Franco, and his appointees in the Spanish Football Federation – all Civil War comrades – did as they were ordered and withdrew the Spanish team from the competition.

The background to the controversy was never reported in Spain's highly censored media at the time other than to belatedly try and shift the blame to the Soviet Union for insisting on playing on neutral ground. The row was taken very badly by some of the players, who privately resented such a blatant intrusion of politics into their sporting activities. As the Spanish international Chus Pereda told me in an interview conducted in 2010 (he was to die of cancer a year later), 'We all returned home with a huge sense of sadness. I and the others had never been to Russia. We were genuinely interested in visiting a country that was a mystery to us and most Spaniards who had not gone into exile in the Civil War or fought there in the Second World War. It was also a great opportunity to play in a major competition final. I remember we were all gathered in the Spanish Federation offices in Madrid when they suddenly told us, the match was off and we could all go home. It was all because of (political) pressure. Some ministers said yes, others said no, but it was Franco who was the boss, and he said no.'

Herrera expressed his disappointment publicly on behalf of the team – without directly raising the issue of politics, still less blaming Franco. The official rumour mill suggested that this had little to do with any sense of patriotic opportunity or love of football but rather the loss of the financial bonuses Herrera had been promised by the Spanish Federation as an incentive to beat the Russians. Abroad it did little to improve Franco's image among his critics. *The Times* condemned what it described as Franco's arbitrary and blatantly political coercive act which had violated the founding principles of the IOC and FIFA. The newspaper suggested, not inaccurately, that Franco was making a point about Spain's credentials as an anti-communist Cold War warrior to impress his military and commercial ally, the United States. It certainly had very little to do with football per se.

Herrera survived for another two years as manager of the Spanish squad, but he made as many enemies as friends and the former eventually caught up with him. The Argentine initially courted criticism for dropping Kubala, first from Barça and then from the national squad, justifying the move on loss of form and lack of discipline linked to the Hungarian's heavy drinking.

Herrera not only forced out Kubala, but another legend of Spanish football – Pepe Samitier, the former star player turned technical director of FC Barcelona. After a row with Herrera, Samitier moved to Real Madrid where he had as many friends as in the Catalan capital, not least Franco himself, and where he harboured an enduring grudge against the Argentine. By the time Spain qualified for the World Cup in Chile in 1962, Herrera had become, as Alfredo Relaño puts it, the 'baddy of the film . . . for many an innovator, for others a real anti-Christ of football.'

On paper the Spanish squad that qualified for the 1962 World Cup, with Herrera as coach, could only impress, such was the talent and experience displayed. It included four naturalised foreigners – Di Stéfano, the Uruguayan-born Real Madrid central defender José Santamaria, Puskás, and Barça's Paraguayan-born striker Eulogio Martinez – together with a coterie of home-grown stardom which included Gento, Collar, Peiró, Garay, Adelardo and Del Sol. Yet Spain did not get past the first round where it was grouped together with Mexico and the two eventual finalists, runners-up Czechoslovakia and Brazil who won the championship.

As Brian Glanville has written, the component pieces of the Brazil team had 'sprung apart, then strangely and steadily come together again'. During the four years since they had last won the World Cup, two key Brazilian players had played at club level in La Liga with contrasting fortunes. Vava, who scored twice in the 1958 final, went on to have two successful seasons with Atlético Madrid. The other was Didi, one of the few foreign stars brought in by Bernabéu who did not prove a success at Real Madrid, partly because he never seemed to be quite up to the energy and speed of his team-mates, and partly because of personal problems involving his wife. She was a journalist who claimed that Di Stéfano was jealous of her husband and mistreated him. Di Stéfano blamed Didi for not fighting enough for the ball, and losing it too easily. 'The Bernabéu stadium likes quality, but it also values effort, work, commitment – it wants a battle. It's a public that is used to winning and to win you have to fight,' Di Stéfano said once. In other words, Didi was a lesser being.

Arguably, bad luck rather than bad football conspired against Helenio Herrera's Spanish squad. It got off to a faltering start, losing 0–1 against the Czechs, their early pressure blocked by a solid defence, their flow of play increasingly interrupted by brutal tackles that crippled Herrera's stars and led one of them, Martinez, out of pure frustration, to lash out with a kick to an opponent's stomach. In the next match against Mexico, the Spaniards rediscovered their rhythm. Again a strong defence resisted the Spanish pressure but this time the gods were smiling, and Peiró scored the winner in the final minute.

In their final match in the group, Spain faced Brazil. The Spaniards needed a draw at least to qualify. It was a game in which Didi had planned to take his revenge on Di Stéfano but Di Stéfano was left out of the Spanish team after pulling a muscle. Before the tournament got under way Di Stéfano's father turned up with a 'magic' liniment, but to no avail. A conflict of egos had led to an enduring rift between Di Stéfano and Herrera. As the then young Spanish international Fusté later recalled: 'Di Stéfano was a guy who liked to lead, to be the boss and he wanted to go on being the boss. The problem was that Herrera wanted to be boss as well and there wasn't room for both of them.'

For the match against Brazil, Herrera took a major gamble, which was also a questionable statement of self-belief, by making no fewer than nine changes from his original eleven. He dropped two star forwards, Del Sol and Suárez, his goalkeeper Carmelo and his centre-half Santamaria. Instead he drew up a traditional attacking five with Puskás and Gento alongside three Atlético Madrid players led by Peiró. In what some commentators regarded as one of the best games of the competition, Spain played with commitment and flair. Those watching the game included the seasoned English journalist Brian Glanville, who noted for the first hour Spain playing a defensive game which had Brazil at full stretch. A swift counterattack led by Puskás helped create a Spanish goal ten minutes before half-time. Spain kept their composure and their lead until the 72nd minute, at which point Brazil equalised. Then, with four minutes of normal time left, Brazil scored the winner.

As Glanville himself concluded, it was a very near thing, and arguably a 'manifest injustice to Spain', which he judged the better organised and more motivated team on the day. Nevertheless Spain's resulting elimination from the 1962 World Cup reignited a national debate about the future of Spanish football, which brought with it some nasty prejudices from Spain's darker past.

Nationalist attacks focused on the foreign influence that had formed part of the Spanish expedition. The state-controlled Spanish sports daily *Marca* led the charge, claiming that Spain had underperformed as a result of not being sufficiently Spanish in selection and spirit. While conceding that naturalised foreign players like Di Stéfano, Puskás and Kubala, and managers like Daučík – Kubala's Hungarian father-in-law – the Paraguayan Manuel Fleitas and Herrera himself had added 'colour and excitement', while also helping clubs like FC Barcelona, Real Madrid and Atlético Madrid win domestic and European competitions, the newspaper argued that the same foreigners were blocking the development of home-grown talent. 'Even worse, the national team is now so full of foreigners and so conditioned by foreign tactics that it no longer plays like a team of real Spaniards, with passion, with aggression, with courage, with virility, and above all with fury,' said *Marca*.

Not even Spain's star international Luis Suárez, a Spaniard born and bred, escaped criticism. The fact that he had chosen to leave his country to play for a foreign club was held against him as anti-patriotic by his detractors. As for Herrera, he had made so many enemies along the way during his time in Spain that he, above all others, became the target of unbridled criticism painting him as a mercenary with no loyalty but to himself.

José Villalonga – coach of 1964 European Champions, Spain

20

An Officer in Charge

Herrera was replaced as Spanish coach by José Villalonga, a Spanish thoroughbred. Born in Cordoba in 1919, Villalonga had, during the Spanish Civil War, enlisted as a volunteer nationalist soldier, aged sixteen, before being promoted to subaltern. After the conflict was over, he entered the Military Academy and in 1947, with the rank of lieutenant, was named professor of physical education before doing a crash course in football coaching.

Villalonga was a soldier the regime could trust politically. But with a decent track record at club level in the post-war La Liga he was also considered a safe pair of hands in football terms. As manager of Real Madrid during the mid-1950s, he coached both foreigners and Spaniards, winning La Liga and the Copa Latina in his first season before taking the club to its first European Cup victory. In 1959 he became coach at Atlético Madrid. The club at the time shone with players like Enrique Collar and Adelardo – both internationals – and Miguel Jones who was brought up in Bilbao, played in SD Indauxtu with

Lezama but was eventually turned down for selection by Athletic on the grounds that his birth in Spanish Guinea disqualified him from the necessary status as a Basque. A similar fate befell two other Indauxtu players, José Gárate and Jesús Pereda, Basque-bred but born outside the region.

Villalonga took Atlético Madrid to two successive victories over Real Madrid in the Copa del Generalissimo in 1961 and 1962 and over Fiorentina in the final of the European Cup Winners' Cup in 1962, so that it entered the history books as the first Spanish club to win a European competition with an unbeaten record during the tournament. These were glory days for Atlético, as good times for the Spanish league's most erratic performers as that earlier period of success when – under Helenio Herrera – the club won the league championship in 1950 and 1951. Two players from Villalonga's period, Joaquín Peiró and Enrique Collar, came to be dubbed *Ala Infernal* (the 'Infernal Wing') because of the combined work ethos, speed and skill they demonstrated down the left flank.

Villalonga's appointment as national coach was not without criticism. Die-hard Real Madrid fans regarded him as a bit of a traitor for moving to Atlético. The Spanish football world generally saw him as what he was – a soldier turned PE teacher with limited technical knowledge of the game whose successes were due more to the individual talent of his players than to any inspiration he might have given them. And yet political considerations appear to have prevailed, and Villalonga was given the opportunity to prove that he was not as bad as some people made him out to be.

He made a virtue of imposing on the national squad the discipline and the physical training he had learned in the barracks, and showed some aptitude in the selection process.

While retaining Luis Suárez as one of his star players, Villalonga drew ambitiously on an emerging generation of young Spanish talent with Athletic Bilbao's Iribar in goal and players like Amancio, Marcelino, Fusté and Pereda – the best crop from the two big clubs, Real Madrid and FC Barcelona – contributing to a team that was both robust defensively and capable of scoring goals. There were no naturalised Spaniards. In fact a new decree announced in 1963 banned foreign players from Spanish football, a policy enforced for the next ten years.

On 21 June 1964, Spain met the Soviet Union at the Bernabéu stadium in Madrid in the final of the European Nations Cup, an achievement in itself, given Spain's failure to make such progress in earlier tournaments. The fact that the final was to be played in the Spanish capital gave it an extra political edge.

Unlike four years previously, both countries approached the event with a good dose of political pragmatism. The Spanish authorities had gone to considerable lengths to strengthen ties with international sporting bodies. Spain, a country that had to depend on its football clubs to break through its diplomatic isolation, was rewarded with the privilege of organising a high-profile sporting event – the four-team climax to the competition – that was televised to fifteen European countries. For the Russians it was also an opportunity to engage with an ally of the US, two years after the debacle of the Cuban missile crisis had brought the world close to nuclear destruction.

Politics played its part in other ways too. An unnamed senior Falange official, a fanatical anti-communist from the Civil War, plotted to secretly drug the Russian players, a plan that was ultimately vetoed by Franco. Before making up his mind to let the event go ahead, let alone attend it personally, Franco consulted one of his more trusted allies, José Solis Ruiz, secretary general of the regime's political movement. Solis Ruiz suggested that football, despite minimal state investment in it, could be used to divert an emerging post-war generation from any ideas of political dissidence. 'Less Latin, more football,' Solis Ruiz told his leader. Franco next talked to his personal doctor Vicente Gil, who fancied himself as something of a football expert. 'Don't you worry, Paco, we are going to win,' Gil told him. Franco gave orders for preparations for the tournament to go ahead.

Villalonga acted as any loyal officer would. He prepared his players for the match as if it was a critical encounter of a protracted war on which the destiny of the nation rested. As one of his star players Pereda recalled:

> Two weeks before the match, Villalonga gathered us in a training camp in La Ventosa on the road from Madrid to Corunna where Franco used to go and shoot. One day he told us all to sit in a circle and watch him draw a miniature football pitch in the sand. He made one side up with stones and the other with pines and told us that we were the stones and the Russians were the pines, before crushing the pines with the rocks. He then said: 'You see pines can't crush rocks; it's rocks that crush pines and you are the rocks because you are stronger in mind and body.' And that is how he psyched us up to beat them. When we played in Madrid, it was pure politics – any fool realised that. It was Franco against communism. For him it was not just a battle, it was war.

Franco needed little persuasion to milk the occasion as only he could. Entering the Bernabéu stadium with his wife Doña

Carmen and a retinue of ministers and officials, the Generalissimo was greeted with pre-arranged cries of 'Franco, Franco, and Franco'. They were initiated by groups of *Falangistas* but soon spread around the 125,000 crowd that had packed into the Bernabéu stadium to support their national team in a kind of collective hysteria. Few relished the occasion as much as Villalonga, who looked on his team as his best regiment. As he declared in a pre-match press conference, he had prepared a 'young, impassioned, aggressive, virile team based on typical Hispanic values.' Football and politics were in perfect synchronicity.

As things turned out, the teams – one representing a totalitarian fascist state, the other a totalitarian socialist one – were a fair match for each other. It was raining and the ground was muddy. With the ball and the players slipping and sliding it was a tough game, although not without skill. Five minutes into the match, Suárez delivered one of his classic visionary crosses which landed at Pereda's feet and produced the opening goal. While elation broke out all over the stadium, Franco in the presidential box raised his arms slightly and smiled. The roar in the stadium had barely died down, though, when the Russians counterattacked and scored. Franco's countenance momentarily darkened as if news had just reached him of a major military reverse. The match from then on became a test of strength and endurance, with each side showing huge resilience in their back lines, as the downpour became heavier and muffled the enthusiasm of the drenched spectators. Seven minutes from the end, Rivilla intercepted an attempted pass from Ivanov to Khusainov, and embarked on a fast run down the right wing. He fed Pereda who crossed to Marcelino, whose header dropped just inside the left post, beating the Russian

Lev Yashin, one of the greatest goalkeepers of all time. This time Franco almost got to his feet and his arms moved further and his smile broadened. The stadium erupted again, this time with a sense that it was all over – and it was. Amid euphoric scenes, Stanley Rous, the UEFA president, handed the Cup to Olivella the captain. Franco had got used to taking centre stage at big football events, personally attending all the domestic finals and handing the Spanish Cup and the League Cup to the victors. But on this occasion he was happy to defer to international protocol, knowing that he would benefit politically anyway. By arrangement with Villalonga and the Spanish Football Federation, in a well-publicised act Olivella subsequently dedicated the Nation's Cup to Franco on behalf of his team and his coach.

The Spanish militarist paper *Arriba* led the media reaction: 'The Spanish fury has returned at last. The victory has demonstrated to the world that *La Furia* is invincible, when enjoyed with passion, aggression, courage and virility.' Villalonga, meanwhile, spoke like a triumphant general dedicating the outcome of battle to his commander-in-chief: 'I think quite frankly that we deserved to win and because it's been a just victory it is only right that we should offer it with all our respect to his Excellency the Head of State who has been a very special witness of how these boys have fought to achieve it. The eleven have been, without distinction, eleven lions who have marked a new milestone in the history of Spain's international football.'

In a series of comments, one proved unconsciously prophetic. 'We have always paid tribute to Spain's great achievement in the Olympics of 1920. Perhaps today's will endure as an example for the next forty-four years,' said Villalonga. The year was

1964. Not until 2008 would a Spanish national team win another major competition.

Two years after winning the European Nations Cup, Villalonga kept the majority of his squad unchanged with the hope of similar success in the World Cup in England. But it proved a typically Quixotic pipe dream. Not only was the squad getting old. It had also run out of luck.

Spain's opening group match provided the great surprise of the first week of the 1966 tournament, when they lost 1–2 to a rough and efficient Argentine side in a match that saw Luis Suárez hacked down on two occasions. In Argentina's later quarter-final encounter with the hosts England, such brutal tactics led to a controversial sending-off of their captain Rattin – the man the English tabloids had dubbed the 'animal'. After being dismissed, Rattin had defiantly traded insults with the Wembley crowd. By then Spain had been knocked out of the tournament. Narrowly beating Switzerland 2–1, Spain went on to lose to West Germany by the same score.

Like the regime that he so loyally personified, Villalonga's grip on the squad was no longer what it once had been. Some of the players had grown resentful of a coach that ratcheted up discipline but seemed lacking in creative ideas. This in turn conspired against the development of a team ethos, with some of the younger players mistrusting Villalonga's motivation. FC Barcelona's Fusté was one of them. He recalled: 'What failed for us in England was the fact that the military still wanted to rule the national squad; for reasons of international prestige they got Villalonga to bring in from Italy highly paid stars like Suárez and Del Sol, although they were already too old. The whole campaign was badly planned and one of the goals was scored by Pirri after he had clearly handled it. It was as evident as Maradona's against England twenty years later and, like Diego did then, he got away with it. The difference was that Argentina went on to become champions in Mexico 1986 – and this time England emerged victorious.'

This was one World Cup in which Spain's stars failed to shine, as Luis Suárez was later honest enough to admit. 'We played very badly, myself in particular,' he admitted when interviewed many years later for a documentary commemorating the centenary of the Spanish Football Federation.

Among the younger players in that Spanish squad was the Basque Iribar. He was just twenty-three when he played in the 1966 World Cup, and was already fast becoming one of Spanish football's goalkeeper legends for his club Athletic Bilbao. But for him the experience of playing for Spain proved a huge disappointment. As he told me: 'We had a league with some great footballers but we just didn't seem to hack it internationally. The truth is that after the 1966 World Cup there were some great national squads – like Brazil, Argentina, Italy and Germany – with a huge potential. Along the way we had some bad luck, but the truth was that other teams were better than ours. They were better trained, and had a fresher outlook. I know the regime liked to talk of *La Furia* but it was a term that was invented by some journalist not by the players. It wasn't fury that we were lacking, it was a clear style, a model – a system.'

FC Barcelona – *Mes Que Un Club* (More than a Club)

21

Rivals

Here is perhaps as good a point as any in the ongoing narrative to examine more closely the rivalry between two giants FC Barcelona and Real Madrid, the one key phenomenon that has straddled much of the history of Spanish football and been fundamental to both its evolution and popularity.

The infamous match between the two clubs in the aftermath of the Spanish Civil War in Real Madrid's stadium in Chamartin, during which an atmosphere of visceral hate led to the visitors being thrashed 11–1, was the first in a series of controversial post-war encounters that would develop as part of world football's most intense and enduring club rivalries. It was a rivalry that, while having its roots in politics and culture, became driven by a momentum of mutual creation. It fed on itself, reflecting the growing popularity of football as a sport, while manifesting most violently at times of maximum political anxiety. The bad blood that ran though every meeting remained a constant for more than half a century. There was rarely an encounter when both sides could claim a level playing field. It did not matter whether the game was played in Madrid or Barcelona, each match was intensely partisan. The occasions when fans set aside tribal loyalties and applauded a player because of how well he played, not because of the shirt he wore, were rare. I have witnessed this only twice – when FC Barcelona's Ronaldinho and later Messi received a standing ovation from the home fans at the Bernabéu in recognition of their outstanding play. By contrast one of the most abusive incidents I can recall witnessing in any *Gran Clásico* was when Figo returned to the Camp Nou in November 2002 for the first time since changing his club colours. While at FC Barcelona, Figo had made 172 appearances for the Catalans and won the league twice. But he had committed the ultimate sin of transferring from FC Barcelona to Real Madrid, setting a new record transfer fee at £37m. The cacophony of jeers and expletitives, together with the cans, lighters and other loose missiles that accompanied the Portuguese international's every move, climaxed with a severed suckling pig's whole head being thrown at him by local fans as he prepared to take a corner kick.

Through much of the history of this rivalry the referee has stood accused of being a fellow-conspirator rather than an arbitrator, hated by one side as much as he was loved by the other. As a general rule the loser would always feel cheated, while FC Barcelona has tended to show itself less magnanimous in victory and a worse loser. In the past this might have reflected a certain inferiority complex FC Barcelona developed during Real Madrid's golden years of the 1950s when it laid justifiable claim to playing the best club football in the world. In more recent times, roles were reversed when José Mourinho characterised his early days as manager of Real Madrid by blaming the supremacy of FC Barcelona on too much diving by the Catalans and too many unjustified decisions given against the players in white.

Battle lines were first drawn in the Spanish capital in 1912 when, twelve minutes from the end of one of their first competitive matches against Real Madrid, the whole FC Barcelona team abandoned the match claiming that the referee was bent against them. During the 1960s, Real Madrid adopted a particular dislike for British referees, holding one of them in particular responsible for disallowing goals by Di Stéfano and Gento and giving FC Barcelona a disputed penalty. On 6 June 1970, the young inexperienced referee from San Sebastián, Emilio Guruceta, was in the eye of the storm when he gave a controversial penalty to Real Madrid during a second-leg quarter-final tie in the Spanish Cup. The penalty was awarded after Real Madrid's Manuel Velazquez seemed to have been brought down well outside the box. The stadium erupted in protest. There was an unprecedented pitch invasion and running battles with riot police.

Although Franco would live and rule for another five years, this was a defining moment in Spanish football. The Guruceta case, named after the referee who made the wrong call in Real Madrid's favour, was the first time that Spanish football had got out of the dictator's control. Until that moment, by allowing FC Barcelona to function he had divided and ruled, exploiting the political confusion of the Catalans, many of whom had fought for him in the Civil War. His intention was never to prevent Barça from winning titles, but to see Spanish football become an ever popular sport thanks to the rivalry between its two great clubs.

It is a conflict I have followed closely for as long as I have been a football fan. It is a subject that has taken up much of my childhood, youth and professional life, and my experience of it has been from the perspective of both camps, having been born and brought up in Madrid, while spending family holiday time in Catalonia, and sharing much of my working life in Spain between Barcelona and the Spanish capital.

It was such a background that no doubt led me to cross paths with the Irish actor Ardal O'Hanlon in 2006, among the countless memorable encounters I have had along my journey into Spanish football. I had never met Ardal when I received a phone call from him out of the blue early that year. The comedy series *Father Ted* in which O'Hanlon plays a goofy young Irish priest called Father Dougal had long been a favourite of mine, so I felt honoured, if surprised, to hear from him. It turned out Ardal was doing another TV series – this time, with a slightly more serious bent, on great football rivalries – and wanted me to help him out in Spain. It was an offer I didn't even consider refusing, and within hours I was sharing some tapas and *vinos* with Ardal and his production team in Barcelona's old quarter, near the cathedral.

Ardal had the disconcerting personality of all good comedians – an intensely private person off stage, both thoughtful and intelligent and far from brash or outspoken. While refusing to be tagged as political, both his father and grandfather were deeply involved in the politics of the Irish state, which gave him a special insight into the divided politics of Spain and its football. Ardal was also a keen observer of the ordinary daily grind of life – as well as its peaks and troughs. His instinctive irreverence was underpinned by intelligence, his laughter mixed in with occasional dark moods. Of his talents not just as a TV actor but as one of Ireland's (and the UK's) most gifted stand-up comedians, I was aware. More of a discovery was his passion for Spanish football, and one club in particular. 'I've been infatuated with football since the age of four,' Ardal admitted. This dated his passion to 1969. 'First it was Leeds, then in 1974 it was the Dutch and then when Cruyff went to Barcelona it was Leeds, Holland and Barça!'

He went on: 'The infatuation grew and then fell off for a while – when I discovered girls and "other things" – but the dream of visiting the Camp Nou never quite disappeared. The first time I came here was about ten years ago on my honeymoon. It was my wife's first ever football match and she loved it.'

This reminded me that my own love affair with the stadium had begun when on a first visit as a young TV researcher in 1976 I had watched Cruyff lead his team out to play in a game against Athletic Bilbao, and the stadium filled with Catalan and Basque flags. It was the first time that such a blatant display of non-Spanish nationalist loyalties had happened in a football stadium since the Spanish Civil War. Franco had banned both flags throughout his dictatorship. Years later I ended up taking one of my daughters to the Camp Nou for the first time and she loved it. It proved a happier experience than that of her younger sister, who on another occasion had to put up with racist abuse from Chelsea hooligans at Stamford Bridge because she was supporting Barça in a Champions League match.

But back to Ardal. I was struck by his familiarity with relevant Spanish history – or at least its mythification – which he commented on with his comedian's eye for the telling anecdote and a knack for synthesis.

'That's Columbus's statue over there,' he observed while walking down by the harbour, 'but you won't find him pointing towards the Americas – this being Barcelona he is pointing towards the Mediterranean. The Catalans claim Columbus as one of their own, which is a bit of a surprise considering it was largely his fault that Catalonia went into a very long and steep decline. Columbus opened up the new trade routes to the west but the King and Queen of Spain forbade the Catalans from using them. Thus Barcelona was thwarted, not for the last time, by the dastardly Spaniards. But they refuse to lie down.'

Over the next days of filming we were on a mutual learning curve and forged a strong friendship around football that belied our age difference – I was twelve years older than he was. Between us I think we tried to illuminate some truths as well as dispel some myths. The fact that neither of us had parents who were particular football fans and were thus without a tribal loyalty helped us view a divisive subject through a more or less objective lens.

So we began to share some unquestionable truths. Of all the regions that constituted Spain, it was the Catalans that historically had been the most forceful in asserting their identity. No matter that their version of history from medieval times onwards exaggerates the extent to which Catalonia was once a nation as opposed to a region. History is perhaps nowhere more argued over and with such passion than in Catalonia, it is a political weapon in the battle for identities. Two centuries ago the English chronicler of Spain Richard Ford commented, with some foresight, thus: 'No province of the unamalgamated bundle which forms the conventional monarchy of Spain hangs more loosely to the crown than Catalonia, this classical country of revolt, which is ever ready to fly off.' The Catalans certainly had a legitimate grievance based on the belief that their history differed from that of the myth of a united nation state ruled from Madrid, and this had fuelled one of their enduring passions.

One can't begin to understand Spanish football's greatest

club rivalry outside the context of Catalonia's relationship with the rest of Spain. Or put another way, one cannot begin to understand FC Barcelona's perception of Real Madrid as the main enemy without taking in Catalan politics, culture and history, and the interrelationship of all three with football. Much of the history of Catalonia, as viewed by a majority of FC Barcelona fans, is a story of humiliation and frustration, the aspirations of this region curbed and stamped on by the central-ising tendencies of Madrid, the potential of Barcelona to be one of the great capitals of the Mediterranean never fully real-ised, and the perceived close links between Real Madrid and the centre of power in the Spanish capital.

Some of the facts of Catalan history are fairly straightfor-ward even if – when seen through the mind of a comedian like Ardal O'Hanlon – hard to take too seriously. 'You can feel the spirit of Wilfred the Hairy here,' proclaimed Ardal late one afternoon in Camp Nou as local fans began to converge for the latest Barça–Real encounter, with their Catalan and Barça flags and shouting in one uninterrupted cry, '*Visca Barça, Visca Catalunya*' (Catalan for 'Up with Catalonia, Up with Barça'). Somewhere in the stadium someone had lifted a large poster with the manifesto: CATALONIA IS NOT SPAIN.

Catalonia was recovered from Moorish occupation in the early eighth century, long before much of the rest of Spain, and had its various fiefdoms united under an inspired count called Wilfred the Hairy (he was indeed called that because he was a heavily bearded bloke, as he is remembered to this day in statue form and the history books of Catalan school kids). While considered by some the founder of Catalonia, this medieval warrior was still a vassal to Charles the Bald (who indeed lost his hair in early adulthood for reasons unknown). It was another

Catalan warrior, Count Borell II, who finally broke his vassal-age from the intruding French King Hugh Capet in what Catalan nationalism would later claim was the birth of political Catalonia in 988.

The Counts of Barcelona became, through a marriage in 1137, the Kings of Aragon, who would later go on a conquering spree that extended south as far as Alicante and east to the Balearics and beyond to Sardinia, Sicily, Corsica and southern Italy – Catalonia's very own days of imperial glory . . .

Fast-forward to the end of the Spanish Civil War, where thousands of Catalans were imprisoned or executed or forced into exile by Franco.

At this point you may well ask what all this history has to do with the militancy that drives football's greatest rivalry. Well, rest assured that Barça fans take their history – however mythological – very seriously. During the late 1990s I toured Spain in a bus filled with one of FC Barcelona's most radical groups of fans. They called themselves the *Almogavers*. Their T-shirts and banners depicted medieval knights in full armour. So what was all this about, I asked Marc, the young secretary of the fan club. 'The *Almogavers* were Catalan soldiers of the thirteenth century (actually they were mercenaries for the King of Greece) who conquered the Mediterranean. They'd go into battle on foot, holding their swords, and fight off whole armies on horseback.'

Then Marc, together with some of his mates, broke into the Barça anthem, '*Tot el camp es un clam, som la gente blau-grana* . . .' (The whole stadium is a rallying cry, we are the people of red and blue), with its emphasis on the Barça colours, blue and red, the colours every club fanatic will insist are the colours of freedom. 'We want Barça to conquer Europe just like the *Almogavers*,' Marc tells me. He is holding a small banner bearing the words '*Barça i Catalunya, sempre al nostre cor*' (Barça and Catalonia, always in our hearts). 'That's what drives me. I've done so much for Barça, missed my exams, missed a whole year at college. You might say I'm fanatical. I like to consider myself someone who loves Barça with all my heart. If that's fanaticism, then I'm a fanatic.'

That such loyalty is often mixed up with a visceral dislike of Real Madrid has to do with the fact that long after Wilfred the Hairy and Columbus had been buried, things got far worse for Catalonia before they got better. First with the united kingdoms of Aragon and Castile moving the balance of political and economic power towards the centre, and then in 1714 when the Bourbon regime of King Philip V deprived the Catalans of their local parliament and other rights, such as the power to raise their own taxes.

And yet Catalonia was to prosper economically over the next two centuries, exporting wool and paper and embracing the industrial revolution before most of the rest of Spain, providing jobs for thousands of migrants from other regions and in effect subsidising the more backwards areas of the country. Catalonia came to look at the rest of Spain, and Madrid in particular, not only as arrogant and intolerant, but also ungrateful.

FC Barcelona drew its strength from troubled times, giving the region as a whole a necessary feeling of collective self-confidence. The collapse of the Spanish Empire with the loss of Cuba in 1898 fuelled Catalan nationalism. The birth of FC Barcelona at the start of the twentieth century gave it a role early on as a central focus of Catalan nationalism along with the re-emergence of a Catalan nationalist party, parliament and newspapers. 'Barcelona became one of the most vibrant and wealthiest cities in Europe, home to the artists Gaudi, Picasso,

Miró and Dali. Dali entered a competition sponsored by FC Barcelona, Miró painted a poster for the club – FC Barcelona was a crucial part of Catalonia's new-found optimism and prosperity,' enthused Ardal O'Hanlon.

It was all change, though, after the Spanish Civil War. In 1942, for all this show of public self-confidence, Spain was a country politically divided within itself. Catalonia was once again denied its local parliament, Castilian was once again imposed as an official language, and the Catalan flag was banned. But although the management of FC Barcelona was hand-picked by the regime, football provided an escape valve for suppressed emotions.

While a majority of Spanish football clubs were purged of political dissidents after the Spanish Civil War, and found themselves with little option but to recruit new members supportive of the new regime, FC Barcelona managed to preserve an identity as a Catalan institution. The official post-war newsreels show the club's stadium Les Corts as a crowded theatre of orderly entertainment, with no anti-regime flags or slogans or chants. But beneath the apparent conformity, a sense of resentment, revenge and resistance persisted.

In 1947 Gregorio Lopez Raimundo, the head of the Catalan Communist Party, returned secretly from exile in France with a false passport and started going to Les Corts, both as a fan and a political militant. He not only enjoyed the football, but also felt more protected from persecution in the stadium than he did on any street corner in Barcelona.

As he told me many years later when I interviewed him about his years in clandestinity: 'Out in the city, fascism was very visible – the names of the streets, the Falangist crests, the portraits of Franco, the flags. But in the stadium you were among the masses and I felt – maybe I was imagining it, but I felt it all the same – that everyone around me was really anti-Fascist deep down, at least in the stands. Maybe things were a little different where people were sitting; the club management was pro-regime, hand-picked no doubt during the early Franco years, but not the fans; they identified themselves with a democratic Catalonia.'

It was not until 1968, a year marking revolution in large swathes of the world, that FC Barcelona's new president Narcis de Carreras took it upon himself to give the club's marketing department a dream motto: *Barça es mes que un club* (Barça is more than just a club). In other words, it could not be compared to any other football club, let alone Real Madrid, because it represented so much more in political, cultural, social terms. Catalans might have been divided over exactly what Catalonia meant – was it a region or a nation? But from now there could be no doubt about Barça. As Bobby Robson, one of its managers, would later tell me: 'Barcelona is a nation without a state, and Barça is its army.'

The politics of Real Madrid do not lend themselves so easily to mottos or manifestos. One of Spanish football's most literate commentators, the Argentine-born former Real Madrid player and manager Jorge Valdano – no old Francoist he – once tried to explain this to me: 'Real Madrid is a team that only thinks in football terms, not political or nationalistic ones . . . I think that is a huge advantage it has over FC Barcelona, which thinks too much in political terms. The worst thing you can do to a football player is to give an excuse to justify his frustration.'

Undoubtedly the 1950s were Real Madrid's golden years when everyone seemed happy, at least in the club. Barça fans console themselves to this day by claiming that one of Real's major stars, Alfredo Di Stéfano, was 'stolen' by their rival in a questionable transfer deal that had a helping hand from the Spanish state. But the legend rests with Real Madrid as the first Spanish club not only to become champions of Europe but to subsequently hang on to the title over several seasons. To Real Madrid fans, old and young, it was Di Stéfano who gave them a sense of identity during a period of history when Spain remained relatively isolated in the world. He came to personify success on a global scale, something that during the 1950s could not be said of any Spanish company, let alone Franco. Di Stéfano, long retired, was asked once by Inocencio Arias, a former Real Madrid director and personal friend, what he thought defined the Real Madrid fan: 'It wants the team to fight . . . it wants it to win . . . but it wants it to win first and then to play.'

During our stay in Barcelona Ardal and I were not short of Catalans prepared to simply dismiss Real Madrid as Franco's team. But Real Madrid fans who belonged to the first generation to be born after the Spanish Civil War and who did not share their parents pro-Franco inclinations feel insulted by this, even more so now that Spain has been a democracy for a while.

In a short memoir published in the Spanish newspaper *El Pais* in 1994, the novelist Javier Marías recalls becoming a Real Madrid fan in 1957, aged six, despite belonging to a group of friends many of whose fathers, like his own, were all anti-Franco.

The enthusiasm I felt for Real Madrid was mainly provoked by one man and he was called Di Stéfano – no doubt. But there was something else – Madrid was a club that neither cheated nor had fear and was blessed with drama. These may seem trivial matters, but in the city of my childhood everything else seemed to lack any worth and only designed to make you fear and everything was sordid rather than dramatic. Real Madrid was like an oasis, like the cinema on Saturday.

But if Real Madrid provided a kind of sanctuary to those who did not consider themselves part of the Franco regime, it has tolerated, long after Franco's demise, among its supporters those of a more politically extreme bent. I remember arriving at Munich airport some years back with a group of Real Madrid fans and seeing a section of them arrested by the police under German's anti-Nazi laws. On another occasion I decided to join a small group of Barça fans at the Bernabéu. As we arrived at the Real Madrid stadium our small group of Barça fans had to run the gauntlet. The *Utra Surs* were waiting with their usual vocabulary of racist abuse against black FC Barcelona players and against Catalonia generally.

Nonetheless, it's no use pointing, as Marías and others do, to the fact that prior to Di Stéfano, Franco ruled the country and Real Madrid never won a domestic championship, let alone an international one, as evidence that this was not the regime's team – that there was no political fix.

The case for the prosecution against football 'collaborators', even of Marías's 'liberal' ilk, collected enough evidence to confirm generations of Barça fans in their prejudice. Real Madrid's 'black book', or its history according to its Catalan nationalist detractors, notes just how trusted Real Madrid was as an ally by the Franco regime when it played in Venezuela representing Spain in an international club tournament in 1952. 'The behaviour of Real Madrid from directors through to players has been irreproachable in all aspects and they have left us with an unsurpassable impression of impeccable sporting good manners and patriotism,' commented the official state bulletin at the end of the tournament.

No such assurance could be given to FC Barcelona, a club whose loyalty to the regime could never be taken for granted as long as there was a simmering undercurrent of Catalan nationalism that fed on feelings of injustice, resentment and envy.

In the 1950s, years during which the Spanish national squad continued to underachieve and Spain remained relatively isolated internationally, Real Madrid, much to the chagrin of Barça supporters, helped promote an image of Spanish success overseas. Santiago Bernabéu's club in effect converted itself, together with emigration and oranges, into Franco's most important export. And because this was a period that saw the expansion of televised football across borders, it put Real Madrid firmly on the map as *the* representative of Spanish football at its best, with its mixture of foreign stars and home-grown talent playing creative, offensive football in a way no other club in the world could match.

The reputation Real Madrid built up beyond Spain's borders was already apparent in the 1955–56 season, which marked the inauguration of a European Cup tournament that would prove its potential not only to get around the diplomatic barriers of the Cold War but also to raise the international profile of major clubs and their revenue-raising capacity. On the eve of the tournament's first final in Paris, the Spanish Embassy in the French capital hosted a reception which attracted an impressive guest list from the French sporting world as well as senior representatives from international bodies like FIFA and the IOC. It was the best-attended reception the embassy had hosted since the days of the Spanish Republican government prior to the Civil War.

In the season before, FC Barcelona, with Kubala as its star, came to Paris and against Nice won the Copa Latina. But this tournament was restricted to southern Europe's clubs and lacked pedigree in the wider football establishment. It was the European Cup, the dreamchild of Gabriel Hanot, a former French international and the editor of the widely respected sports daily *L'Equipe*, that established itself as the most prized trophy in world club football, setting a marker for a new age in which football became a matter of celebrity as much as success. The legend of Real Madrid as the most successful sporting institution in the world is bound up with it because no other institution can claim to have won it so many times – five successive championship victories between 1956 and 1960.

Such a record has been absorbed by Barça fans over the years, nurturing their loyalty rather than diminishing it, and ensuring that the rivalry between FC Barcelona and Real Madrid not only strengthens but becomes more intense as each new encounter approaches. In 2006, four days before *El Gran Clásico*, Ardal O'Hanlon signed up as a member of Barça football club. He called it the proudest day of his life, as good as, probably better than, the day he got his first Irish passport.

Johan Cruyff – Dutch international and FC Barcelona star player

22

The Death of Franco

On Thursday 20 November 1975, Spain's prime minister Carlos Arias Navarro tearfully announced the death of General Francisco Franco, the man who had cast a long shadow over the nation's destiny for four decades, and influenced every aspect of Spanish life, not least football.

Vicente Marco, a presenter with the then hugely popular radio programme *Carrusel Deportivo* (The Sport Carousel), told his listeners that players in all La Liga matches would wear black armbands as a sign of mourning and respect. 'They will pay tribute to the late head of state, Francisco Franco, and a landmark in our history who will be a point of reference from now onwards. Fans and players will pray an Our Father together in his memory.'

Before dying, Franco had decided to formalise the succession of the Bourbon dynasty – out of power since 1931 – and decreed that his successor as head of state would be Prince Juan Carlos, the grandson of King Alfonso XIII. But the hopes of die-hard Francoist loyalists that the young prince would meekly follow in Franco's footsteps proved remarkably short-sighted. As the new King of Spain, Juan Carlos would convert into a constitutional monarch and oversee the restoration of democracy for the first time since before the Spanish Civil War. While the expectation of reform of the Spanish state – with a restoration of autonomy to the regions – stirred enduring rivalries, Spanish football was now set to evolve within the context of profound political and social liberalisation.

When Franco died, the season of La Liga was in its tenth week. Earlier in the month Real Madrid, coached by the Montenegran Miljan Miljanić, had progressed into the quarter-finals of the European Cup after beating Derby County 6–5 on aggregate in the second round. Miljanić was not to every Real Madrid fan's taste because of his tendency to focus on defending rather than attacking. But as long as the team went on winning, he had a job. Madrid had secured its lead at the top of the table, ahead of Hércules, Athletic Bilbao, Atlético Madrid and FC Barcelona after a controversial away victory over newly promoted Sevilla at the Sánchez Pizjuán stadium. Real Madrid's German midfielder Paul Breitner scored a goal through a hole in the side of the Sevilla net. The referee claimed it was a straightforward goal. After a sports newspaper published a photograph showing the ball indeed entering through the net, the home crowd declared it the most scandalous phantom goal in history.

On the Sunday following the death of Franco, Real Madrid and Zaragoza players wore their armbands as they faced each other in the Bernabéu. In the Basque Country and Catalonia not all players similarly mourned. While some Franco loyalists had wanted La Liga to be temporarily suspended as a further sign of respect towards the old dictator, King Juan Carlos decreed the games should go ahead. It was his way of infusing a sense of normality among the masses but also a sign that the young king was his own man.

Spanish football, meanwhile, adapted itself to the changing political environment with remarkable ease, not least in Real Madrid, the club whose enemies had always tarnished them with the brush of collaboration with the Franco regime. One of the most respected Real Madrid players was Vicente Del Bosque, who had joined the first team five years earlier. He had earned a reputation as a playmaker in midfield. Del Bosque was also a discreet anti-Francoist. Born in 1950, he had grown up amid memories of his family suffering as a result of being on the losing side of the Civil War. Del Bosque's father was a Republican railway clerk who had served a prison sentence under Franco for his political beliefs.

'Inside the club we all took the news of Franco's death pretty calmly. We were, after all, politically independent,' Del Bosque told me many years later, the first time we met. 'I remember that in those days everyone in Spain was talking about whether there was going to be *rupture* or *reforma* (a total break from the past or just an orderly reform); fortunately we took a path of reform that allowed us to live our lives normally.'

Del Bosque had willed himself to believe in football's potential to break through the barriers of politics. He always disapproved of the caricature of Real Madrid as 'Franco's team'. He believed that even in the Franco years, Real Madrid had fans of all political tendencies but with a common belief that the club, along with the Spanish national team, could and should play the best football in the world. When Santiago Bernabéu, the club's long-serving president and a Francoist civil war veteran, died in June 1978, Del Bosque was one of the players that honoured his contribution to the game by carrying his coffin. Bernabéu outlived Franco by nearly three years. But while statues of Franco and street signs named after him were torn down, the stadium Bernabéu built would remain named after him, an enduring monument to one of the great figures of Spanish football.

The death of Franco produced mixed emotions, none more so than in Catalonia, a region that had grown economically during the regime while having its political and cultural identity repressed. At FC Barcelona, the club president Agustin Montal sent three telegrams to Madrid. One to Franco's private office, expressing 'sadness at the irreplaceable loss of the Head of State'; a second to Franco's widow, Doña Carmen Polo de Franco, and her family, 'with our most heartfelt condolence'; the third, to Franco's appointed successor King Juan Carlos, declaring 'the personal loyalty of our club, and the hope of a future of peaceful and democratic coexistence represented by your Royal Highness'.

At FC Barcelona there was a touch of tragicomedy the day Franco died. 'Gentlemen, the *Caudillo* (leader) is dead,' the concierge announced solemnly after interrupting a meeting Montal was having with some of his senior officials. Among others present was Jaume Rosell, the club secretary and father of a future club president Sandro, and he provided me with his eye-witness account. 'There were two reactions: those who said, "Let's open a bottle of *cava*," and the others who stayed silent and were evidently scared shitless, (given their Francoist tendencies). Among the latter was a director who said he didn't feel well and who went home. Poor guy, it seems the news gave him a stomach upset. Among the happier reactions was that of his brother – he was a communist!'

Later, after the main meeting had dispersed, Rosell stayed behind with the chief secretary of the club, Joan Granados. Alone in Montal's room, they found their eyes focusing on a bust of Franco that was perched high on a shelf. Instinctively, Granados got up on a chair, picked up the bust and threw it across the room at Rosell. By accident Franco nearly hit him on the head, before striking the ground and shattering into little bits. Rosell had feared it might be made of bronze. In fact it was made of plaster. He exclaimed, 'Fuck me, we thought this was so solid that it could never break, and now it turns out it's nothing but shitty plaster!'

A few minutes later some Barça fans turned up. Rosell had an enduring memory of that moment. 'They were in a state of high excitement. We handed them some photographs of Franco that were hanging up in another room. Then we gave instructions for the removal of a sign that was in the stadium remembering the Francoist members of Barça who had fallen during the Civil war – "For Spain and for God", it stated. We put the sign in a box and took it down to the basement where we put it well out of the way, hidden from view, for it seemed to me that such a sentiment did not belong to the history of Barça, although I didn't think we should destroy it as other things were destroyed.'

By the time of Franco's death, the administration of FC Barcelona had come under the increasing influence of the Catalan nationalist movement, headed by Jordi Pujol. The two men who had toyed with Franco's bust before seeing it shatter – Rosell and Granados – were active members of Pujol's party Convergencia Democratica de Catalunya. And it was the bank which Pujol controlled – Banca Catalana – which helped finance one of the most important transfers in Spanish football history – that of the Dutchman Johan Cruyff – after the Spanish Football Federation lifted the ban on foreign players, allowing two per team, on 26 May 1973.

Cruyff was already something of a legend as a player with Ajax and the Dutch national team. It was under Ajax's coach Rinus Michels that Cruyff emerged as the star performer of what the Dutch called total football. The concept, which had seen earlier manifestations in South America, was one in which every player was supposed to have the technical and physical ability to interchange roles and positions at will. At its best, the system was supposed to have players in a seemingly effortless collective flow for most of the game: an exciting mixture of dribbling, first-touch passing and creatively executed goals, rather than long balls or kicks into touch.

The number 14 Cruyff was the personification of total football. While he might play centre-forward, he was often seen playing through the midfield or out on either wing, his ever-changing position on the pitch playing havoc with any conventional concept of defence or counterattack. A profile by a local Dutch journalist published in the 1970s noted: 'Wherever he plays, with his radius of action, his ability to run past defenders at speed, his inimitable movement, his hard shot with both feet, his running for every ball, his stamina and his sense of positioning, he makes defences despair . . . His greatest pleasure is playing beautiful football.' Another chronicler of Dutch football, David Winner, notes how the idea took hold that what Cruyff and the other players at Ajax were doing was something more than football. 'It was no longer men kicking a ball around a muddy field. It was something refined and intriguing. It was Art.'

On 18 August 1973 Cruyff was bought by FC Barcelona in

a record US $1m transfer – the highest price ever paid at that time by the Catalan club for any player. The club had as its coach Rinus Michels, the fellow Dutchman Cruyff would describe as his 'first and only football master'. The key deal maker was Armando Caraben, an economist and lawyer who was then serving as the FC Barcelona secretary. Married to the Dutch writer Marjolijn van der Meer who he had met one summer as a student in the Costa Brava, Caraben had got to know Holland and its football well, and had established a friendship with Cruyff and his wife. A committed Catalan nationalist and opponent of the regime, Caraben saw a political opportunity. He gambled, correctly as it turned out, that the Dutchman's inspiration would increase Barça's popularity at a time of historic political change from dictatorship to democracy. Caraben had watched Cruyff play many times and was convinced not only of his goal-scoring abilities, but also his capacity to organise a team around his talent.

Cruyff's arrival in Barcelona fuelled a sense of huge expectation in Spanish football that mirrored the hopes that many Spaniards, not least Catalans, had of a better Spain post-Franco. An article in the magazine *Dicen* described Cruyff's coming as a key moment in the club's history, on a par with that of the arrival in the 1950s of the great Hungarian Kubala. It predicted a new period of glory. While Kubala came as a vehicle of Franco's anti-communist propaganda, Cruyff came from a European country that had pioneered some of the social freedoms and cultural innovations of the 1960s.

Fans were not disappointed. Cruyff electrified the Spanish league in his first season. He was dubbed *El Salvador* – the Saviour – lifting FC Barcelona from bottom of the table to top, thus making them La Liga champions for the first time since

1960. After Barça had easily crushed Granada early on in the season, the club magazine reported:

> Cruyff not only plays for the rest of the team, he makes the team play. His quality brings out the best in those other Barça players whose quality was never in doubt but who sometimes stumbled rather than show the true measure of their worth. The team has turned into a homogenous unit, full of ideas and at ease with itself. And what all this means is that football has begun to be fun again, it's recovered that special grace which makes it the favourite sport of the masses.

Michels as coach had concerns that Cruyff's diva status might demoralise his team-mates and there were rumours that Marcial was among those who resented suddenly being projected as mere appendices. But for every team colleague in whom Cruyff provoked envy, there were others who felt only admiration. As the Spanish international Charly Rexach told me: 'We all had our sense of pride that made us feel that we were as good as the next one and that meant that for a while Barça had a team that wanted to prove it could play football.'

FC Barcelona played some wonderful football that season and delivered where it most mattered, beating Real Madrid 5–0 in the Bernabéu, with two goals by Asensi, and one each by Cruyff, Juan Carlos and Sotil. Cruyff's goal was, well, pure Cruyff. Picking up the ball from just inside Real's half, on the turn, the Dutchman dribbled first with the uncluttered, floating speed of a gazelle, and then weaved in and out of the Real defence, his nimble frame turning at sharp angles, and then skipping effortlessly over a final desperate sliding tackle. Cruyff took the ball on his left foot, and then struck home, easily beating the goalkeeper.

The *New York Times* correspondent later wrote that Cruyff had done more for the spirit of the Catalan nation in ninety minutes than any politician had achieved in years of stifled struggle. A few days before the game Cruyff had gone to the Franco authorities and insisted that his newly born son be registered as Jordi, the Catalan for George and the local patron saint, in defiance of an official ruling that only Spanish/Castilian names could be used in official documents. 'It took me some time to understand what was happening politically in Spain although I realised soon enough how important the club was in Catalan terms,' Cruyff told me. Unwittingly, the birth of a son transformed itself into the Dutchman's first political act in Spain.

Following the death of Franco, there were other instances when Spanish football took on an even more blatant political symbolism. Cruyff and Iribar, as FC Barcelona and Athletic Bilbao captains respectively, led their teams out at Camp Nou. The stadium was bathed in the colours of the Catalan and Basque nationalist flags as the stadium united in giving the players a standing ovation. It was the run-up to 1977's free elections – the first to be held in over forty years. Iribar, who had played as a Spanish international during the Franco years, had by then nailed his colours to the cause of the Basque people, actively campaigning for the release of political prisoners.

On 5 December 1976, just over a year since the death of Franco, the Athletic captain Iribar and the captain of Real Sociedad Kortabarria walked out into a packed Atocha stadium in San Sebastián holding the banned Basque flag the Ikurriña. The flag had been smuggled into the stadium by Josean del la

Hoz Uranga, one of the Real Sociedad players, hidden in his kit bag. It was publicly displayed only after each captain had consulted with their teams in the dressing room and obtained unanimous approval.

Uranga recalled later:

We were all in Real Sociedad at the time native players who had come up through the youth team and we all had our concerns and feelings. The majority of us were Basque nationalists, with a few in favour of all-out independence from Spain. Democracy had yet to find a firm foundation and we were in a transition period with the Basque people demanding change . . . When we came out into the stadium with the flag it was a very emotional moment. There were a lot of people who cried. There were about 16,000 spectators in Atocha and the stadium erupted.

Such was the popular support for the Basque flag that the local police chief ordered his men not to intervene rather than provoke a riot of incalculable consequences. Times were changing anyway in Spain now that Franco was dead and the old die-hards of the regime were fighting a losing battle to keep the country under authoritarian rule.

In January 2001 I interviewed Iribar at Athletic's training ground of Lezama (named after the player who had been a boy refugee in the UK during the Civil War) in the highlands outside Bilbao. Much water had flowed under the Spanish political bridge over the previous twenty-five years. The years of terrorism by ETA in post-Franco Spain had fuelled deep divisions in the Basque Country. Iribar had long since retired from football and had been put in charge of 'institutional relations' by Athletic after his potato merchandising business had fallen on bad times. It was rumoured locally that a key contract to supply members of the security forces had been cancelled by the client on political grounds. Iribar remained a popular figure in Bilbao, but in Madrid he had made enemies because of his support for Basque nationalism.

'I am writing a book about Spanish football and trying to put it in a political, sociological context . . .' I began. Iribar interrupted, 'Well, I am telling you that here we talk about football and nothing else, exclusively about sport.' It was of course nonsense and we both knew it. Three months later the Spanish newspaper *El Pais* published an extensive conversation between Iribar and another Basque football legend, Real Sociedad's Roberto López Ufarte, who played the day the banned Ikurriña flag was brought out in Atocha stadium. As the two veterans walked along the beach of Zarautz, they pondered on the historic significance of that event. 'I think it marked an important step which helped a great deal the process towards the legalisation of the Ikurriña . . . the fact is that it was that derby between our two teams that had endured as my best football memory – and that is despite the fact that we (Athletic) lost 0–5!' Iribar recalled.

During our earlier encounter, Iribar remained cautious before opening up slightly when I told him that as a young journalist I had filmed that day in the Camp Nou when he and Cruyff had come out to a sea of Basque and Catalan flags. How had he felt?

'Well, the dictatorship had ended and we were in a transition towards democracy and there was a general expression of joy in the stadium that day, a real hunger for liberty on both sides so that the game became a reflection of all that was happening.

You could feel a real sense of happiness of being part of a democratic process and of winning freedom – you could feel it in the
stadium, in the streets . . .'

And yet for all the political euphoria and expectation of
change stimulated by the death of Franco, Spanish football
struggled to dominate internationally. The loss of hegemony of
Spanish clubs at European level reached its most striking
moment in April 1973 when Ajax, the reigning champions,
thrashed Bayern Munich before destroying Real Madrid in the
semi-finals of the European Cup. Ajax won 2–1 in Amsterdam
and faced a hostile 110,000 crowd for the return leg at the
Bernabéu. Gerrie Mühren scored in the first half to give Ajax a
1–0 lead. But it was Mühren's brilliant display in the second
half that drew a rare tribute from the massed host fans.

Mühren later spoke of how as a child, like so many fans
around the world, he had idolised the Real Madrid team of the
golden years and how it had always been his dream to play
good football against the Spanish champions. On that day in
the Bernabéu, Ajax and Real Madrid changed positions. As he
put it, 'Before that it was always the big Real Madrid and the
little Ajax – but when they saw me doing what I did, the balance
changed. The Real Madrid players were looking. They nearly
applauded. The stadium was standing up. It was the moment
Ajax took over.'

It was not just Real Madrid that bowed to greater opponents
in this period. Having failed to qualify for the 1974 World
Cup, the Spanish national team coached by Kubala reached the
quarter-finals of the 1976 European Championship before
losing on aggregate 1–3 to a strong West Germany. Returning
to the World Cup in Argentina in 1978, Spain failed to get
beyond the first-round group stage, although once again a

certain bad luck was blamed for Spain's underachievement. Spain lost 1–2 in a tougher than expected opening game with Austria. Next, when facing Brazil, the Spaniards kept level at 0–0 before the midfielder Julio Cardenosa, the Real Betis midfielder, was faced with an open goal and fluffed it. In their final group game Spain met Sweden needing a win to pressurise Brazil. Cardona this time partly made up for his earlier give-away with a good second-half performance while his team-mate, FC Barcelona's Asensi, another attacking midfielder, scored the winning goal. But it was not enough to go through to the next round, and Spain were eliminated.

In the aftermath of the 1978 World Cup, the country's two biggest clubs, FC Barcelona and Real Madrid, competed for supremacy in an increasingly charged political environment. Of the two it was Real Madrid that had change forced on it from within its own organisation rather sooner than it would have otherwise hoped. Change at Real Madrid tended to come slowly, with right-wing elements deeply entrenched in the club's administrative structure. The death of the long-ruling club president Santiago Bernabéu in June 1978, the year after Spain had celebrated its first post-Franco parliamentary elections, led to a carefully manipulated transfer of power to a 'steady-as-you-go' candidate, Luis de Carlos, another Francoist war veteran who had served the club loyally as its treasurer. De Carlos's deliberate strategy of administrative continuity, while in effect disengaging Real Madrid from the evolving political process, was relatively risk-proof as long as the club continued to be successful. Real's record during the seven years of his presidency was mixed, and fell short of the high benchmark set by the golden years. The club won two successive league championships in De Carlos's first two seasons at the helm, but then lost its dominance in La Liga as Basque football staged a revival. Athletic Bilbao and Real Sociedad shared four league titles between them, with another going to FC Barcelona.

Nonetheless, De Carlos had pledged that Real Madrid would regain its European crown under his presidency, so it was in an atmosphere of huge expectation that 30,000 of its fans descended on Paris's Parc des Princes stadium on 27 May 1981 to face Liverpool in the final of the European Cup. Real Madrid had not won the competition in fifteen years. Most fans dreamed of reliving that day, 13 May 1956, when the legendary Di Stéfano had led his team of superstars to victory in the European Cup, ushering in an extended period of unrivalled excellence in Spanish club football.

The 1981 final involved players of considerable stature on both sides. Liverpool had Graeme Souness, Alan Hansen and Kenny Dalgish. Real Madrid fielded their own English 'star' – Laurie Cunningham – along with German Uli Stielike and talented Spanish players like Carlos Santillana, Vicente Del Bosque and José Antonio Camacho. The side also included one of Spanish football's legends – the fast, highly skilful winger from Malaga, Juan Gomez González – popularly known as Juanito. The player had a spirited temperament – he was always associated with leading heoroic fight-backs by his team. During his ten years with the club (1977–87) it won five league championshoips, two Spanish Cups and two UEFA Cups. He never recovered psychologically or professionally from the five-year ban he received from UEFA in April 1987 for infamously stamping on the head of Bayern Munich's Matthäus in a European Cup match. He retired the following year and was killed in a car crash in 1992, aged thirty-seven. Ever since then, in honour of the number 7 shirt Juanito wore, the seventh minute of every game Real Madrid play at the Bernabéu is marked by the radical *Ultra Surs* with the commemorative cry: '*Illa illa illa, Juanito maravilla*' (roughly translated: 'Hey, hey, hey, Juanito is simply great').

The 1981 Real Madrid–Liverpool encounter proved an anticlimax, entering the collective memory of die-hard *Madridistas* as the 'final of fear', with each side more concerned with defending rather than scoring goals. Liverpool won 1–0 thanks to a goal by Alan Kennedy. 'It was a pity that we lost but to have got that far was quite an achievement for the team we had then,' recalled Del Bosque many years later. In the aftermath of the 1981 European Cup final, the infamous neo-fascist hooligan brigade the *Ultra Surs* emerged as a distinct pressure group within Spanish football, named because they occupied the south stands of the Bernabéu while delivering provocative, often abusive, chants against visitors, particularly against Basque teams and FC Barcelona, and their city rivals Atlético Madrid, each of whom also had their contingent of hard-core fans.

The genesis of the *Ultra Surs* is disputed to this day, even by its own members. One told me that it was the assault that some Real Madrid fans, including their wives, had suffered at the hands of Liverpool thugs in the 1981 final. 'There were a few among the younger Real Madrid supporters who saw what happened, and how Spaniards reacted, and vowed from thereon to never surrender again, and be prepared if necessary to be as violent as the English.' But other *Ultra Sur* veterans recall an earlier encounter with West Ham fans, and other matches against Italian clubs.

The imitation of foreign cultures along with a rebellion against the more orderly traditional forms of club support organisations imposed by old hierarchies – the fan clubs known as the *peñas* – was perhaps an inevitable consequence of Spain's transition from dictatorship to democracy. The *Ultra Surs* based in the capital of Spain, associated as they were with Spain's most successful club, had the largest following among the radical Spanish fans and yet represented a mish-mash of political and social backgrounds. They included neo-Nazis and skinheads, many of them unemployed and united by a common attitude of generational rebellion and inherited prejudice against rival clubs, in particular, although not exclusively. As Fernando Carreno, a Spanish journalist who has investigated the darker side of Real Madrid, points out: 'The *Ultra Surs* are neo-fascist because although their space is theoretically open to anyone according to the basic requirement that he is a fervent Madrid supporter, in reality anyone who is not politically and socially to the right of Genghis Khan stands to have a bad time in their midst.'

Other significicant radicalised elements would grow in clubs like Rayo Vallecano associated with post-war industrial neigh-bourhoods (anarchists), and towns with a reputation for militant politics like Pamplona in Navarre (considered by some of its inhabitants as belonging to the Basque nation) where Osasuna *ultras* picked up the flag of radical left-wing Basque separatism in response to the more conservative Basque nationalist supporters of Athletic Bilbao. Similarly in the Catalan capital, FC Barcelona saw the emergence within its stadium of the *boixos nois*, who came to be associated with a violent expression of Catalan nation-alism in contrast to what they perceive as the right-wing Spanish followers of Espanyol, the *Brigadas Blanquiazules*.

These radical fans, together with fan clubs across the coun-try, developed in post-Franco Spain around long-standing rivalries between clubs and the resurgent regional standard-bearers. By contrast the relative lack of popular support for Spain's national team reflected the absence of an agreed national identity given the continuing and unresolved political tensions between Madrid and the regions. It was also the inevitable consequence of the poor performance of the national squad.

One of the consequences of the Franco period – its cultural insularity and socio-economic backwardness, including poor communications and infrastructure – meant the absence of a critical mass of fans prepared and able to travel to away games. While this was common to both club football and national football, it was particularly pronounced in the low numbers that traditionally accompanied the national team, in striking contrast to other European countries.

Spanish club football rivalries intensified as Spain's nascent democracy swam in troubled waters. In February 1981, the country survived an attempted extreme right-wing military coup.

Spain was being governed by a caretaker prime minister, the centre-right Leopoldo Calvo Sotelo, in the lead-up to fresh elections when it hosted the 1982 World Cup. The tournament, played as it was across stadiums in different regions of Spain, should have provided a showcase for the still relatively young democratic state, and might have galvanised a larger measure of support had it not turned into a national embarrassment, on and off the pitch. The gods seemed set against Spain from the moment the draw held in Madrid turned to farce. Scarcely had FIFA president João Havelange praised the hosts for taking on the challenge of organising the biggest football tournament 'in the heroic spirit of Don Quixote' when the revolving drums from which the balls representing each team were supposed to be drawn got stuck. Widespread complaints about tickets and hotel arrangements followed, as did allegations – in the opening games – that the cards, including refereeing, might be stacked so as to ensure that Spain progressed towards the final.

Questions about the probity of referees were not new in the world of football. But in Spain it had developed almost into a national pastime. The advent of democracy and the lifting of censorship fuelled an acrimonious debate about the extent to which Real Madrid's success during the Franco years and beyond could be partly explained by biased refereeing. It was Sporting Gijón fans that in 1979 had responded to the expulsion of one of its players in a game against Real Madrid with cries of '*Asi, Asi gana el Madrid*' ('That is how Madrid wins'). It was a cry that would echo across the stands of other stadiums in subsequent seasons. In fact Real Madrid's success was generally achieved by good teams, not bent referees, and it never enjoyed a monopoly of championship titles that might have been the case had they been able to count on friendly referees. There were numerous examples of critical decisions that had gone against the club.

Unquestionably during the years of the dictatorship, anger against referees was an escape valve, a diversion, a necessary counterpoint within the stadium to the political suppression outside it. Even after Franco died the referee remained a convenient target for abuse, as old football rivalries were kept alive, and the hopes Spaniards had for their democracy gave way, on occasions, to disillusionment, on and off the field.

In the 1982 World Cup held in Spain, the host nation's squad was of such poor quality in football terms that it had to seek the help of referees simply to survive. This became evident in the opening game Spain played against Honduras in Valencia, a town with a club named after it that, while never achieving anywhere near the international respect of Real Madrid and FC Barcelona, had during the 1950s and 1970s drawn on the talents of foreign stars like the Argentine Mario Kempes, Dutchmen Faas Wilkes and Johnny Rep, and the Austrian Kurt Jara to produce some exciting football.

Four times La Liga champions by 1971, Valencia went on to win the Copa del Rey in the 1978–79 season, and then to win its second international trophy the following year, beating Arsenal in the final of the European Cup Winners' Cup.

The people of Valencia were used to watching class football. But what they got instead from the Spanish team was a performance worthy of a village scrap from a team always rumoured to be in a state of permanent dysfunctionality from the moment they entered the dressing room. Conceding a seventh-minute goal, the Spaniards struggled against the unrated Hondurans, and ended up resorting to diving and appealing for penalties. Eventually they were awarded a disputed one, which allowed them to secure a draw without any honour.

In the next match, it was again mainly thanks to a referee that Spain prevailed, this time with another controversial penalty (awarded for a cynical foul committed on Juanito, but outside the box) helping them to an unimpressive 2–1 victory against Yugoslavia.

Spain then returned to Valencia only to be beaten by Northern Ireland thanks to a goal by Gerry Armstrong. The Irish won considerable plaudits from the international media, overcoming all the odds – sweltering Mediterranean heat, a hostile crowd, rough tackling by the Spanish, and a referee that did them no favours. As for Armstrong, he was nicknamed 'Don quick quote' for the ease with which he dealt with the press requests for comments. He was destined to eventually become a Spanish football pundit with Sky TV after a career that included playing with Real Mallorca.

Spain managed to progress through to the next round, second in its group, behind Northern Ireland but just ahead of Yugoslavia on goals scored. But they ended up bottom of their next group after losing 1–2 to West Germany and drawing 0–0 with England, in the Santiago Bernabéu stadium of all places.

The former Real Madrid player who had coached the team, José Santamaria, was sacked after shouldering the blame for a lacklustre performance by his players. The debacle sparked a national debate about the nature and future direction of Spanish football, nowhere more so than at Real Madrid, a club that had belatedly acclimatised to the new democracy.

Raul – Spanish international and Real Madrid star player

23

The Vulture Squad and Raul

In late October 2010, some 2,000 fans gathered in the Salto del Caballo, a municipal stadium (capacity 5,000) on the outskirts of the once imperial Spanish city of Toledo, to watch a charity match between a team of Real Madrid veterans and the local football club.

Some well-known Madrid stars who had long retired from the game muscled in, more for fun than hard work, but with a hint of strutting arrogance, like privileged overgrown schoolboys. Their opponents were a rag-tag collective of physically rather less healthy and underpaid individuals, downtrodden representatives of CD Toledo, a club that had never got beyond the Third Division since joining the Spanish league after the Civil War.

Amid the beer paunches and ruddy faces, Real Madrid's Emilio Butragueño, a small trim figure with the chiselled handsomeness of a middle-aged Robert Redford, directed play from midfield with distinction, his quick and accurate passing and positioning of the ball, as well as killer instinct near the goal, proving a constant threat to the defence of the amateur hosts, and an inspiration to the veterans and onlookers alike.

Football fans in Toledo, like much of the country, were still basking in the memory of Spain's recent World Cup win, and the crowd had come in no mood to see a simple kick-around. Thanks to Butragueño's enduring skills and work ethos, they were treated to an entertaining spectacle well worth the money they had given to the Catholic charity Caritas. Butragueño's grace on the field, his deft touch with the ball and intelligent positioning off it, was watched by a predominantly young crowd of reverential fans. Butragueño's gentle artistry contrasted with the imposing architectural severity of the nearby Alcazar, the military museum – a former barracks – that during the 1930s had been the setting for one of the bloodiest encounters of the Civil War. Spain, like its football, had entered the modern era. The veterans beat Toledo 9–0.

My friend Inocencio 'Chencho' Arias, a Spanish diplomat and Real Madrid fanatic, tried, even in his busiest periods as a government official based in Madrid during Butragueño's heyday in the 1980s, to see every game in which he played. 'It was like following a famous matador – you had to hurry and see Butragueño for fear that an injury, like a bull's goring, might deprive you of relishing his art forever,' said Chencho. 'He played four and a half good years but he had something few players in the world have – an ability to play with the ball in a very reduced area, which electrified the fans. In my case he'd make me cry with sheer emotion.'

The Dutch international Leo Beenhakker, who managed the great Real Madrid team of the late 1980s, once praised what he called the ruthless winning streak he encountered in Spanish football compared to the creative yet underachieving school of Dutch football favoured by Cruyff and others. As he told David Winner:

> Every Dutchman has an opinion about everything. When you go to a hotel with the Dutch, one player says, 'Hey, it's too big', and the other says, 'It's too small', 'It's too hot', 'It's too cold', 'It's too . . .' We are busy with everything, ev-er-y-thing! But when I went to a hotel with a Spanish team – and they're all big stars, Hugo Sanchez, Butragueño, Gordillo, Michel, Camacho, Santillana, Juanito, great players – they come and it's: 'OK, this is fine. Where's my room? OK. Bye.' They sit quietly and they don't talk about the bus, and about the driver and the driver's wife. No! Come on! They think: 'We are here to play a football match. We play and we kill them. And then we go home.' That's the difference.

Beenhakker was speaking ten years before *La Roja* may have suggested a different thesis. He was right at the time – up to a point. That generation of Real Madrid players expressed the spirit of *La Furia* at its most effective. But to watch *El Buitre* (the vulture) play for Real Madrid at his peak was to experience the excitement of a new generation of players full of creative ideas. They were a mirror image of the outpouring of new cinema, theatre, art and media during Spain's transition to democracy – the so-called cultural *Movida* or 'Movement' – which represented a liberation of mind and body from many of the taboos imposed by the Franco regime. Was there a connection between the football and the cultural 'revolution'? Yes, in football terms, it meant style and spirit, as well as success. Leo Beenhakker may have believed in aggressive attacking football but he was no Captain Villalonga clutching a military manual. *La Furia* had entered the modern era.

To watch *El Buitre* – nicknamed this because of his scavenging instinct in most parts of the park, but particularly when the goal was in sight – was to follow his swerves and acceleration through defenders, his explosive speed inside the penalty box, an ability to reach, in a split second or two, a place where you least expected him, and to create a goal out of nothing. As well as knowing how to exploit a good pass from a colleague, he had an ability mercilessly to make good use of a loose ball. Other people's mistakes were among his favourite pickings. He forged the core of an inspirational football quintet, named after him as the *Quinta del Buitre* (The Vulture Squad). The four others were Manuel Sanchis, Rafael Martin Vázquez, Miguel González Michel and Pardeza .

As Sanchis told me: 'We were young guys from Madrid who shared a similar view on how football should be played – we wanted it to be bold and attacking – and we saw ourselves as part of what was happening in Spain more widely at the time, part of a generation that wanted change, that was prepared to take risks.'

It was the mid-1980s. The first socialist government in Spain in more than half a century was reaching the end of its first term, and was about to be re-elected on a manifesto of deepening democratic and social reform based around the country's protracted admission into the European Community. During the late 1970s the arrival of Johan Cruyff as a player had raised FC Barcelona's profile and popularity, making it *the* cool club, football at its most creative and bold when Barcelona itself was enjoying a major cultural revival. In May 1979, FC Barcelona won the European Cup Winners' Cup, beating Fortuna

Dusseldorf 4–3. By contrast Real Madrid had dragged its feet culturally and socially, with the Bernabéu stadium for a while turning as grey in spirit as the concrete slabs that supported its structures. Worse, between 1982 and 1984, with the Bernabéu still tainted as the stadium where Spain lost the World Cup, Real Madrid was in danger of making its reputation for invincibility look like a bad joke. The old legend Di Stéfano survived just two seasons before being sacked as Real Madrid coach when the club finished runner-up in the league championship but failed to win any trophies.

A new post-war generation of Real Madrid fans who had watched Di Stéfano play as young boys had grown up disillusioned with the club's inability to repeat those glory days and to suffer instead the humiliation of seeing Barça lay claim to being more in step with the country's overwhelming desire for change. Then, in May 1985, Real Madrid caught up with Spanish society and appointed as president of the Spanish 'White House' Ramon Mendoza, three years after his candidacy had been rejected by the club's old guard.

Mendoza, a controversial businessman, blamed his earlier defeat on dubious tactics employed by a self-serving conservative clique within the club and their right-wing political allies. They included leaks to the media, emanating from Spanish intelligence sources, suggesting that he had been employed as a Russian spy by the KBG while trading with the Soviet Union during the latter years of the Franco regime, and allegations that he at one point helped finance the Spanish Communist Party. Britain's MI6 and the USA's CIA shared suspicions about Mendoza's political links at a time when Spain was settling in as a relatively young member of NATO. What is certainly true is that Mendoza shared a drink with the legendary communist veteran firebrand of the Spanish Civil War, *La Pasionaria*, while she was in exile in Moscow and helped publish the Spanish translation of the Soviet president Leonid Brezhnev's memoirs.

And yet Mendoza's buffoonery was perhaps best epitomised by his self-description as a 'political independent with a full belly'. Certainly his reputation as a political opportunist may provide an explanation as to how he managed eventually to take power at Real Madrid. Once in the hot seat he continued to make some questionable allies. For example he openly courted Madrid's hooligan pack – the *Ultra Surs* – finding in FC Barcelona's president Núñez a willing sparring partner who was only too happy to stir up the antagonism between the two clubs. On one occasion Mendoza accompanied a group of *Ultra Surs* to Barajas airport in Madrid, to greet a Real Madrid team after a game against Barça. President and fans together chanted abuse at Catalonia.

Mendoza never quite fulfilled his dream of enjoying the international high profile of his two great friends, the Italians Silvio Berlusconi and Gianni Agnelli who so skilfully exploited their political, business, media and football interests to forge, for many years, an unrivalled power base, at least in their own country. But the fact that Mendoza's hair, while silvery grey, was on the long side, that he dressed in flashy jackets without a tie, and liked fast cars, intelligent women and partying, was for a while a most suitable and influential addition to a new cult of dazzling celebrity spawned by the power-bloated socialist government. More importantly, he was appointed on a pledge to reverse the declining fortunes of Real Madrid.

Mendoza's most positive legacy is that under his presidency the *Quinta del Buitre* – the vulture squad of young Spanish players led by Butragueño – was allowed to flourish from its early beginnings in the club's youth teams (even if he may have been motivated by a need to save money on expensive foreign players). *La Quinta* became hugely popular for a while, drawing together players of different personality and background, as well as undoubted talent. Such was the case of the agile Mexican-born Hugo Sanchez, who coined the phrase *Quinta de los Machos* – the virile squad – just to remind the fans that Spanish football had not abandoned *La Furia*. Sanchez relished provoking opposition defenders and goalkeepers as well as their fans, an attitude that won him the fervent support of the *Ultra Surs*.

For years Real Madrid had lacked what its rival FC Barcelona seemed to have built from early times into its DNA: a sense of itself, its history, its place in society, its style of football that could puncture the myth perpetuated by its enemies that it was a club that owed its claim to greatness and its popularity to Franco. Only after Franco died did the club begin to develop a counter-narrative capable of reaching out to a broader fan base, one that not only took pride in the football achievements of the past in a way that depoliticised them but also laid claim to an enduring and privileged presence in the heart and soul of Spanish football.

Emilio Butragueño had passed his peak when Raul González – popularly known as simply Raul – another Spanish star, rose in his footsteps. Raul was born in Madrid in 1977, two years after David Beckham was born in Leytonstone, and seven years before Fernando Torres was born in Fuenlabrada, Madrid. Raul played as a junior with Atlético Madrid before moving to Real Madrid in 1992 aged fifteen. At the time Cruyff's FC Barcelona was the team everyone wanted to watch in Spain.

Raul contributed to Real Madrid's greatness, and became a pivotal figure in the national squad just as *El Buitre* had been. What separated the two stars was temperament and circumstances. Of the many tributes that have been paid to Butragueño over the years, few have been as eloquent as that made by his team-mate Michel, part of a group of Spanish players that in their heyday were as loyally supportive as a band of brothers. 'His talent lay in intuition, in the always intelligent spark of his play . . . His time was perfectly structured. The ball didn't surround him day and night. He found it quite easy to disconnect from the sound of football, he was untroubled by the media . . . Perhaps there were people who would have liked to have seen him more involved in his profession, but Emilio was genuine and unique. He had his own personal vision of what football should be.'

While *El Buitre* was infused with Zen, Raul sweated his shirt like a fundamentalist. While *El Buitre* felt himself one more of a team, Raul took his role of captaincy very seriously – too seriously in the eyes of some of his team-mates. They found him *pesado*, hard work. He provoked confrontations and simmering resentments in the dressing room. These became more acute at Real Madrid with the imposition by club president Florentino Perez of his *galactico* model, yearly superstar foreign signings and endless managerial changes that led to clashes of egos and fuelled resentment among the aspiring home-grown talent.

Part of Raul's problem was that he was a very traditional Spanish kid who at Real Madrid landed in the deep end of football as a global money-spinning enterprise with its sponsorship deals and endless media events.

It takes a thick skin and a steady mind to survive in a football environment where Spain's two biggest clubs have two mass-circulation sports dailies printing up to ten or more pages on each of them every day. Add to that the coverage in TV, radio and other broadsheets and it's constant judgement day. Raul functioned, but in way that denied him *El Buitre*'s popularity.

In June 2002 Raul's record at club level among the players attending the World Cup in Japan and South Korea marked him out as a special case. Turning twenty-six years old, Raul had won three European Cups, two Spanish championships, and had scored more goals than any other player in the Champions League and for the Spanish national side. A profile of him at the time by author and journalist Simon Kuper asserted, now that *El Buitre* had long retired, that at the highest level of the game there was no more proven match-winner than Raul, who 'may confidently be expected to keep performing the way he is now, or better, for another five or six years'.

Kuper wrote: 'If there is any love or loyalty behind those eyes (of Raul) it is only his inner circle of family and one or two friends who know about it. Otherwise he is humourless, pitiless, calculating and ferociously single-minded. Think Al Pacino in *The Godfather*. The one who systematically annihilates his enemies as his child is being baptised. That's Raul.'

My fanatical Real Madrid friend Chencho Arias put it somewhat differently. 'He had balls, he played his heart out, and surprised people with his devil's trickery.'

Raul scored his first goal for Real Madrid on 5 November 1994, one week after making his debut in the team, in a 4–2 derby win over Atlético. Over the next fifteen years he was to go from promising youngster to Real Madrid's joint top scorer of all time, along with Di Stéfano. Having played alongside and outlasted the likes of Zidane, Ronaldo, Figo, and Roberto Carlos at the Bernabéu, the number 7's status as a *Los Merengues* legend seemed beyond doubt.

Certainly there were moments destined to live long in the collective memory of Real Madrid fans: his part in May 1998 in ending the club's 32-year wait for another European Champions club title in the renamed Champions League as part of the team that beat Juventus in the final 1–0; the moment, celebrated to this day in the club's more militant fan clubs, when following a crucial equaliser against FC Barcelona he celebrated by lifting his finger to his lips and quite literally reducing the Camp Nou to a stunned silence; that same season when despite his club missing out on the La Liga title, he was crowned his country's Pichichi, or top scorer; the final goal he scored in his club's 3–0 Champions League victory in the all-Spanish Champions League final against Valencia in May 2000, when after receiving a long pass from Savio well inside his own half, he ran the length of the pitch before dribbling round the goalkeeper – not just any goalkeeper but Canizares, a Spanish international and among Europe's best – and stroked the ball into the net. Five weeks earlier, in the second leg of the quarter-final against Manchester United, Raul, still aged only twenty-three, had lit up the night at Old Trafford with a brace of briiliant goals, earning from Alex Ferguson the rare accolade of 'the best player in the world'. Two seasons later, in 2002, Raul was one of the goal-scorers in Real Madrid's 2–1 victory over Bayer Leverkusen, the club's ninth European Cup success and a new record.

Raul's reputation had grown as a proven match-winner. He had the ability to turn a game around thanks to his rock-hard single-mindedness and what Jorge Valdano called his 'insolent self-belief', qualities he employed with the sole purpose of winning.

To his most loyal fans, who saw the true native Spanish Real

Madrid player as the personification of the traditional values of Spanish nationhood, Raul was totemic and thus untouchable. When the player celebrated sweet moments of conquest like in the victory over Valencia in the Champions League in Paris, he did so by taking a bullfighter's cape to show that he was both a *matador* and a *torero,* a killer and fighter.

And yet in October 2007, in a season during which he captained Real Madrid to a league title, thus ending a three-year major trophy drought, he was dropped from the national squad just before a game that could make or break Spain's qualification for the European Championships.

In a thirteen-year career, Raul had won five league titles, three European Cups and two Pichichi awards, but he was no different from any other Spanish player in that during this time he had never won anything with Spain. This fact divided Spanish fans between pro- and anti-*Raulistas,* a debate which for a while seemed as irreconcilable and destructive as that which had led the country to civil war. The fact that Raul's form had markedly deteriorated just as his identity as a player had been lost in a Madrid side put in the hands of foreign superstars, mattered little to those who had mythologised him as the latest version of their knight in white armour.

Chencho Arias claimed to have cried only three times in his life: at the funeral of the Spanish Jesuit priests murdered by a death squad in El Salvador; during the final scene of some movie he'd seen in New York; and after the goal Raul scored during the 1998 Intercontinental Club Cup against Vasco de Gama of Brazil in Japan. Clarence Seedorf had struck a long pass from midfield, from right to left. Raul received the ball, controlled it perfectly with the left foot, beat one defender, next another, before pushing it to his right and striking it home to clinch the trophy. 'Proust's exquisite cake was cattle shit compared to what I relished in that moment – Real Madrid in all its glory,' recalled Chencho.

But such memories had faded fast among those who instead of looking back were looking towards the future to see if Spain's reputation as Europe's great underachiever could be corrected. Luis Aragonés became the first Spanish coach to act on the basis that if *La Roja* was to succeed, he could do without a player who, in addition to no longer being able to hit the target, had a reputation for alienating team-mates and celebrating too often his own personal achievements. At his prime Raul proved himself an instinctive lock-picker, and could be trusted to take up his own position anywhere in the forward area. But he lacked *El Buitre's* good grace and selfless artistry. Spain had to move on without Raul.

To that extent Raul's rise and fall marked a period of transition for Spanish football: when a new generation of players took over from the old and the best lessons learned at youth and club level were transferred to the national team.

Jesus Gil – Mayor of Marbella, President of Atlético de Madrid

24

Of God, Mammon and Philosophy

When the former Real Madrid president Ramon Mendoza died on 4 April 2001, it was widely reported that he had expired while enjoying a massage on a Caribbean island. He was seventy-three years old and was holidaying with his latest lover, an attractive female lawyer forty-two years his junior. He was buried three days later in Madrid's Almudena cemetery, named after the capital's favourite Virgin to whom generations of Real Madrid players have paid homage. His coffin was covered in the flags of the club and Spain. The many dignitaries and celebrities who personally gave their condolences to his family included King Juan Carlos.

At the time the Spanish people had fallen out of love with the socialist government of Felipe González, whose third term in office had fallen apart amid mounting allegations of corruption and incompetence. The centre-right led by José Maria Aznar was about to take power. Spain had clearly moved a long way in matters of public morality, not least in the football world.

But for the presence of priests and bishops at the Almudena, one could have been forgiven for thinking that the Real Madrid of Mendoza's time was from another social planet to that which had existed in the days of Franco and in the aftermath of his death.

In 1969, when the democracies of the Western world were immersed in sex, drugs, protest and rock and roll, Real Madrid's long-serving president Santiago Bernabéu reflected on his duty as a servant of the Francoist state: 'What we want is to keep people happy. People like football a lot and with football Spaniards can deal better with their everyday problems. We are living at a time of such misunderstanding and such horrible confusion that what people want is calm.'

A highly moral man, Bernabéu's own success pre-dated the get-rich boom years of the 1960s. While a visionary of global football, he shared none of its material obsessions. His enduring popularity stemmed from his apparent ability to remain uncorrupted by the power his position gave him. Bernabéu was never accused of personally enriching himself on Real Madrid's account. He paid his players what he thought they deserved and no more, and kept a tight hold on their expenses – which some of them found difficult to swallow amid the increasing conspicuous consumption that characterised the 1960s.

He was at heart a traditionalist. While delegating the day-to-day administration of the club, he liked to treat his players like members of a family, and was helped in that by his inseparable wife Maria. She used to recite the rosary each morning for her husband and his team. She would also give prayer cards of St Teresa and jerseys to the newborn children of the players.

One of the Real Madrid veterans from the 1960s, Ignacio Zoco, told me once that Bernabéu found it increasingly difficult to come to terms with the changes that began to impact on his country. Zoco recalled: 'He didn't like long hair, beards, players who played with their shirt hanging out of their shorts or their socks halfway down their ankles . . . He liked to see a team play in its uniform and wanted to see us all keep on the straight and narrow.'

Bernabéu was not pleased when Pirri, one of his star players during the 1960s, became the first at Real Madrid to marry an actress. Until then, any show woman – whether actress or flamenco artist – involved in the life of a Spanish football player was seen as a negative influence, better kept on the sidelines, and certainly not legitimised. Some ten years earlier, Spanish football had been rocked by the very public and controversial affairs that one of the most famous singers of the Franco era, the sultry and outspoken gypsy Lola Flores, had with at least two leading players, FC Barcelona's Gustavo Biosca and Atlético Madrid's Gerardo Coque. As a result Flores was demonised by the traditionalists in the world of Spanish football as an unprincipled whore who not only undermined family life but also impacted negatively on the playing performance of the men concerned.

The memory of Lola Flores played heavily on Bernabéu's mind so that he tried to control his players' sex lives. When it came to Zoco's choice of lover and wife, Bernabéu approved. She was Maria Ostiz, a soft-spoken and modest folk singer who represented Spain at its most morally disciplined. The childless Bernabéu treated her like a daughter-in-law after adopting Zoco as one of his favourite players. Zoco shared with me a telling anecdote of Maria's first encounter with Bernabéu, soon after the player's marriage to the singer. She and Zoco were walking in the Real Madrid training ground when he spotted Bernabéu and decided to introduce her to him. The president's first words to Maria, who he had never spoken to until then, were these: 'Maria, the day Ignacio retires you will have to leave him with me as a breeding bull.' Unsurprisingly Maria was speechless.

I remember many years later interviewing Butragueño about his time during the 1980s when Spanish players became seriously rich for the first time and certain foreign imports drew them to the wild side and into the flash guns of the paparazzi. 'At first I used to get followed all over the place by press men to see if they could catch me with anybody, but when they always saw me with the same girl I think they got bored,' he recalled. He had a long-term girlfriend, Sonia, who later became his wife.

While Real Madrid took a while to shake off its traditionalist image, FC Barcelona had long been anticipating the death of Franco. On 17 November 1974, almost exactly a year to the day before Franco's death, Barça fans took part in a political demonstration in the Benedictine monastery at Montserrat, in the mountains outside the Catalan capital. The monastery had lost some of its monks to anarchist execution squads during the Spanish Civil War, but during the years of the Franco regime had become increasingly involved in the campaign for democratic rights.

On that autumn day some 6,000 people gathered at the monastery as part of a series of events organised to celebrate the 75th anniversary of FC Barcelona's foundation. Among those present was the future president of post-Franco Spain's first democratically elected Catalan government, Jordi Pujol, then a 42-year-old banker and former political prisoner of the Franco regime. Pujol was taken to his first Barça game, in the old Les Corts stadium, aged four, in the spring of 1936 just days before the outbreak of the Civil War. Pujol would later write: 'Barça is like other folkloric manifestations of our people – Montserrat is another example – a reserve we can draw on when other sources dry up, when the doors of normality are closed to us.'

After the Spanish Civil War, Franco came to Montserrat on a number of occasions to pray before the Virgin there. It was his way of telling the Catalans that the Virgin was Spanish first and foremost. But FC Barcelona's devotion to the Virgin of Montserrat long outlived Franco, as did its tradition of dedicating every cup won to the Virgin of *La Merce*, the 'Mother' of Barcelona and for players – if they wished – to pray in the Camp Nou chapel prior to a big match.

No Spanish club worth its name has abandoned its holy icons over the years. Even Real Madrid, whose fans celebrate victory before the goddess Cibeles, do so only out of convention rather than any deference to a pre-Christian deity. The square surrounding the eighteenth-century statue depicting the Goddess of Nature on her chariot stands firmly in the centre of one of the capital's busiest commercial, administrative and residential neighbourhoods. The club's patron still remains the Virgin of Almudena and each major victory is marked by floral offerings to her as well as Cibeles being covered in Real Madrid scarves and embraced by players and fans.

Spanish football's enduring propensity to mix sport with religion suggests that the Catholic faith has remained deeply embedded in the collective subconscious however much Spanish society becomes laicised and the Catholic Church loses its traditional powers. But it is money rather more than religious faith that has arguably shaped some of the key developments of Spanish football in the modern era.

In May 1978, FC Barcelona elected a construction magnate,

the non-Catalan native Josep Lluis Núñez, as its new president. Núñez had made his first millions during the Franco era. He ran a rather nasty election campaign in which he mixed black propaganda against his opponents while boasting of his own ambition to break with tradition and move full-square into the modern era – '*Romper con el porron*' (break with the wine jar). Previously the running of FC Barcelona had been passed from one textile boss to another just as peasants pass their wine from one to the next.

The winning candidate owned the biggest construction company in Catalonia and was especially well known in Barcelona for his involvement in more than two decades of redevelopment in the city. He had made a fortune out of the unconstrained and unplanned urban growth that had taken place in Catalonia in response to an influx of migrants from other parts of Spain.

Núñez was a migrant himself from the Basque Country, the son of a customs officer working for the Spanish state. He managed to get his hands on Catalonia's great sporting institution by playing the left against the right and marketing himself, with the aid of a group of influential local journalists, as the only candidate who represented a real break with the past, the new rich taking on the old bourgeoisie.

Núñez was being somewhat economical with the truth. He had made his first fortune under Franco. Nevertheless, during his campaign Núñez promised he would find the money not just to buy some of the best players in the world, but also for the expansion of the Camp Nou, in effect making FC Barcelona as big as if not bigger than its arch rival Real Madrid. Another election slogan promised a 'triumphant' Barça.

One of the architects of his campaign, journalist Domingo

Garcia, told me: 'Núñez was a product of a rebellion by a small sector of Barça against the establishment, against those families who had between them maintained control over the presidency for decades. The club had become a political instrument (for Catalan nationalism) but had been a disaster in football terms for most of the time. It was true that a lot of people felt sentimentally attached to the club as an expression of their nationalism, but there were also people who were fed up to the back teeth of seeing Real Madrid win the league too often and calling itself the best team in Spain.'

If Núñez had pledged a triumphant Barça he had done so anticipating what was to become one of the guiding principles of the most wealthy clubs in Europe: success is only possible with star players and star players cannot be bought without money. So a search began for a player who could fill the Camp Nou's increased capacity – from 90,000 to 120,000 – and win titles in a way that Cruyff the player had failed to do while at FC Barcelona.

In 1982, the club signed up Diego Maradona. The Argentine, like the rest of his squad, had had a lacklustre World Cup campaign, distracted by his country's doomed war with Britain over the Falklands, and finally humiliated when he was shown a red card in the closing minutes of his team's group stage match against Brazil. But FC Barcelona's talent scouts had done their homework and had identified Maradona's huge potential. In Madrid, the cautious men of football, and a few conservative politicians, accused FC Barcelona of mindless extravagance when they paid $7.3m for the 21-year-old who had not played club football outside Argentina. Núñez boldly proclaimed, 'Maradona is going to revitalise football and thanks to him we're going to avoid a financial crisis. We deserve a monument to be built in our honour over this.'

On 28 July 1982, three weeks after Argentina were knocked out of the World Cup, Maradona took to the field of the Camp Nou for the traditional start-of-season presentation ceremony. There were 50,000 fans present to honour him along with Bernd Schuster, the star of West Germany's 1980 European Championship victory. Once the season was under way, Maradona's impact was immediate, inspiring his colleagues and bringing many afternoons of palpable enjoyment to Spanish fans generally as they marvelled at a player of such unique talent. One of his team-mates, 'Lobo' Carrasco, told me: 'He was like a chameleon. On the football pitch he was transformed. He was so sure of himself. He seemed to have total control of the ball. When he ran with it and dribbled through the defence, it seemed he had it tied to his boots. In training sessions the rest of the team would just stop and watch him. No one seemed to generate such interest. We all felt it was a real pleasure just to be able to witness what he could do.'

Maradona not only brought a new excitement on the pitch, but also ushered in a period of unprecedented personal wealth and power in Spanish football. During the early 1980s FC Barcelona not only benefited from increased ticket sales, merchandising and sponsorship receipts but from the creation of new Catalan media groups, led by the regional TV channel TV3. Across Spain, the evolution of a new style of newspaper freed from official censorship and appealing to a politically diverse readership encouraged the development of a sports journalism of analysis, criticism and debate, alongside match reportage. Styles of play, team systems and management were put under closer scrutiny. Meanwhile a distinct whiff of scandal began to be smelled in Spanish football.

Few figures in Spanish football were to prove as controversial as Jesús Gil, the property magnate who took over the presidency of Atlético Madrid in 1987. Gil was elected on a populist pledge to transform the club of also-rans into a serious challenger in La Liga and a competitor in Europe. His initial investment in new players like the Portuguese international Paulo Futre, López Ufarte from Real Sociedad, and Goikoetxea from Athletic Bilbao raised Atlético's quality as a team. However, the club's organisation and reputation was destined to be severely damaged by Gil's volatile character and dubious business practices. During his time as president, Gil erratically dealt with a selection of managers like Ron Atkinson, César Menotti, and Javier Clemente – with none seeing out his original contract. In one season alone Gil got through a record of five managers!

In football terms Gil produced mixed results. Atlético improved its competitiveness in La Liga in the first two seasons under his presidency, only to end up relegated to the Second Division in the third, on the fiftieth anniversary of its earlier reincarnation as Atlético Aviación, when during the first period of the Franco dictatorship the club had become Spanish champions. It was a reminder that whatever political influences the club might have once had, Gil no longer had it all his own way in a democracy. On the contrary, beyond Atlético's Calderon stadium, the construction magnate who tried to create his own political fiefdom as mayor of the luxury resort of Marbella increasingly became a judicial outcast, pursued by tax inspectors and the courts. In the late 1990s Atlético Madrid's headquarters were raided by police acting on orders from

Spain's special anti-corruption prosecutor investigating alleged diversion of municipal funds. Other prosecutions would follow, drawing an array of public personalities from bullfighter's wives to footballers and actors into a complex web of opaque property deals, alleged bribes and personal favours. In the midst of ongoing prosecutions, Gil was banned for two years from travelling to European matches with his club after calling a French referee a homosexual.

In 1991 Gil's many detractors in the press and the political establishment lost no time in labelling him a fascist. Gil preached non-corruption, although his own style and his criminal record reduced the credibility of this message. His insults attracted a stream of libel writs from Spain's great and good. The one memory he was unable to flick away with a curse was of the fifty-eight people who died in 1969 when the roof of a restaurant he was building near Madrid collapsed on a party of 300. Gil was sent to prison for five years for being responsible for the structural 'economies' that caused the collapse. He served eighteen months before paying a 400m peseta fine and being pardoned by General Franco.

Gil died before he was ever imprisoned in democratic Spain. His funeral on 17 May 2004 provoked a mass outpouring of collective mourning from 40,000 followers, many of them Atlético fans who remained grateful for the fleeting and unexpected triumphs he helped secure for them, and the way he seemed to make a virtue of taking on Real Madrid and FC Barcelona against the odds.

But the cast of characters drawn from the higher echelons of Spanish politics and football that joined his more identifiable fans to pay their last respects at his funeral suggested a darker narrative in which there was no clear separation between saints and sinners in the evolving democracy of post-Franco Spain. They included Atlético, Real Madrid and Athletic Bilbao players – among them Spanish internationals – foreign players and managers who had played and worked in La Liga, past and present presidents of Real Madrid, FC Barcelona and Real Betis, senior officials of the Spanish Football Federation, and elected politicians of Spain's centre-right Partido Popular and PSOE socialist parties.

While Gil came under intense media scrutiny, Spain's two biggest clubs remained answerable, according to their statutes, to the fans. In practice both clubs became powerful fiefdoms within Spanish football, a duopoly backed by the country's leading banks and businesses as they secured sponsorship and marketing deals, TV contracts, and star players at a value which left the majority of Spanish clubs behind and unable to compete.

In Madrid, a broader debate about how Spanish football was played – its lost potential and enduring prejudices and the need to overcome them – began to emerge in the sports pages of *El Pais*, a newspaper published for the first time in 1978, three years after Franco's death. It had as its specific mission that of helping the nascent democracy affirm itself while banishing the old demons that had cast a shadow over all aspects of society, including club and national football. It would take time before Real Madrid and Spanish football more generally found in Jorge Valdano, a philosopher as well as a player, a new voice capable of articulating a vision of Spanish football less as a test of virility than an art form.

Valdano immigrated to Spain in 1975, months before a bloody military coup in his homeland of Argentina. He played first for Alaves and then for Zaragoza before joining Real

Madrid in 1984. Three years later he retired as a player after being felled by hepatitis. But by then Valdano had played with two of the most talented players in the history of football. He had played alongside Butragueño in the *Quinta del Buitre,* and with Maradona in the 1986 World Cup. In formulating his views about how football could best be played, Valdano was also influenced by his compatriot César Menotti, the manager of the Argentine squad that won the 1978 World Cup, and failed to retain it in 1982, before signing up with FC Barcelona.

Menotti had grown up in his native Argentina in Rosario, a town with a tradition of radical politics and stylish football. In the 1960s he had developed a reputation as an anti-establishment figure. Tall, long-haired and with sleepy good looks, *El Flaco* (the thin one) as he was popularly known developed a creative style of football based on a slow tempo and elegant touches. He did not fit in easily with the heavy marking and kick-and-run tactics that characterised the two Argentine teams he played for during those years: Racing and Boca Juniors. In 1967 he opted for temporary exile, playing first for the Generals in New York and then in 1969 with Santos, the Brazilian team Pele had put on the world map. After a brief time as a journalist he returned to football in 1973, when he was appointed coach at Huracán. His year there coincided with a period of growing political upheaval in Argentina.

Menotti became widely known in Argentina as an articulate defender of a style he claimed was an original native creation responsible for improving the quality of football in Europe, not least Spain where such talents as Real Madrid's Di Stéfano played with a mixture of carefully choreographed technique and instinctive daring.

One of Menotti's philosophical tracts, *Football without*

Tricks, sold well in Latin America and Spain during the early 1980s. In it he contrasted his admiration for a free and creative style of football with the 'tyranny' of the defensive, destructive play favoured by authoritarian managers. Within days of his arrival as the new coach of FC Barcelona in 1982 Menotti engaged in a widely publicised verbal slanging match with Javier Clemente, the then manager of Athletic Bilbao. Basque born and bred, and politically conservative, Clemente was distrusted by the left, but regarded as something of a legend by many Athletic fans because of his three years as a player during which he had heroically struggled against injuries with the kind of resilience and spirit of self-sacrifice the club had traditionally made its trademark.

In the year after Spain failed to win the World Cup it had hosted, Clemente set about creating one of the most successful teams in Athletic's history, drawing from the club's trail-blazing youth academy players such as Santiago Urkiaga, Miguel de Andrés, Ismael Urtubi, Estanislao Argote and Andoni Zubizaretta to play alongside respected veterans like Dani and Andoni Goikoetxea. The Basque was in no mood to be given football lessons by the Argentine. Clemente regarded Menotti as a womaniser and chain-smoking hippy who had been on a downward professional curve since winning the World Cup. But Menotti was focused on his target, blaming Clemente for personifying all that had gone wrong with Spanish football in the past. 'The day Spain as represented by Clemente decides to be a bullfighter rather than a bull on the pitch it will play better football,' Menotti declared.

The row between the two men intensified after a league match in the Camp Nou on 24 September 1983 in which the Athletic defender Goikoetxea tackled Maradona from behind, breaking a run that could easily have ended in a goal. The tackle, one of the most brutal ever seen in Spanish club football, so shocked Edward Owen, a Spanish-based English tabloid journalist, that he dreamed up the memorable description of Goikoetxea as 'the butcher of Bilbao'. Barça won the match 4–0 and a second league encounter at San Mamés by 2–1. This was no consolation to Maradona, who spent three months recovering from a severe injury to his left ankle. And what particularly angered Menotti was that Athletic went on to win La Liga in 1983. This was a huge achievement for a club that had in previous years suffered one of its periodical dips with an enduring and painful memory of the 1976–77 season when it had lost the (by now re-named) King's Cup final against a resurgent Betis, and weeks later suffered a further blow, losing to Juventus in the UEFA Cup final.

By the following season, relations between FC Barcelona and Athletic had fallen to an all-time low, the mutual acrimony banishing to a distant past the political and social synergies of Catalans and Basques in their opposition to Franco and mutual respect for the other's national identities. 'The shooting season was declared open and two clubs with a huge sense of history and who for years had shown exemplary mutual respect, threw everything they had at each other,' wrote the Bilbao-based journalist Jon Agiriano, one of Athletic's most incisive chroniclers.

FC Barcelona in those days fell well short of a 'dream team'. For all its individual talent, it was a hardened contingent, less beautiful than vengeful, and determined to destroy Athletic by fair means or foul. For all his musings about the beautiful game, Menotti could and did draw on the brutal tactics he had learned in his early days as a player with Racing and Boca Juniors.

'Barcelona is prepared to respond to a determined violence with the same violence,' Menotti declared on the eve of his team's King's Cup final encounter with Athletic. 'Clemente hasn't the balls to look me in the eye and call me stupid,' Maradona threw in for good measure. Clemente hit back: 'Maradona is both stupid and castrated. It's a shame that a player like him who earns so much money has no human qualities whatsoever.'

On 5 May 1984, the two sides met at the Bernabéu. Nearly 100,000 fans divided between followers of each team turned the stadium into a cauldron. While Menotti chain-smoked and Maradona rallied the troops, in the Bilbao dressing room, one of the players, Natxo Biritxinaga, tried to break the unbearable tension by dressing up in drag. A few minutes before the start of the game, he disappeared only to return dressed as Eva Nasarre, a popular TV presenter. The team broke into fits of laugher, then fell silent again and prepared themselves for battle.

It was a dirty match from the outset. Bilbao took an early lead and then held on to it with an uncompromising defence that frustrated Barça's flow of play. Menotti's players, led by Maradona, became increasingly angry, with their few shots at goal easily dealt with by Andoni Zubizarreta, Spain's international goalkeeper. By the time the referee blew the final whistle, the fuse had been lit for an explosion. Maradona was in the thick of it, hitting out at Sola after the Athletic player gave him a 'fuck off' sign. Then several players from each side joined in, with kung-fu kicks and Wild West punches.

The brawl, viewed by millions on TV, was eventually brought to a stop by club officials. But the enduring image was to be that of the total horror on the face of democratic Spain's constitutional monarch, King Juan Carlos, as if his country was disintegrating before his eyes, just over three years since he had successfully seen off an attempted military coup. It was certainly the worst act of violence to involve players ever in the history of Spanish football. It precipitated Menotti's and Maradona's exit from FC Barcelona and the Spanish league, while elevating Clemente to hero status among Athletic fans for winning the double. Both trophies were dedicated – as tradition demanded – to Bilbao's patron Virgin of Begoña.

FC Barcelona – winning the European Cup at Wembley 1992

25

The Cruyff Factor and Venables

With a history made up of more disappointments than victories and the humiliation of the 1982 World Cup a recent memory, Spain had much to prove in the subsequent European Championships. Given the bitter rivalries in Spanish club football, it was no small miracle that in 1984 Spain's underachieving national squad enjoyed something of a revival. The credit was largely due to the management of Miguel Muñoz, who had come to the job with an impressive track record as a player and coach with Real Madrid. As a player, Muñoz had been part of the golden Di Stéfano years of the 1950s, scoring the club's first ever goal in the European Cup against Servette FC and subsequently serving as captain in two consecutive competition wins.

His time in charge of Real Madrid as coach (1960–74) was one of the club's most successful eras in La Liga as under his guidance they won the league nine times, while winning the European Cup twice. After leaving Real Madrid in 1974 he worked for seven more seasons at club level (for Granada, Hércules, Las Palmas and Sevilla) before taking on the challenge of moulding Spanish football's disparate talent base into a national unit.

His initial squad managed to reconcile Barça (Julio Alberto, Victor Muñoz, Carrasco) and Athletic players (Urkiaga and Goikoetxea) alongside the key Real Madrid figures like Gallego, Camacho and Santillana. It also counted on the talent of Zaragoza's Juan Senor, Sporting de Gijón's Maceda, and Betis's Rafael Gordillo. Under Muñoz the Spanish side relied on a tradition of spirited rather than elaborate play, a collective work ethos rather than any individual skill.

In the European Championships of 1984, the Spanish side started well, finishing top of its group, above Portugal and West Germany, before beating the Danes in the semi-finals. Then they lost 0–2 to France in the final.

Two years later, Spain got off to a good start in the 1986 World Cup in Mexico, and proceeded well thanks to the technical brilliance of Emilio Butragueño and Michel, stars of Real Madrid's 'Vulture Squad'. The Spaniards qualified from a group that included the bookies' favourite Brazil and went on to thrash the Danes 5–1 in the second round with an entertaining and lethal display of offensive football that overwhelmed the opposition. Then Spain was knocked out in a quarter-final penalty shoot-out against Belgium. The defeat was blamed by the team on bad luck. As Michel would reflect in its aftermath: 'Did we do something bad to create that penalty shoot-out and end up eliminated from the tournament? Well, no. But in that combination of detail that separates success from sadness, we always lacked good fortune.'

And yet after the 1986 World Cup, whatever self-confidence Muñoz had instilled in Spain as a competitive national squad disappeared. It not only underachieved but also underperformed in the 1988 European Championship in West Germany, outplayed and beaten in matches against Italy and the hosts. In the World Cup in Italy in 1990, hopes were raised with Luis Suárez as the new coach. Suárez was widely remembered as one of the great Spanish players. The Golden Galician, as he was nicknamed, had enthused fans with his amazing talent for moving the ball, his great vision and explosive shot. He had also developed a reputation for his elegant style. It was often said that he was such a graceful sportsman that he could have played football just as well in a dinner jacket.

And yet despite Suárez's proven track record as a player, Spain's experience of Italia 1990 under his tutelage was not a happy one. As Michel later recalled: 'The World Cup in Italy in 1990 was one of those experiences that you don't want even your worst enemy to have to go through.' Relations between the squad and the media were fraught. As pressures mounted, the chemistry between coach and players became equally tetchy. Suárez gambled by including players whose stars had shone in the past but who were now approaching their sell-by date in competitive football and who journalists viewed as spoiled and overpaid. Any appeal to Spaniards' sense of patriotism was handicapped by the growing unpopularity of Spain's socialist government amid revelations of alleged financial impropriety and suggestions (later proved) that sectors of the Spanish security forces had been involved in a shoot-to-kill policy against ETA sympathisers in the Basque Country.

Michel, the number 8 of the legendary *Quinta del Buitre* with a great skill for crosses, personified the disaster that hounded the national squad when he let slip through his place in the wall the Yugoslav free-kick that booted Spain out of the tournament before the quarter-finals. As the player later recalled: 'I came under attack from all sides. I emerged from that World Cup as if from an acute emergency ward, battered and bruised, publicly beaten to pulp. I tried to keep face, for the sake of the other team members – but inside I felt destroyed.'

And yet brighter days were ahead. Pre-planning for the staging of the Olympics in Barcelona in 1992 had involved the biggest state investment in Spanish competitive sports ever, with a new, much improved nationwide structure for training football players from primary school to La Liga. With Spain's nascent democracy flushed with EU funds, new stadiums popped up in almost every municipality in the country. Major clubs like Real Madrid and FC Barcelona followed the example set years previously by Athletic Bilbao and Sporting Gijón and began to strengthen their development of teenagers with the potential to become first-team players.

The 1992 Olympics were memorable for many things – the physical transformation of Barcelona as a city, the duet recorded in 1988 by Montserrat Caballé and Freddie Mercury, the brilliance of the US basketball team led by Michael Jordan, Cuba's participation after boycotting the previous two Games, the dignity shown by the athletes from Ethiopia and the new post-apartheid South Africa, but perhaps most of all by the way that the tournament generally showed off the potential of democratic Spain. While the smooth running of the Olympics was a showcase for the organisational skills of Catalonia's autonomous government, they were exported to the world as a Spanish event, very much framed by the high-profile presence of the Spanish royal family. This was no celebration of fascism as in the days of Franco but confirmation of a pluralist society held together, however tentatively, by a constitutional monarch who claimed to represent the rights of all Spaniards. At the Games' opening, the Spanish team was led out by the young heir to the Bourbon throne Prince Felipe, while his father and mother – King Juan Carlos and Queen Sofia – took centre stage in the VIP box with government ministers and local politicians. In a show of genuine enthusiasm, they all celebrated Spain's impressive clutch of medals. One of the memorable triumphs of those Olympics was the Spanish athlete Fermin Cacho winning the final of the 1,500 metres. But it was the gold won by Spain's young football team that proved most symbolic, marking a new era full of potential. The defining moment came in the final minute of Spain's bruising encounter with Poland in the football finals when Francisco Miguel Narvaez Machon, better known as Kiko, picked up a deflection from the goalkeeper and struck it home to secure Spain the gold medal.

Among the other players in the winning Spanish team that day was a 21-year-old called Pep Guardiola. Two years earlier Guardiola had been promoted from the youth to the first team of FC Barcelona by Johan Cruyff to fill the 'number 4', the Dutchman's version of a quarterback – one with the capacity to buzz around midfield distributing passes, a pivotal figure in the Dutchman's updating of the 'total football' of the 1970s. The promotion would prove providential, setting Guardiola on a career path that would lead him one day to coaching one of the best teams in the history of football, at FC Barcelona.

But before Guardiola, there was Johan Cruyff, whose playing days formed only half of the legend. Cruyff says of himself that it took him until he was thirty to understand why he did the things he did with the ball. He has since spent much of his life inspiring others with his philosophy of how football should be played. As a coach at FC Barcelona and as Guardiola's mentor, Cruyff can rightly claim ownership over the club's golden years, and to infusing Spanish football generally with an example worth following.

The first time I met Johan Cruyff, he was relaxing in his family home up in the hills outside Barcelona. Somewhat in awe of the 'flying Dutchman' I had first seen leading out his Barça team at the Camp Nou circa 1976, I had been brought to my first personal encounter by a Catalan friend, Armando Caraben, the economist and lawyer who during the 1970s had been instrumental in negotiating the Dutchman's transfer from Ajax to Catalonia.

The meeting, towards the end of the 1990s, was several years after Cruyff had retired from the front line. But if there was a style of Spanish football that took shape and achieved glory in the new millennium, it was Cruyff that planted some important seeds.

Over cold beer and a selection of Dutch cheeses and Spanish ham, Cruyff settled into our interview with his rapid-fire accented and curiously constructed English punctuated often by insightful musings on a sport not overwhelmed with literacy. 'I like positioning of the ball, I like attack, I like to see the team dominating the situation . . . The "other" game was basically: play the long ball, close it down, and take it from there. It's a different approach but I think my way brings out individual skill.'

Before the Cruyff era, Barça had had three (foreign) managers in five years, each importing a star player or two that tended to dominate the team's overall strategy and performance – Schuster under Lattek, Maradona under Menotti, Archibald and Lineker under Venables. Cruyff thought that such a system undermined the club's sense of collective identity and ill-fitted the social and cultural context of Catalonia. He had learned enough from his own experience as a player to want to put it right. He came, after all, from Holland, a football country that had long stimulated young talent. So he focused on encouraging a new generation of Barça players that were coming through the club's youth training programme, and mixing them into teams with quality Basque players and a sprinkling of foreign stars. Such an initiative helped to bring about a general resurgence of Spanish football.

Cruyff explained how he spotted local talent that he knew he had to build on so as to give the team a sense of identity. 'It just happened that when I arrived, there was a new crop of players who had come through the *cantera* (the youth team) and were ready to join the first team. There was the kind of availability that comes at the end of a cycle, every five or six years. But there was another situation that I understood. Fans the world over like to see good players who share their mentality, and preferably come from their country, and if a coach has to choose between a foreign and a local with equal qualities, he should go for the local. That way the fans are less likely to whistle him if things go wrong. In Barça, people like seeing players from the *cantera* in the first team; it makes them feel that the coach somehow is more a part of Barcelona that way. So I tried to do it the way they liked, to produce a game that they could claim as Catalan. Because I'd been here as a player I think I knew what they wanted.'

Fellow Dutchman Rinus Michels influenced Cruyff during their time together, as coach and player respectively, at Ajax. Cruyff was impressed by the rigidity with which Michels stuck to his system. In Barcelona such rigidity brought Cruyff success but not without some internal dissent. For example, tension was provoked by Cruyff's determination to play Gary

Lineker out of the position he had occupied for most of his playing life. 'I knew that Lineker was a goal-scorer and that is good for any team. But I also knew that with a more attacking system, and more players moving forward, the field was smaller up front. That is why I moved him from the centre to the right side, to give him more space in which to use his spring,' Cruyff told me.

Lineker saw it rather differently. As he told me: 'It became pretty apparent to me relatively quickly that Cruyff basically wanted his own people in, and me out. But instead of coming along and saying to me, "You're not my type of player," he tried to mess me about by making me play on the wing . . . I was just one of two wide players. I wasn't an individual, I was just a number, just like number 4 – the centre-back – was part of the system too. You wouldn't have thought in a million years that Gary Lineker could play on the wing, but I know why he did it – he did it so I would kick up a fuss, then the crowd would turn against me and he'd get rid of me that way.'

Lineker was not without sympathisers. According to his agent John Holmes, he was much admired on a personal and professional level by the 'Brian Clough of Spanish football' Javier Clemente, who during his passage through a succession of Spanish clubs prior to being put in charge of the national squad tried, without success, to poach the English 'matador'. 'Clemente always told Gary that Cruyff didn't really understand how football should be played, and didn't value him as he should,' Holmes told me. While there was a mutual personal and professional respect, Lineker spurned Clemente's advances as he similarly turned away an approach from Alex Ferguson, who wanted to have Lineker play alongside another former Barça player, Mark Hughes.

The Welshman Hughes had transferred to Manchester United via a loan to Bayern Munich after finding it hard to adapt to life in Barcelona (where he lasted no more than a season), unlike Lineker, who loved the climate and food and learned Catalan as well as Spanish while earning the nickname *El Matador* for his goal-scoring abilities. In bullfighting, the word *matador* describes the bullfighter at the point of death, rather than involved in its elaboration. It is the *torero* who uses his skill with the cape to confront the bull, and gradually overwhelm him. Lineker was viewed as a classic striker, with a killer instinct up front but lacking the multi-tasking that Cruyff demanded from his players. In the end the Englishman's disagreements with Cruyff proved irreconcilable, and Lineker left Barça for Tottenham Hotspur in a deal negotiated with the Spurs coach Terry Venables.

It was Venables who had brought Lineker to FC Barcelona – along with Steve Archibald – when he was appointed coach in 1984 in succession to César Menotti. Venables had played for and coached several English clubs before coming to Catalonia, where he had the most rewarding time of his career, taking FC Barcelona to its first league title in more than ten years in the 1984–85 season and the European Cup final and Spanish League Cup victory in the following season. Venables provided me with a valuable insight into the differences there have been between English and Spanish football in an interview at the FA headquarters in 1995 during his time as manager of England, eight years after he quit FC Barcelona.

He recalled: 'When I was at Barcelona we would travel to San Sebastián by coach, a journey of seven or eight hours, and the players would just drink water, all the way there and back. In England, the players would drink water and Coca-Cola on the way to a match, but on the way back they would be swilling beer. In Spain, I did not see a single player smoke or drink until we won the league, and then they all got absolutely smashed. They were professional and the job was done. In England we do it every Saturday, after the match . . .'

Venables went on, 'The Spanish footballers care about their condition, their fitness and their behaviour. They enjoy showing off their skills. The British are more functional, they get the job done, and are professionals from that point of view, and if they lack the technical ability of the Spanish players, they do have resilience . . . We both have our strengths and weaknesses, but the sight of a squad of highly skilled, motivated and disciplined footballers waiting for me at my first training session with Barcelona was a very welcome one.'

The exception was Maradona, who was already negotiating a transfer to Napoli having fallen out with FC Barcelona President Núñez over pay and conditions. Núñez, who had exploited Maradona's early years at FC Barcelona to make the club a lot of money, couldn't wait to see the back of him after the Argentine lost form and private detectives discovered mounting evidence of his debauched private life.

El Tel, as Venables was nicknamed in his native UK, became a popular figure at Barcelona, earning a respectful place in the list of English managers that have graced Spanish football with their presence.

But it was Cruyff who within a year of Venables' departure had initiated one of the most exciting and entertaining periods in Spanish club history, taking FC Barcelona to its first ever European Cup victory against Sampdoria at Wembley in 1992, and winning with the club a further ten domestic and international titles between 1988 and 1996. At a time when European clubs were limited by UEFA rules as to the amount of foreign players they could sign up, Cruyff built his team around a small number of key star signings – the Brits were replaced by the likes of Koeman, Laudrup and Stoichkov, while young Spanish players like Luis Milla and Pep Guardiola were promoted after being developed through the club's youth system.

In Guardiola, Cruyff tapped a footballing talent who not only fitted seamlessly into Barcelona's cultural and political mystique but who was also destined to personify its periods of greatest success, as player and coach. Years would have to pass before Guardiola came to be respected more generally by Spaniards regardless of their political leanings and their divergent views as to which nation they owed their ultimate allegiance to.

Javier Clemente – Athletic Bilbao and Spanish national squad manager

26

The Bruiser from Barakaldo

The year of Cruyff's Dream Team's apotheosis was also the year when Javier Clemente, a very different character to the Dutchman, was appointed as the new manager of the Spanish national team.

Clemente was born among the steel mills of Barakaldo, the industrial suburb of Bilbao, the same neighbourhood where José Luis Núñez, the president of FC Barcelona, had once lived. But while the Núñez family abandoned the Basque Country for Catalonia, the Clementes felt part of its social, political and religious fabric. Javier's father worked as a foreman in the metallurgical conglomerate Altos Hornos de Vizcaya in a region that during the late 1970s was hit by the onset of recession – with factory closures fuelling a tense political and social situation provoked by the violence of the Basque terrorist group ETA.

Clemente began playing for Athletic Bilbao from the age of sixteen, where he earned a reputation as a dedicated workhorse whose fighting spirit, passing skills and vision off the ball defied his small five-foot-six stature. As a player, he came to personify Basque football at its best – a mixture of guts and gift, aggression and talent with the ball. He was a member of the Athletic team that won the Copa del Generalissimo in 1969, but his playing career was subsequently cut short at the age of nineteen by a crippling tackle from behind by a Sabadell player called Marañón, which he accepted with seemingly disarming stoicism.

'I don't blame Marañón for anything,' he would tell Alfredo Relaño of *El Pais* in 1977. 'It was a very tough tackle, but there are many like that. It had been a tough match, and we were all a bit *picados* (stirred up like fighting bulls who have been lanced by the *picador*). We were a minute away from the final whistle and I had the ball at my feet; he came in and broke my leg.' His determination to try and recover from his injury turned into a personal odyssey with his repeated attempts to recover form frustrated by a series of botched operations and compulsory military service over an agonising three-year period before he finally threw in the towel.

He retrained as a coach, despite being scarred physically (and some would argue mentally) for life. He would continue to show interested journalists the ten centimetres of discoloured and hacked skin on his leg for many years, like a veteran showing off his war wound or a bullfighter his worst goring. It fuelled the myth of another icon of the Spanish fury, with Clemente, while at Athletic, making much of his distinctive Basque credentials.

In an extensive interview with a Bilbao journalist in 1985, Clemente proudly told the story of how as a schoolboy during the Franco years he had painted a picture of the banned Basque national flag, a gesture for which he was punished by his teacher with a black mark against his exam sheet. Nevertheless, he claimed not to bear an enduring grudge against the nuns and

Salesian brothers who ran the school. His enduring loyalty – next to football – was to the Catholic faith.

After serving his apprenticeship with Arenas Club de Getxo, CD Baskonia, and Athletic's youth training academy he was promoted to the first team in 1981 where he set about putting together one of the most successful Athletic teams in the club's history. For the next five years he took the club into its last golden period, winning two league championships (1982–83 and 1983–84) and a Copa del Rey and Super Cup (both 1984). The celebrations of the triumphant two seasons coincided with a particularly nasty period of political violence involving ETA and the Spanish security forces. As has occurred for much of Spanish history, football was celebrated both by those who genuinely enjoyed the game and those who sought to strengthen their political identity through their team. Add to this tribal loyalties based on family affiliation and you had a combustible mix where football could as easily become a demonstration as a party.

Athletic's triumphs in the early 1980s were marked by the ringing of church bells, nuns applauding from the windows of their convents, and factory workers and militant students joining in the collective party as the team was transported along Bilbao's Nervión River on a barge. For a short, very short, time the guns fell silent, at least in Bilbao. It was with Clemente that Athletic won their last league championship of the twentieth century in 1984. From the balcony of the palace of the Bilbao mayor's office, Clemente declared that it was a victory for the people and not just the team. Just who 'the people' were was kept deliberately vague. After all, Athletic fans ranged from old Franco die-hards to ETA sympathisers. If there was something that united them it was the myth of some imagined racial purity that could only be found in that region of Spain. A popular song at the time held up the club's Basque-only selection process as an example that other clubs were condemned not to follow: 'We always fight with our own weapons, because we do not like imports,' went its defining verse.

Clemente had a bust of Sabino Arana, the father of Basque nationalism, in pride of place in his Bilbao home. Lest we forget, Arana was a controversial figure in Spanish history, initially claiming that the only true homeland or *patria* was Vizcaya, the province based around Bilbao, before deciding that his *patria* extended across several northern provinces and even across the French border. Arana claimed that the basic principles of Basque nationalism – as he saw them – were revealed to him on Whitsunday, a key date in the Catholic liturgical year commemorating the descent of the Holy Spirit on the disciples of Christ following his resurrection. Arana called his nation Euzkadi, one in which some Basques were clearly more equal than others. Before he died he penned some racist articles against the *maketos* – an offensive slang used to identify immigrants from other parts of Spain, including those in Barakaldo where Clemente's father lived and worked. Arana was not to every freethinking liberal's taste, but then Clemente was, well, Clemente.

The rest of Spain continued to look at most Basques as terrorists and remained distinctly unimpressed by Athletic who, it was claimed, had won more by the mistakes of its betters than any superior skill of its own. But in Bilbao, frustrating the big clubs at that time – the Real Madrid of Martin Vazquez, Sanchis, Santillana and Juanito, the FC Barcelona of Maradona and Schuster and the then powerful Valencia led by the ageing Argentine world champion Mario Kempes – was seen as a noble achievement for a club with only modest resources based on home-grown talent.

During this period, Clemente was courted by the Basque Nationalist Party that Arana had founded – his professed cultural identity ('Us Basques are a race apart,' he declared in a controversial interview with Spanish state TV), no-nonsense work ethos and religious convictions seemingly epitomising the best traditional values of the Basque nation. In 1985, the then president of the PNV, the former Jesuit Xabier Arzallus, said this of Clemente: 'For me he is an example. Not because he is a coach of Athletic. Not because he is famous. Simply because he is a whole man, of the kind that Diogenes looked for with a candle in the agora of Athens in daylight. And he is a complete Basque.'

Later a friendly journalist asked Clemente to imagine the team he would most like to have in his life. Clemente volunteered just three 'players' he would like to have with him in his version of a quasi political and spiritual 'dream team'. He named as two of his key players the Basque nationalist leader Arzallus, and the auxiliary Bishop of Bilbao. Only one other person was 'selected' by Clemente and that was Pope John Paul II, in the position of goalkeeper. Why? 'Because he can save everything,' said Clemente – such was his religious conviction and his loyalty to one of the most charismatic figures in papal history, who had himself been a goalkeeper in his youth.

Clemente, the son of poor immigrants who grew up speaking Spanish and not *eusquerra* – the Basque language – was distrusted as a reactionary by the left-wing sympathisers of ETA, and became a controversial and divisive figure in Spanish football, hated as much as he was loved, generating particular resentment among the Cruyff-inspired stylists of FC Barcelona. During Athletic's glory period, Clemente would make a habit of ensuring that the San Mamés stadium was conditioned to undermine any visitor whose game was predicated on swift passing and rapid movement off the ball. He made famous the *manguerazo* (the sprinkler), even when it rained – as it often does in that part of Spain. The method involved soaking the pitch prior to the game to ensure that the turf covered at least half the boot, and turned muddy within minutes of the game getting under way.

One of his favourite players was Andoni Goikoetxea, whose devastating tackle on Maradona's left ankle on 23 September 1983 had an eerie resemblance to that suffered by Clemente fourteen years earlier, as if the coach's tactics had been motivated by some psychological need for revenge.

Goikoetxea was banned for eighteen games, later commuted to ten, after which Clemente brought him back into the team for Athletic's European Cup tie against Joe Fagan's Liverpool. With Liceranzu and Txema Noriega, the 'Butcher of Bilbao' formed part of an uncompromising defence that with a great deal of cynical time-wasting held Liverpool's star attacking line-up of Dalgish, Souness, Ian Rush, Craig Johnston and Michael Robinson to a frustrating goalless draw at Anfield. But Athletic lost 0–1 in the return leg at San Mamés, thanks to a 66th-minute header from Rush.

Clemente thus failed to repeat the success of fifteen years earlier when he had played in a team that eliminated one of the greatest Liverpool teams ever from the European Fair's Cup. During the 1968–69 season, the two teams played each other in the first round of the tournament, a forerunner of the UEFA Cup. Both legs were 2–1 for the home side, which meant that the tie had to be settled by the toss of a coin at Anfield. The toss was successfully gambled by Athletic captain Koldo Aguirre.

Even in defeat, Clemente, who in his best playing days was compared by his faithful admirers to 'the blond Englishman' Bobby Charlton, showed little remorse, sticking obsessively with a style of play he claimed to have learned from his other English heroes Bobby Robson (when at Ipswich) and Ronnie Allen, his coach at Athletic. He never apologised for his side's brutal treatment of Maradona in the King's Cup final against Barça in 1984. In 2010 he told the journalist and author Orfeo Suárez: 'We fought like dogs in that final of 1984, because with Maradona and Schuster we had to do some dirty work so they couldn't play against us. If we allowed them to play, we wouldn't have had a chance. As a result neither of them could get a touch on the ball, and we scored a goal and won.'

The philosophy of the ends justifying the means evidently brought Clemente the results his fans wanted – but once Athletic's performance began to decline in La Liga and failed to deliver any major international trophy, the coach's arrogance and authoritarianism began to be viewed as a liability. In January 1986 Clemente squandered the collective good faith generated by Athletic's championship victories by relegating to the subs bench one of the team's most successful and best loved players, the striker Manu Sarabia. The move was justified by Clemente on the questionable grounds that it was best to keep even the better players for the decisive minutes of the game. It proved hugely divisive among the fans, and was widely criticised in the local media. Clemente was sacked and became coach at Espanyol.

His move to a club that had traditionally been viewed as Barcelona's non-Catalan club, with many of its members drawn from the central government's civil service, may have seemed somewhat at odds with his Basque credentials, but they did no harm to Clemente's career, however controversial it remained. After Espanyol qualified for the UEFA Cup, the team beat Milan and Internazionale before losing in the final to Bayer Leverkusen in a second-leg penalty shoot-out. The defeat followed another of Clemente's bloody-minded and unthinkable decisions – this time leaving out two of the team's best players, John Lauridsen and Ernesto Valverde.

And yet Clemente's reputation was such that he lived to fight another day. After a further successful spell at Atlético Madrid and a brief return to Espanyol in the 1990–91 season, Clemente was appointed coach of Spain's national team in a move celebrated by his die-hard loyalists in the working-class districts of Bilbao, Barcelona and Madrid, but greeted with trepidation by a new generation of wise football commentators – among them Johan Cruyff and the then coach of Real Madrid, the Argentine philosopher of football Jorge Valdano. They wanted the beautiful game of flowing attacking football with the emphasis on quick passing and interchangeable positions to dominate Spanish football and feared the unpredictable consequences of Clemente's impulsive character on the development of a winning team.

Clemente's trademark was to pick players for his squad best known for their toughness and 'efficiency' in defence. He had great faith, for example, in the Real Madrid powerhouse Fernando Hierro, a player who was equally at ease as a central defender or defensive midfielder with a talent focused on his range of passing skills and use of his height to score goals. At the same time, Clemente didn't hesitate to exclude from his squad all five components of the legendary Vulture Squad, a move that soured his relations with large swathes of Real Madrid fans. It was almost as if he saw star players as a challenge to his authority.

Clemente initially defied the pessimists, by taking Spain on a relatively smooth run – eight wins and one loss in twelve matches – into the 1994 World Cup in the US before losing to Italy in the quarter-final when Roberto Baggio scored a late goal. In England in the European Championships two years later, Spain fell at a similar stage.

In the 1998 World Cup in France, Clemente's strategy of remaining loyal to a select group of trusted players regardless of their form proved costly, with the ageing Zubizarreta no longer able to protect the Spanish goal with the brilliance of his earlier years. Clemente did bring into the squad the twenty-year-old Raul, a rising star in La Liga, but his inclusion failed to lift the team spirit. Clemente was widely criticised as having lost his own killer instinct as Spain failed to even reach the second round. He was eventually sacked during qualification for the 2000 European Championships in Belgium and Holland. In its time of need, the Spanish Federation recalled former Real Madrid player José Antonio Camacho as his replacement, but he too was destined to fail.

Fernando Torres – Euro 2008

27

The Wise Man from Hortaleza

By the time of the World Cup in Germany in 2006 Spain had a new coach, Luis Aragonés. Spain had disappointed under Clemente's successors Camacho and Iñaki Saez. But with Aragonés, expectations once again rose that the Spanish Federation had finally picked on someone who could motivate an emerging generation of players to combine in a team capable of seriously challenging the best in the world, casting off the demons of the past that had condemned Spain to the status of football's great underachiever.

Aragonés was born three years into the Spanish Civil War in Hortaleza, a small rural Castilian community northeast of Madrid, in an area held by the Republican forces. During the post-war years, the area was developed into one of the satellite towns that surrounded the capital. Aragonés, a heavily built youth with a reputation for speaking his mind and showing leadership in games, began playing with Getafe before joining Real Madrid. However, it was at the unpredictable if always entertaining Atlético Madrid that he spent the longest time

(1964–74), sharing a Pichichi in 1970 as one of La Liga's top scorers, and reaching the European Cup final in 1974 before losing to Bayern Munich.

Aragonés came to the job of national coach with a track record as one of the best-known names in Spanish football, thanks to his involvement, often successful, as player and later coach in a variety of Spanish clubs including FC Barcelona. The sheer scope of his experience meant that Aragonés over the years came to acquire a rich knowledge of the full potential of Spanish football, the varying styles and strategies of individual clubs, identifying what he thought worked best, and keeping a keen eye on emerging talent.

Those who appreciated Aragonés came to see him as a major football 'mind' and dubbed him *El Sabio de Hortaleza,* the wise man from Hortaleza. There was talk of him becoming national coach in the 1980s. That the Spanish Federation delayed his appointment was partly due to Aragonés' unpredictable mood swings and a tendency to buckle under pressure. In 1988, while serving as a coach for one season at FC Barcelona, Aragonés had shown his weakness when the club was confronted with an unprecedented players' rebellion during which the seamier side of Spanish football had surfaced. The prelude to the rebellion was a rare investigation by Spain's tax inspectors into the complex arrangements Barça had conjured up to keep its foreign players in particular well remunerated.

The investigation, which surfaced after Aragonés' predecessor at Barça Terry Venables had left for Tottenham, initially found that the German international Bernd Schuster had signed two contracts with the Catalan club, although only one had been declared to the tax authorities. Further probes uncovered similar tax avoidance deals involving other players, including elaborate payments to offshore companies, designed to minimise the amount of tax they had to pay on their earnings. When the club was ordered to pay to the Spanish Inland Revenue what was owed, the president José Luis Núñez passed the bill on to the players.

The reaction of the players was swift and very public. They called a press conference in Barcelona's Hotel Heredia pointing out that the double contracts had been drawn with the club's full approval and encouragement, and that it was therefore the club's responsibility to make provision for the loss. In what came to be known as the Mutiny of Heredia, the players issued a joint statement. 'Núñez has deceived us as individuals and humiliated us as professionals,' the statement declared. One of the Barça players absent on the day was Gary Lineker, who was away on duty for the England squad and who felt he had nothing to gain from being associated with the row. 'You just couldn't imagine such a mutiny taking place in England, the fans just wouldn't buy it,' Lineker told me when we discussed the incident.

Aragonés decided to get involved, and suffered as a result. During a pre-match strategy meeting with the players, he broke down in tears, the stress of managing one of the biggest clubs in the world exacerbated by the strained relationship between the team and the president. The mutiny eventually fizzled out with the players failing to secure the support of the fans, and the club engaging in some imaginative accounting. Then Núñez delivered a masterstroke by bringing back to Barça, as Aragonés' replacement, the one person who seemed to be able to guarantee the success and spectacle that so many Barça fans pined for: Johan Cruyff.

As he grew older – and Aragonés was one of the oldest

characters in modern Spanish football – his love of the game came to sustain him as he struggled with his dark moods and his weakness for drinking and gambling, and saying exactly what he felt in public. In October 2004, Aragonés was embroiled in a public controversy of a distasteful kind when a Spanish TV crew filmed him coaching José Antonio Reyes and making a reference to the Spanish wing-forward's Arsenal team-mate Thierry Henry. Aragonés was heard telling Reyes: 'Tell that *negro de mierda* (that black shit) that you are better than him. Don't hold back, tell him. Tell him from me. You have to believe in yourself, you're better than that *negro de mierda*.'

The comments caused a wave of protest in the British media and consternation elsewhere in the football world, although within Spain the media's reaction was generally muted. Aragonés himself was unapologetic for an offence he claimed not to have committed, insisting he had a 'very easy conscience'. In comments that echoed the less diplomatic period of the Clemente era, Aragonés stated: 'I'm obliged to motivate my players to get the best results. As part of that job, I use colloquial language, with which we can all understand each other within the framework of the football world.'

A month later black English players Ashley Cole and Shaun Wright-Phillips were subjected to racist abuse from the crowd at the Bernabéu during an England–Spain 'friendly'. The Spanish Football Federation was initially fined £44,650. But it took the Spanish Football Federation another five months to take any further action of its own and when it came it horrified anti-racism campaigners by its levity. Aragonés was fined €3,000, equivalent to his estimated day's wages. The Director General of Spain's Sports Council Rafael Blanco dismissed any link between the reaction of isolated groups of fans and Aragonés' comments.

Immigration was still a relatively recent topic on democratic Spain's social and political agenda. At the beginning of the 1990s the population was made up almost entirely of Spaniards, with immigrants accounting for less than 1 per cent of residents. But the past decade has seen an influx from around the globe, mostly from other European countries, South America and North Africa. With a buoyant economy and historically low birth-rate, Spain had in the early years of the 21st century become the main destination for immigrants into Europe.

Aragonés unwittingly put Spanish football's attitudes towards race under international scrutiny, exposing a culture at best of ambivalence, at worst of collective denial within Spain itself at a time when its politicians were struggling to formulate a national consensus around how best to deal with the issue. Henry himself described the ineffectiveness of the fines as 'absolutely ridiculous'. He declared, 'You really have to look at the Spanish authorities and they must take a long look at themselves. They obviously don't care about racism. It is laughable. They fined Aragonés for the sake of it, not because they felt he did something wrong.'

By contrast Henry's other Spanish Arsenal colleague Manuel Almunia, along with players from La Liga, black and white, including the Brazilian-born Spanish international midfielder Marcos Senna, followed the line adopted by Spanish officials, insisting that Aragonés was really a decent guy but a victim of overreaction and misunderstanding. He had been lost in translation, in other words.

Aragonés was not sacked, after the Spanish media further

excused the monkey chants. Writing in *El Mundo*, the Spanish journalist Carlos Carbajosa claimed the British reaction was part of a conspiracy typical of the deceiving Perfidious Albion. 'Because the Spanish coach had been attacked as a racist by the English press, the counterattack had to be jeering at the blacks because, if the blacks did not exist, none of this would have happened,' he wrote. Thus the problem, according to Carbajosa, was not the Spanish racism but the aggressive imposition of a 'politically correct' agenda by the hypocritical English tabloid press.

While a minority of Spanish commentators were critical of Aragonés, the episode, as the seasoned Irish hispanist Paddy Woodworth pointed out, revealed 'deeply contradictory attitudes to race in the Spanish psyche, which go back a long, long way'. However, perhaps the most surprising thing about the British media's response to the anti-black racism displayed by elements of the Spanish football world was that they should have been so surprised.

As any British journalist, player or coach who has been closely involved in Spanish football over many years has witnessed, Spain has been no more immune from racism than any other country. Long after the Franco dictatorship had given way to parliamentary democracy in Spain, it was not uncommon to hear monkey chants and other racial abuse greet black players in Spanish stadiums. In 2006, the FC Barcelona player Eto'o walked off the pitch after suffering continual racist abuse from Zaragoza fans. Three years later Barcelona fans were shown on national TV repeatedly abusing Espanyol's Cameroon international goalkeeper Carlos Kameni, with the club's stewards doing nothing to deal with the situation.

Modern Spain has struggled to come to terms with itself as a multicultural society when faced with the huge rise in immigration of recent years. Nevertheless, a growing number of Spanish-born sons of immigrants were making their way through the youth academies to the first teams of major clubs and competing for places in the national squad. Perhaps one of the most interesting recent examples was the promotion in December 2009 of Jonás Ramalho – the son of an Angolan father and a Basque mother – to the first team of Athletic, the last-remaining major Spanish club to incorporate a black player, because of its long-standing policy of having only totally Basque-blood players.

Three years earlier, Spain, under Aragonés, went to the World Cup in Germany with few friends among the British press. The 'racism' issue was not so easily dismissed. FIFA used the tournament to make much of its own impeccable credentials as world football's moral arbitrator, by promoting a somewhat superficial initiative to 'kick out racism'. Despite the campaign, FIFA was criticised by some commentators not just for turning a convenient blind eye to the presence of the Ukrainian manager Oleg Blokhin, who had escaped any sanction after making an unashamedly racist attack on black footballers in his country, but also for providing similar immunity to Aragonés.

And yet Aragonés had come to the world stage with an impressive unbeaten record and a different narrative with which to win hearts and minds. It was Aragonés in an early encounter with the Spanish media who referred to his squad as *La Roja*. Ever since most Spaniards could remember – and that dated back to the Franco years – the squad had been called simply *La Seleccion Nacional* (the national team). But the definition of nationhood became a complicated business in post-Franco

Spain, with various regions claiming increasing autonomy if not independence from Madrid. Only a minority of Spanish fans of an extreme-right persuasion objected to the national team being branded and marketed with the colour red that for them conjured up memories of communists in the Civil War. There were others – again a minority – who took the cynical view that Aragonés wanted to ingratiate himself with the incumbent socialist government of José Luis Zapatero, which was still living in a pre-crisis honeymoon period.

But Aragonés played down any deeper significance than the fact that the Spanish team had played in red shirts (and blue shorts) even during the latter years of the Franco regime, and no one could accuse him of political correctness. Spain was simply following in the steps of other successful football nations who had made a trademark of their shirt colours – Italy (*Azzurri*); France (*Les Bleus*), the Dutch (Brilliant Orange). For those with marketing ambitions, or of a more philosophical bent, *La Roja* transformed the somewhat destructive and negative *La Furia* of old into something as vital as but more life-giving than wine or even blood, transfused rather than spilled. From such synchronicity, the best Spanish tourist posters had been made. Spain was not only different, it was now potentially better by far.

Spain got off to an impressive start, beating Ukraine 4–0, and ending up unbeaten at the top of its group after defeating Saudi Arabia and Tunisia. With Marcos Senna a bedrock in midfield, supported by two of the most versatile and hard-working defenders in La Liga – Barça's Carlos Puyol and Real Madrid's Sergio Ramos – the squad's strike capability was beefed up with the inclusion of three 'young Turks', two from the Valencia stable – David Villa (a future Barça player) and

David Silva – and Atlético Madrid's Fernando Torres, who would subsequently join another Spanish international, Xabi Alonso, and Spanish coach Rafa Benitez at Liverpool, before moving to Chelsea. Silva would later move to Manchester City.

But predictions in the Spanish media that *La Roja,* which had had an unbeaten run of twenty-five matches, would go on and beat France in the next round – *Marca* headlined 'WE ARE GOING TO SEND ZIDANE INTO RETIREMENT!' – proved overoptimistic. Spain lost and exited the tournament. That autumn, following defeats by Northern Ireland and Sweden – seemingly making qualification for Euro 2008 difficult – Aragonés struggled to hang on to his job. The fickle Spanish media turned and called for his resignation, forcing the Spanish Federation's president Ángel Maria Villar belatedly to come to his defence in public.

Behind the scenes the Federation had contacted other managers about taking over, but the plan was shelved after Spain beat Argentina 2–1 in a friendly and the players united behind Aragonés. 'When one loses, everything is a disaster, there is a lot of criticism, and most of it at the *Mister* (the coach). That is unfair and that is how we all saw it. We became stronger and more united around him,' recalled Puyol.

In the coming months it became clear that far from contributing to another Spanish football disaster, Aragonés had laid the foundations of a predominantly youth-based and dynamic project that deserved time to mature. Aragonés moved from being lampooned as an eccentric geriatric to living up to his legendary reputation for wisdom. At Euro 2008, he took Spain to its first major international trophy (outside the gold of the Olympics) in forty-four years, a Torres goal securing a precious 1–0 victory over Germany in Vienna.

Spain was finally victorious. And it had been achieved in a way that seemed to encompass all the best currents of style that had hitherto developed in a dysfunctional manner, and mainly at club level. Spain played with the high-tempo virility that had been the badge of the English since they first arrived in Rio Tinto, but with the technique and inspired creativity that had shown itself over many years, moving back and forth across the Atlantic. With players like Iniesta, Xavi, Cesc Fàbregas, Ramos, Torres, Villa, Silva, and Iker Casillas, Spain had a vibrant and harmonious organisation, with movement, speed, offensive intent and collective self-belief that made them hugely exciting to watch.

So what had brought about this transformative fusion? The answer lay partly in Aragonés' pragmatism, and partly in the nature of the players themselves. Perhaps Aragonés' most defining moment was when he decided to exclude Raul from his squad.

A watershed was reached when in the run-up to Euro 2008, Aragonés dropped Raul and brought in Tamudo Montero, the captain of Espanyol. With Torres and Villa injured, Aragonés gambled on another newcomer, Raúl Albiol, in defence along with Xavi as the backbone of his team. Spain played sensationally in a key qualifying match against Denmark, beating them 3–1, with the victory rounded off thanks to a superb debut international goal by Albert Riera after Aragonés had substituted Joaquin in the 69th minute. The match proved a huge morale boost for the Spanish squad as it ensured their qualification for a tournament they believed they could win. As Xabi Alonso later recalled, 'After Denmark, the squad's spirit, optimism and confidence markedly improved. That victory helped us to believe in ourselves and to boost our sense of self-worth.'

Drawing on the legacy of Cruyff, among others, Aragonés had finally embraced *tiki-taka,* the style that prioritised passing, patience and possession above all else, and for this he drew on players for whom such beauty in motion came naturally. For years, Spanish commentators had tried to excuse their country's failure with talk of bad luck, without ever quite admitting that the country just did not have a collective unit of native players capable of delivering the successes they achieved at club level. But now the talk was of an exciting unprecedented talent pool that transferred seamlessly from club to national squad, and could coalesce to play football that was both aesthetic and effective.

A mixture of bad luck and bad play had combined to deny the Spanish national squad (with the exception of Olympic gold in 1992) any major tournament victory since Marcelino's winning goal against Russia in the European Nations Cup final at the Bernabéu on 21 June 1964. Now the gods smiled on a team that felt it deserved to win, and could. A synchronicity between coach and team translated into a powerful force.

Minutes before the start of Spain's game against Germany in the finals of Euro 2008 Aragonés took Torres to one side in the dressing room and repeated a ritual he had once performed when he and the rising young star were both at Atlético Madrid. 'You are going to score two goals,' Aragonés told Torres, and then drew the sign of the cross on his forehead.

As things turned out Torres scored only one goal, but it was the goal Spanish football had been waiting forty-four years for. Inside the German half, Xavi picked up a pass from Senna, faced Ballack and Schweinsteiger, turned and, with his back to them and seemingly with eyes in the back of his head, twisted and passed the ball forward on his right to Torres, who with a burst of acceleration, ran on to it, switched direction to beat Lahm, then leaped, gazelle-like, over Jens Lehman, and stumbling, but without falling, struck it home.

As Torres would later recall:

The ground was very wet and that new Adidas ball was very fast. I miscalculated its arrival and it seemed to get away ahead of me a little. Perhaps Lahm was too confident or just surprised by the ball's trajectory because it was going fast, very fast, and he gave me space on the right. I drew him out towards the left, he blocked me and then didn't look back. I decided to change direction and went to his right. At that moment I saw that Lehman was coming out late and I realised there was a gap there. I thought the goalkeeper would reach the ball first, but on seeing the space, I lifted the ball and it turned in. I thought it might be going out because the ball was spinning, and because in the direction it was going, it looked as if it was going to go on the outside of the post. But the ground was so wet that the ball skidded and went in . . .

That Torres goal in the 33rd minute of the Euro 2008 final at the Ernst Happel stadium in Vienna was a defining moment in a tournament in which *La Roja* had finally proved themselves worthy Champions of Europe with their formidable attacking football. The creation of the goal epitomised the artistry Spain had stood for from the outset of the tournament. It was the moment when the Spanish squad's brightest young *matador* dispatched an ageing bull that had lost its fire and nobility. The Germans tried to resist a team that passed the ball like gods.

But this was a plodding veterans' Germany well past its best, that in the end conceded the winning goal to a much better team, full of promise.

In an important sense this was an emblemic parting of the ways for Spanish football. Torres saw his star rise just as another legend of Spanish football, Raul, saw his fall. But the new Spanish football of *La Roja* was only partly built on Raul's demise, and Torres' maturity. It also came into being thanks to a generation of young and extremely talented Spanish players suited to a *tiki-taka* style in which passing, patience and possession was never taken to a slow, directionless extreme, but formed part of a rich choreography of attacking, winning football, built up in midfield by the likes of Iniesta and Xavi, and in which players such as Villa and Torres provided the cutting edge.

As Xavi explained on being asked by the *Guardian*'s Sid Lowe to explain the secret of success: 'Think quickly, look for spaces. That's what I do: look for spaces. All day. I'm always looking. All day, all day. (Xavi starts gesturing as if he is looking around, swinging his head.) Here? No. There? No. People who haven't played don't always realise how hard that is. Space, space, space. It's like being on the PlayStation. I think shit, the defender's here, play it there. I see the space and pass. That's what I do.'

High-tempo virility had long been the badge English football liked to flash, and Torres in particular had learned something of this after moving to play in the Premier League at Liverpool. To the extent that his goal against the Germans owed as much to pace, faith and strength, as to touch and class, it was quintessentially Spanish, drawing on the best of the past and throwing it into the future as a vibrant, creative hybrid.

Statistically, the margin of Spain's victory in Vienna was the same as Greece's victory in Euro 2004, with the two tournaments goal tally equal at seventy-seven. But it was widely accepted that this was an infinitely better tournament. It wasn't about statistics, but the sheer flair and panache of the build-up, and the beauty of the goals scored. It was also about a team's spirit, how players connected with each other, making the whole even better than its constituent parts, and rewarding a manager's faith in Spain's ability to perform and achieve. *La Roja* had come into its own.

Los Galacticos – Beckham and Capello at Real Madrid

28

From Beckham to Guardiola

Spain's impressive performance at Euro 2008 rekindled a sense of optimism about the future of international football, which had been eclipsed since the beginning of the millennium by the inexorable rise of clubs like Manchester United, Real Madrid, AC Milan and Barcelona as global superbrands. There was a fear that this new club superiority had come at the expense of national cultural identity. Globalisation had raised the attraction to talented players, their agents and their clubs to sell or be sold to the highest bidder. Everything seemed to have a price, even loyalty to one's roots. Cultural identity appeared to increasingly matter less than the business of winning the most lucrative deals, whether they be sponsorship or TV.

A watershed moment was the European Court of Justice ruling in 1995 in favour of the Belgian player Jean-Marc Bosman, who challenged the restrictions placed on footballers from European Union countries playing within the national leagues of Europe. The ruling allowed professional football players in the EU to move freely to another club at the end of their contract, in accordance with the new competition rules established by the EU's single market in 1992. While destined to have a far-reaching impact on the business of international football, the extent to which globalisation, and the freeing up of the market post-Bosman, shaped Spanish football was most evident in the Real Madrid side that the construction magnate Florentino Perez created after winning the presidency in 2000.

Real Madrid at the time was not short of trophies, but was short of cash. Perez believed that the club's weak financial situation reflected fundamentally a glaring imbalance between its spending on players and the underdeveloped exploitation of its image as one of the most successful clubs in the world. Modern football is littered with examples of clubs brandishing cheque books only to end with headaches. Perez seemed to work even bigger miracles with Real Madrid's balance sheet than with its team sheet. Over four seasons, he took advantage of the speculative and overheated Spanish economy to sell off high-value real estate at a huge profit, and built Real Madrid's marketing strategy around the purchase of a major new international star per year with the ability to appeal to consumers across frontiers.

Over three years Real Madrid developed its 'brand' as a global club of *galacticos* – superstars – with record transfer deals led by Figo, Zidane and Ronaldo. Not only were millions of new shirts sold, but the club negotiated upwards its TV and sponsorship contracts. It also became a formidable force on the pitch – less a team than a group of individual high-quality, hugely talented performers capable of putting on a fantastically entertaining show, and also winning. With Figo, Real Madrid won the league championship, with Zidane the European Champions League and the World Club Championship, and with Ronaldo the league again and the European Super Cup. Then it was time for David Beckham to come to Spain.

The Manchester United star's falling-out with manager Alex Ferguson had become the club's worst-kept secret, so that it was no longer a question of if Beckham would leave but when. From early on in the saga United had no doubt that Beckham wanted to go to Real Madrid and that the club was determined to buy him. But that summer Joan Laporta, an ambitious young Catalan lawyer, spun the rumour that Beckham would transfer to FC Barcelona no sooner had he been elected president. Laporta was elected after boosting his poll ratings with a news item on the Manchester United official website that appeared to give the story some credibility. As one of Laporta's top aides told me, 'We knew that Beckham was going to Real Madrid, but we wanted to win the presidency, and the Beckham "story" was helpful.' Manchester United's complicity was in using Laporta's political ambition to help raise the price Real Madrid was willing to pay.

As things turned out Beckham's transfer from Manchester United to Real Madrid was officially announced with a masterly sense of timing just hours before he and his pop star/model wife, the ex-Spice Girl Victoria 'Posh' Beckham, flew to Japan on a promotional tour for their sponsors. Thus at a stroke Beckham's red-shirted Asian fans from Tokyo to Bangkok rushed into buying up the white merchandising of his new club. Back in Madrid, the latest modernisation of the Bernabéu stadium was given the green light. A key element in the planning was the expansion of the number of high-value corporate VIP seats, with multinational companies based in Madrid lining up to write off the costs, in tax terms, as client entertainment. That August of 2003, Beckham emerged from the

Bernabéu dressing room and into a building site, and there amid the dust, like a proverbial phoenix rising from the ashes, calmly ran the gauntlet of the world's media.

Outside, along the ramp that leads up to the adjoining street from the club's private garage, hundreds of young, mostly female fans, screamed with excitement, and shouted '*Guapo*' – handsome – repeatedly as Beckham and Posh emerged in their car. Spanish newspapers carried photographs of the couple on their front pages. Lengthy reports focused on Beckham's glittering celebrity lifestyle and marketing power. Beckham came to Spain with the support of an army of legal advisers, agents and PR men – a streamlined commercial operation the likes of which Spanish football had never witnessed.

At his official signing ceremony, Beckham held up his new Madrid shirt to a packed gathering of the world's football media. At his side was Real Madrid's most admired veteran Alfredo Di Stéfano, the player who fifty years earlier had helped transform Real Madrid into the most successful club in the world. It looked as if Di Stéfano's smile would disintegrate like wax any minute, such did the old man struggle with the sense that his beloved football club had become a circus.

All everyone knew was that it had never been like this in Di Stéfano's time. Beckham – a master of the photo-op and the ingratiating marketing phrase – uttered his only words so far learned in Spanish – *gracia*s and the club's traditional *Hala, Madrid.* The cry had been first uttered many decades previously by a young member of the Spanish royal household. Beckham later allowed himself to be photographed with a small Spanish boy called Alfonso, allegedly the son of a long-term Madrid fan. But all this had very little to do with preserving the identity of one of Spain's oldest and greatest clubs. It was instead part of a carefully managed choreography suited to the ambitions of the club's 21st-century moneyspinners.

In December 2003 I went to see Real Madrid's head of marketing José Ángel Sanchez to talk about Beckham in Spain. A smooth dynamic salesman who operated in plush offices off Madrid's Castellana Avenue, Sanchez showed me spreadsheets of his marketing projections around the world in which territories beyond Spain were disputed with Manchester United and FC Barcelona. This was football played out like a game of Risk. He then told me about Beckham: 'Buying Beckham is like buying into a business. He brings with him a whole range of customers, not just because of his value as a footballer but also as a celebrity, he is an icon of modern society . . . Real Madrid is not going to abandon its Spanish roots but right now it's a club with many followers around the world and this is a source of pride.'

Looking at the global context of the Beckham phenomenon, and having watched, not least in the UK, 'playing fields, pitches and open spaces consumed by the voracious property booms of the 1990s', David Goldblatt gloomily predicted youth football retreating 'to teenagers' bedrooms and the pixilated images of football played out on a video game console'.

Wanting to check out further the impact of Beckham on Spanish football, I visited one of Real Madrid's youth training schools, not in Madrid but in Barcelona. Funding the school in a territory historically monopolised by Real Madrid's arch rival was a bold move by Florentino Perez. It reflected the ruthless streak of an entrepreneur that relished hostile bids. But this was not so much a dawn raid as a calculated subversion from within. Ignacio Marquez, the school's director – no bearded academic but a slick young lawyer who read the *Financial Times* – was my host when I visited the school halfway through Beckham's first season in Spain. He talked about his academy as if it was part social-network site, part business school. He told me: 'It is run according to the administrative and financial arrangements between Real Madrid and an educational foundation dedicated to the investigation and development of the teaching of football. It is state-of-the-art stuff – the development of spectacular individual skills with the tactics and strategies of play of an international standard.'

The Real Madrid academy was conceived as a template for similar schools in Asia, South America, the US and the Middle East. It clearly served a particular social and political motive in Catalonia. Many of the school kids I saw that day were the sons of Spain's growing population of immigrants – Asians, South Americans, Africans, Arabs, Eastern Europeans. I watched some of them in action. Kids, some not much older than seven, played with disarming skill and speed. Their part-time teachers included first-team players from the other Barcelona team, Espanyol. Football at the school was in addition to a normal curriculum, I was told – although I soon discovered that the word 'normal' had to be qualified. While in Catalonia's state schools Catalan was taught as an obligatory first language, here in this small enclave of Real Madrid different rules prevailed: pupils not only dressed in white but were taught as a priority in Spanish, along with English and French.

Marquez strongly rejected my suggestion that, faced with a majority of Catalan nationalists in the region, this might be seen as a recipe for social division and alienation. 'What we are doing here is helping the process of belonging to Spain which an immigrant needs, by not only showing them how to play football but to be good in human terms – values like sacrifice, generosity, companionship,' he insisted.

He wanted converts to the cause of Real Madrid. But I don't think the concept of nationhood really bothered him and he wasn't in the business of being provocative for provocation's sake. Marquez was no *Ultra Sur*. The pupils were encouraged, for their own safety's sake, not to walk out on the streets of Barcelona dressed in Real Madrid's white shirts and pants. 'To be honest, it's not recommended to go around Madrid sporting the colours of FC Barcelona either,' he added for good measure. 'There are extremes on both sides and we don't want to play into their hands.'

But just how much and what kind of a role model was Beckham turning out to be here in this conquered territory of Spain? Marquez replied, 'I think Beckham is a difficult example. His image is not an easy one to replicate. You could say that to be like Beckham is impossible in reality and that can make kids here feel as if they are underachieving, depressed even.'

Outside the school, Beckham did have an impact on Spanish football in the four seasons he played at Real Madrid, but most of it was to do with money. Spanish football journalists like the hugely knowledgeable Santiago Segurola tended to view Beckham as a pop celebrity first and foremost, whose skills as a footballer fell well short of those of several Spanish players past and present. Another Spanish journalist friend of mine, *Marca*'s long-serving Real Madrid specialist Ulises Sanchez Flor, while admiring Beckham for his talent with the dead ball, felt he fell well short as a playmaker. His ability in one-touch play and dribbling was less apparent than his tendency to chase balls unnecessarily around the pitch, and to occasionally tackle in a way that in the theatrical Spanish league was destined to end in grief.

Marca dubbed Beckham *Forrest Gump* on account of his perceived lack of genuine creativity or intelligence, even if

Beckham's attempt to reincarnate the *Furia* of such Real Madrid legends as Juanito earned him some support from the *Ultra Surs*. The club's most fanatical fan-base had warmly applauded him in January 2004 when he was awarded his first red card in Spain midway through Real Madrid's King's Cup quarter-final first-leg victory over Valencia at the Bernabéu.

In Spain, taking on the referee – a symbol of officialdom in a country ruled for large chunks of its history by dictatorships, but also prone to rebellion – was often seen as a badge of honour, and on that occasion Beckham's anti-referee *hijo de puta* – another Spanish phrase he had learned – was applauded by thousands of supporters watching in the stadium and on TV. His second dismissal of 2004 proved less popular at a time when Real Madrid's performance as a team was floundering, not least because he took the opportunity of his suspension to turn out for Martin Keown's testimonial in London. After receiving an angry phone call from Perez, not best pleased with the temporarily, allegedly unauthorised, absence of his star *galactico*, Beckham played for only three minutes at the Arsenal stadium then was forced to dash back to Madrid.

When at the end of Beckham's first season in Spain, Real Madrid lost 2–3 to Mallorca at the Bernabéu, their third successive home defeat, paving the way for Valencia's La Liga title win, Mallorca's then coach and future creator of *La Roja* Luis Aragonés made this disparaging remark about one of the most expensive players in the world: 'Beckham is finding it difficult to play in the middle. He passes acceptably and works hard, but he doesn't think quickly. In the centre of midfield it's very important to know where you are going to place the ball before it comes to you. He doesn't think in a hurry.' In other words, Beckham was still Forrest Gump.

In fairness, Beckham was too easily a whipping boy for a deeper malaise affecting the *galactico* project. Real Madrid as a team, far from representing an exciting constellation, seemed dysfunctional and nearly burned out. Beckham was failing to click, while causing some friction in the dressing room. Some Spanish players appeared to resent the media circus built up around him in the run-up to and the aftermath of every match. But other superstars were failing too. The great Frenchman and one-time World Cup hero of *Les Bleus* Zidane had ceased to live up to his earlier status as the crown jewel of the *galactico* project. He could not remember having ever played as badly as he did in the last game of the season.

Some Spanish commentators blamed Real Madrid's Portuguese manager Carlos Queiroz for not rotating enough, and making little use of native-born players, including those who had come up through the club's youth academy. Queiroz had succumbed to pressure from President Perez to make full use of his investment by playing the *galacticos* as often as possible, even if they were out of form. The show had to go on. The global audience demanded nothing else, the marketing men believed. Controversy also lingered over the circumstances of the former Manchester United assistant manager Queiroz's appointment, which had coincided with Beckham's arrival.

Queiroz had replaced an unceremoniously sacked Vicente del Bosque, a mild-mannered and popular former Real Madrid player, as Beckham arrived in Madrid. In his four seasons in charge Del Bosque had led Real Madrid through its most successful period in modern history: two Champions League titles in 2000 and 2002, two La Liga titles in 2001 and 2003, a Spanish Super Cup in 2001, a UEFA Super Cup in 2002, and an Intercontinental Cup in 2002, as well as reaching the last four of the Champions League in every year he was in charge. Not since the golden years of the 1950s had the club had such a consistent record of success.

Del Bosque had patiently overseen the first intake of *los galacticos*, over whose transfer he had no say, and merged them into a coherent team. But he was sacked in a shake-up of the club that also involved the exit of eleven players, among them Spanish internationals like Fernando Hierro and Fernando Morientes, the Englishman Steve McManaman and the Frenchman Claude Makélélé. 'Del Bosque was showing signs of exhaustion. I want to be sincere about this – our belief was that he was not the right coach for the future,' Perez told the BBC.

Queiroz survived one season in the job before he too was sacrificed. Beckham's second season in Spain began with new head coach José Antonio Camacho, another former Real Madrid player who had been in charge of Spain's national squad. His tenure lasted only three matches as Real Madrid slipped to eighth spot in La Liga. A succession of lacklustre and luckless coaches followed over the season, and Perez resigned on 27 February 2006. (He would later be re-elected as president.) Under his successor Ramon Calderon, the new coach at Real Madrid was the Italian Fabio Capello, with a track record of trophy success in Serie A and a former stint at the Spanish club.

Capello's return to Spain was not universally welcomed by local fans. The last two trophies he had won, at Juventus, had been declared null and void after several players at the club had been embroiled in a match-fixing scandal in which Capello denied any involvement. Moulded in the tradition of uncompromising defensive play and opportunistic goal-scoring, Capello declared that the days of 'beautiful football' were over and what mattered were results.

While researching those days at Real Madrid, I discovered the roots of a common love that Capello and Beckham came to share. I was told by a Real Madrid veteran that when Capello began his first stint as coach at Real Madrid in 1996, he told his players that Spanish ham was unhealthy and ordered them to cut it from their diet. Only later did he come round to admiring its medicinal properties, judging Spain's *pata negra* ham of better quality than Italy's Parma *prosciutto*. When in an earlier interview with *Marca*, memorable only for its total lack of substance, Beckham was asked by a young work-placement British graduate what he liked best about Spanish culture, the superstar replied that he had discovered a liking for Spanish cured ham, *jamon serrano*.

Whatever their common interests, Capello and Beckham did not have an easy run of their shared time in Spain. In January 2007, just five months into his new contract, Capello sensationally vowed that Beckham would never play for Real Madrid again after the player agreed a deal to join LA Galaxy the following summer. Already the newly selected England manager Steve McClaren had made it clear that his future team had no place for Beckham either. It looked as if Beckham's career in the top flight of football was effectively over. Beckham bounced back – his continued efforts in training and proven work rate convincing Capello to recall the Englishman within a month, much to the delight of the club's marketing department. Beckham went on to help Real Madrid in a dramatic late-season surge to win La Liga on the final day of the season.

Following his departure to the US, Beckham's celebrity in Spain proved ephemeral. He disappeared from the attention of the local sports media and the marketing world generally almost as quickly as he had once taken dominance over it, much in the manner of a shooting star. However, there were a growing crop of Spanish players who had learned a thing or two from him about marketing themselves. Advised by agents, they attempted to increase their net worth by posing for fashion photographs, appearing in style magazines and advertising hoardings, and generally branding themselves on and off the field.

From Beckham's early days in Spain, Fernando Torres provided an early native response to the celebrity status of the expat Brit. While still playing for Atlético Madrid, Torres' seemingly innocent charm and youthful good looks (he was eight years younger than Beckham) ensured him a popular following among Spanish fans. But *El Niño* (the kid), as he was affectionately called, was much more than just a pretty face. Torres was a key element in Atlético's fight to return to La Liga after their humiliating demotion and he became a growing presence in the Spanish national squad. By the start of the season of 2004–05, Torres had emerged as one of the most attractive goal-scoring talents among a new generation of Spanish players who had the skills, energy and projection to rival the superstar imports.

That autumn of 2005, fame landed through Torres' letter box in the form of a letter informing him that Madrid's waxwork museum was going to make a model of him as they had of other sporting greats. When Christmas came he was asked to inaugurate Madrid's Christmas celebrations from the balcony of the town hall. In 2007 he joined the former Valencia coach Rafa Benitez and a group of Spanish players at Liverpool, where he became the fastest player in Liverpool history to score fifty league goals for the club. In January 2011 Torres joined Chelsea for a record British transfer fee of £50 million, which also made him the most expensive Spanish player in history.

For Torres a defining moment in his career was when in May 2007, during his last season with Atlético Madrid, his club was beaten 6–0 at home by FC Barcelona. 'I reflected on the match and could not avoid the conclusion that Barcelona was a big club and Atlético were not yet,' he later recalled. 'The thought went round my head and I reached the conclusion that to compete with Barcelona – to really compete, as equals – we'd need five to eight years.' It proved an overoptimistic forecast.

By 2007, FC Barcelona was on its way to affirming itself as the world's top club. It was also drawing together a generation of players that were to have a profound impact on the character and fortunes of Spanish national football. The seeds for this transformation were planted during the dream team years of Johan Cruyff, when special emphasis was placed on developing the club's production of home-grown talent at its youth academy. The school was founded in 1978 and until just after the 2010 World Cup was housed next to the Camp Nou in a converted traditional stone farmhouse, named La Masia – Catalan for home – in recognition of the club's identification with local culture, before moving to more modern premises more in keeping with its global marketing ambitions.

To visit and talk with those involved in the project was to be reminded not just why FC Barcelona prided itself on being *mes que un club* – more than just a club – committed to engage with football as much more than a sport. In La Masia it was a whole way of existence – and, of course, about how to play beautiful football.

La Masia was the icing on the cake of Barça's version of *fútbol base*, Spain's well-financed and impeccably organised national football training programme. The learning curve began to take shape in early kick-arounds on beaches, neighbourhood streets and waste grounds, but then became more focused as kids evolved through highly competitive football games at primary school and beyond, and teachers were contacted by club scouts, looking for those with real potential to be top-flight professionals in their late teens.

In any one year some one hundred teenage kids – the youngest is eleven but a majority are teenagers aged between fifteen and seventeen – were attached to La Masia either as boarders or daytime attendees after being selected, with their parents' agreement, for an education that includes the curriculum followed by the region's state school system but which places a special emphasis on a philosophy of excellence, both sporting and human.

During one of FC Barcelona's most recent golden periods, La Masia's director Carlos Folguera was a quiet-spoken if intense former hockey player turned sports teacher specialising in child and youth psychology. In early 2011 he received me in a spartan office that could have otherwise been occupied by an abbot. The whole building was inauspicious, in stark contrast to the looming presence of the nearby stadium. La Masia prior to its current plusher headquarters had the air of a modern monastery about it, simply decorated and furnished, with touches of functionality like the computer screens, but an underlying air of austere discipline. It reminded me of the quarters inhabited by the Benedictines of Montserrat, the mountain shrine outside Barcelona, where the Catalan virgin, her face darkened by the flames of votive candles, remains a key place of pilgrimage for Barça fans.

Catalonia would not have produced artists like Gaudi, Dali and Miró if it didn't appreciate the creative force of the extrovert, and Catalans have popularised the word *rauxa* to describe the irrational or crazy. But as central to the Catalan psyche

– perhaps as a necessary counterbalance – was the equally popular term *seny*, which translates into an air of sense and reliability. Folguera was a definite advocate of *seny*. The tiny and nimble-framed Andrés Iniesta, the monk-like midfielder who, despite his humility on and off the pitch, came to display extraordinary touch, pace and vision, with FC Barcelona and *La Roja*, was La Masia's Spanish role model, while Lionel Messi was its most famous non-Spanish old boy, looked on as probably the best player of his generation.

Brought here as a young teenager from his native Argentina, Messi had turned into one of the greatest footballers of all time, finding in the team ethos and style of FC Barcelona and the personal security and support offered to him by the club, the perfect context for his talent to flourish. Undoubtedly one of La Masia's greatest achievements was in ensuring that Messi was protected from any demons that might have threatened him from within or without at a critical point in his evolution as a human being. The club had enough of a history of brilliant South Americans – Maradona, Romario, Ronaldinho among them – who had buckled under the pressure of fame and allowed their personal lives to jeopardise their professional careers, to know it had to continue to be particularly mindful of ensuring that Messi's private life was safe and secure and that he was content with his treatment within the team. But it had the advantage of having brought Messi over to Barcelona when he was relatively unknown and at a young impressionable age, and of having paid for the hormonal-boosting treatment without which his talent for the game would have remained unfulfilled. His best support staff included first-team players who had grown up with him and the principles and conduct which La Masia has instilled in him.

Folguera explained La Masia's mission: 'I and the teaching staff try and engage with the pupils as much as possible to instil in them a set of fundamental values that have to do with respect for others, regardless of whether he is the cook or the director of the school. We then get them to realise that not everyone who comes here makes it, so they don't take their stay here for granted. It's important that a pupil knows that his talent is in the end on a hiding to nothing unless it is accompanied by values such as commitment, discipline, solidarity, comradeship . . .'

Discipline extended to a zero-tolerance policy on class absenteeism, drugs, alcohol and uncontrolled website surfing, although Folguera swore that these problems never arose thanks to effectively enforced rules and regulations combined with an enlightened programme of workshops, consultative assemblies, brainstorms and lectures by outside specialists on subjects ranging from the destructive qualities of cocaine to the security risks inherent in social networking.

'We try and get our kids to understand that simply because you have 800 "friends" on Facebook, this is not a guarantee of support and loyalty. Trust is knowing that a friend is not going to take a picture of you in the bathroom and then distribute it round the world. It's a question of privacy and respect,' Folguera told me.

So was this a religious education, I asked. Folguera replied: 'No, religion doesn't play a part here. This is a lay education, it's about respecting the rules of the game, about leadership, about team building . . . At the end of the day the kids who come here tend to take care of themselves because they don't want to squander the opportunity of fulfilling their dream, that of playing for Barça's first team one day.'

It was that vision which also influenced the way La Masia

went about choosing its pupils. The selection was divided into equal parts of three territories: Catalonia, the rest of Spain, and the rest of the world. It was thus less racially exclusive than Athletic Bilbao's Lezama School, which insisted that its pupils should have Basque blood. Far from diluting Barça's identity, Folguera argued, the mix was a faithful reflection of the society in which the club played, enriching it with talent and moulding it in the club colours. Moreover, Folguera claimed that this one-stop in-house education was La Masia's strength as an institution, compared for example to Real Madrid, which contracted out many of its courses to state schools.

So what about football? Well, I didn't need to be shown the carefully protected and secret lessons in skills, tactics and strategy to realise that perhaps this well-financed no-go- area to visitors was precisely the one that gave La Masia the edge over other reputable training schools such as those at Athletic Bilbao, Villarreal and Sporting Gijón, although it continued to face tough competition for young hearts and minds from Real Madrid given the club's huge exposure on TV and the web.

When I visited La Masia, the list of some of its former 'star' pupils was the most striking testimony to its success. In addition to the Argentine national Messi, the Castilian-born Iniesta, and Pedro from the Canary Islands, they included its most famous Catalans –Puyol, Xavi, Busquets, Fàbregas and Piqué. But of the old boys of La Masia, one more than any other had earned a special place in the history of Spanish football – Pep Guardiola.

Guardiola's Catalan identity and football skills were defined at an early age. He was born in the small rural village of Santpedor, some fifty kilometres north of Barcelona, where locals spoke the Catalan language during the Franco years, and poor local kids like him learned to kick a ball around in the

narrow streets, playing off the stone walls. Guardiola was thirteen years old when in 1984 he arrived at La Masia.. '*Mare
meva* (Mamma Mia)' he marvelled in Catalan on his first day,
'Every morning when I open the window, I will see the Camp
Nou,' he said on his first day as a boarder. He was there for the
next five years. There were four bedrooms and ten talented
youngsters in each of them. Guardiola shared a bunk with
another village kid from a similar poor background. His name
was Tito Vilanova. He was two years older than Guardiola and
became a kind of mentor.

Tito never really made it as a player. He stayed in the lower
divisions, where the grounds were not so good, the 'playing
fields of poverty' they called them in Spain, even if some of
their facilities put many sports grounds elsewhere in Europe to
shame. Guardiola was promoted through the ranks, but he
never turned his back on his old friend Tito. When it came to
managing the first team he called on Tito, just as he had done
when he was at the B team, to be his assistant and to remain
one of his trusted friends. Both Guardiola and Tito shared an
unflagging faith in La Masia's contribution to a football of style
and grace. They also believed that its youngsters had an inde-
structible Barça strain in their DNA, which could be passed on
to others, whatever their background or nationality.

While at La Masia, Guardiola learned Catalan poetry and
listened to the songs of Lluís Llach, whose protest songs had
become popular in the final years of the Franco regime. But
much of his time was spent getting as close as he could to the
Camp Nou, developing his own skills while spying as much as
he could on the first-team players. He would in time look up to
the Basque Andoni Zubizarreta and the Dane Michael Laudrup
as his role models – examples of noble characters on and off the

pitch. But the earlier and clearest image a lot of older Barça fans have of Guardiola is of a skinny, unshaven water boy running out from the touchline and embracing Pichi Alonso the day Terry Venables' team qualified for the European Cup.

Guardiola was promoted by Cruyff to the first team. Jorge Valdano, who would become one of many huge admirers of Guardiola, would famously remark that in the Catalan's game one noticed the pride of the neighbourhood kid. Guardiola remained forever conscious of his Catalan village roots but also had luck on his side. At the time Koeman was injured, Guillermo Amor was suspended because he'd collected too many red cards, and Milla had left the club, leaving a gap that needed filling in midfield. In the end Guardiola got his big break because Cruyff had faith in him. 'Cruyff believed I could do it and gave me the opportunity. I think there are a lot of people who sometimes miss out simply because they are not given the chance. I owe it to Cruyff,' Guardiola said.

Cruyff certainly would not have picked Guardiola if he hadn't believed in him. As the Dutchman told me: 'Guardiola could control the ball quickly and pass it quickly. He could deliver the ball in good condition so that another player could do something with it.' In the legendary 'dream team' that won both the league and the European Cup in the 1991–92 season, Guardiola formed part of an array of talent and skill that would for a while have even hard-core *Madridistas* watching in awe. It was arguably the best Spanish club side since the golden years of Real Madrid in the 1950s. Its triumph at Wembley brought over a million people out onto the streets of Barcelona. Pep Guardiola waved the Catalan flag from City Hall and the offices of the Generalitat. '*Visca Barça, Visca Catalunya!*' cried Jordi Pujol, the regional government's president. He was neither the first nor the last local politician to transform a football event into an act of political affirmation, the rallying cry for the club uttered in the same linguistic breath as the declaration of Catalan nationhood. But it was Guardiola who struck the most passionate and emotional note that day, declaring, '*Ciutadans de Catalunya, ya la tenim aqui!*' (Citizens of Catalonia, you have it here!) as he raised the European Cup. Everyone there knew he had paraphrased the historic words of the former Catalan President Josep Tarradellas on his return, after Franco's death, from post-civil war exile, and many Catalans loved him for it.

Guardiola's close involvement with *Barça* from his days as a young pupil, through to playing with Cruyff's dream team and later, as a young coach, leading the B team to promotion from the Third to the Second Division, turned into a major asset. As well as experiencing, as a Spanish international, the peaks and troughs of an underachieving national squad pre-Aragonés, Guardiola had also learned a lot about emerging talent, tactics and strategy at one of the world's most successful football clubs. *Barça* was in Guardiola's DNA. 'OK,' he told club president Joan Laporta on being offered his new job as manager of FC Barcelona in the spring of 2008, 'but only if I can do it my way and with my people.'

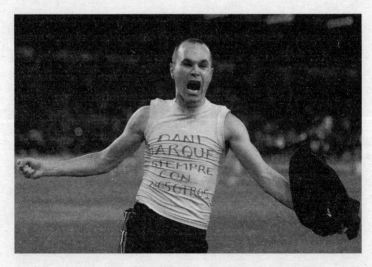

Champions of the World

29

Champions of the World

When Guardiola took over at FC Barcelona, the club had gone two seasons without winning trophies under the tutelage of Dutch international Frank Rijkaard, in striking contrast to an earlier record of two successive La Liga championships (2005 and 2006) and a Champions League victory (2006). A sense of crisis had begun to infect the club. The team's Brazilian star Ronaldinho, who had been instrumental in reviving Barça's fortunes, had lost form. He was suspected by senior club executives of drawing other players, including the young Argentine international Lionel Messi, into his wild night life. They also thought Rijkaard was running out of ideas and losing control.

In picking Guardiola, Laporta was taking a gamble. A former Spanish international and FC Barcelona captain, Guardiola had also played in Italy and for a short period in Qatar, but his management experience was limited to Barça's B team.

However, Guardiola was one of football's great thinkers and although reticent about giving interviews was disarmingly articulate whenever he spoke in public. He published his equivalent of a book of proverbs, *Escoltant Guardiola* – Listening to Guardiola – which was subtitled '150 Lessons in Football and Life'. It showed that for him football was much more than just about Barça – it infused his sense of how football should be played by any team. As the Catalonia-based Dutch writer Edwin Winkels put it: 'This book was unlike anything Cruyff, in dreadful Spanish, had ever written. Guardiola's Catalan was far superior to Cruyff's Dutch (or indeed to most English players' English). It was flawless, perfectly crafted, incisive, often very serious, and occasionally light-hearted. Guardiola was intelligent.'

With his tall, thin frame, and dark, brooding, biblical looks, Guardiola cut an almost mystical figure – a perfect model for one of El Greco's religious pictures. Guardiola confessed that of all the teams he learned most from, it was the Dutch Ajax – the three times European champions of the early 1970s – who had an enduring influence with their creative 'total football'. As he recalled: 'They played great football collectively. They built up a line of attack from the rear with great ease . . . all players were fully aware of their role on the pitch and exercised discipline. Ball possession was their mantra. They were ready at all times to assist. They are capable of touch and movement with simplicity and brilliance . . .'

Hardly anything escaped Guardiola about his players. He believed the face was the mirror of the soul. In other words he put the person before the footballer and was constantly on the lookout to ensure his wellbeing off the pitch as well as on. He was to show himself ruthless with those he lost faith in like Ronaldinho, Eto'o, and Bojan, all of whom he encouraged to transfer to another club. But with others he felt were essential to his mission, like the majority of La Masia-educated stars, not least Messi, he was prepared to go that extra mile in terms of encouragement.

Hours after Messi's latest night out with Ronaldinho, when the Argentine's form had clearly dipped, Guardiola confronted him with a life-defining choice: either he went on following the Brazilian's hedonistic lifestyle and risked ending up like Maradona, a huge talent destroyed physically and mentally before realising his full potential, or he remembered the values and discipline he had learned at La Masia and continued at Barça on his way to being one of the best players in the world. Messi agreed to resubmit himself to a disciplined regime of early nights, a healthy low-alcohol diet, and training.

Later, in May 2009, just before Guardiola's players walked out in Rome's Olympic stadium to play Manchester United in the final of the Champions League, he gathered them one last time in the dressing room and there, to their surprise, got them to watch a video he had had specially made by a TV journalist friend. The video showed the Barça players intercut with scenes from the film *Gladiator,* with Russell Crowe substituting for Guardiola as the team cheerleader. The message to the players was that they should face the imminent contest with courage and without fear, knowing that their best chance of survival and victory lay in unity and playing the football they had mastered. And so it was. Manchester United were systematically outplayed, as they struggled against the effectiveness and elaboration of Barça's shifting geometry, of players constantly swapping positions, while linking with each other, and passing the ball from one to the other, one touch at a time, in a flowing and ever-changing display of creativity. Among them Messi was the linchpin of Barça's attacking trio, contributing to the first goal from Eto'o after only ten minutes. But it was in the seventieth minute that the little big man educated by La Masia showed his true genius. Having sneaked into space between Ferdinand and O'Shea, Messi received a perfect cross from Xavi and, lifting himself to the skies, delivered a header into the top corner with effortless accuracy. No 'Hand of God' here, just sheer determination and brilliance. Messi offered the goal up to God anyway, having first embraced his team-mates. Barça won 2–0 and were crowned European club champions.

Eighteen years had gone by since Cruyff, in his third season as FC Barcelona coach, had brought Guardiola into his first team. Under Cruyff's regime, Guardiola became a number 4, Barcelona's equivalent of a quarterback, and was encouraged to control and pass the ball quickly, and to fight to get it back. Guardiola would later keep a copy of a book by Cruyff, like a bible, always by his bedside. His better-known sayings came to echo those of his guru – and had to do with attacking, owning the ball, collective effort, and the importance of passing the ball. 'Without a pass, there is no ball control. Without ball control, there is no Barça,' Guardiola stated.

It was a philosophy that was destined not only to bring Barça further success as one of the best club sides in history, but also to help transform the Spanish national team for the first time into worthy and widely admired world champions.

Another contributor to Spain's success, Luis Aragonés, had quit as national coach at the end of the European Championships. Despite his achievement, the controversial coach's gruff and uncompromising manner had made him as many enemies as friends when he was in the job. He had people gunning for him in the media and within the Spanish Football Federation. Even in the immediate euphoria of victory, Aragonés told friends he didn't relish the continuing stress linked to the job, and felt it was worth quitting while his reputation was on an up.

He was to miss the Spanish players more than they missed him. His subsequent season working as coach for the Turkish club Fenerbahçe went from bad to worse. Turkish fans nick-named Luis Aragonés *dede* or 'granddad' – at first to convey the respect they wanted to show a wise and experienced elder, but with time to express their fury at a man they viewed as an incompetent geriatric.

Calls for his resignation increased after Fenerbahçe lost the Turkish Cup to Istanbul rivals Besiktas. Then Fenerbahçe, Champions League quarter-finalists in 2008, failed to reach the knockout stages of the competition and finished bottom of their group with just two points. The club then headed for their lowest league finish in years, at which point Aragonés' days in Turkey were over. The wise man from Hortaleza was suddenly transformed into a dejected Don Quixote figure, humiliated and misunderstood when once his Spanish players had looked up to him like a warlord.

But Spain's football authorities had made a wise choice for his succession in Vicente Del Bosque, a less controversial figure and with a reputation in Spanish club football for winning the loyalty of his players with his patient and unassuming style.

Del Bosque was born in 1950 in Salamanca, in Castile, the same region as Madrid. I asked him once if a sense of geography was important to him. 'I think the climate, the society in which you're born into, defines much of your life – in that sense I've considered myself a classic Castilian all my life,' he answered. What did he mean? I thought of what the legendary Real Madrid president Santiago Bernabéu had once said about what made Castilians better – that they had bigger and more rounded *cojones* than other Spaniards. But Del Bosque put it slightly differently. 'I would say we are people with a sense of responsibility, somewhat august, cold and quite serene, without great eccentricities.' In other words, the Catalans did not have a monopoly on sense and sensibility, what they called in their language *seny*.

Del Bosque's humility belied an impressive track record during his time at Real Madrid. While never a great goal-scorer – in fact he scored only one goal in the eighteen games he played for the Spanish national team – Del Bosque was a hard-working player in a Real Madrid that won five league titles between 1974 and 1980. Later, in his four seasons as a coach of Real Madrid, he presided over one of its most successful periods in modern history. With him as coach, the club won two Champions League titles, two La Liga titles, a Spanish Super Cup, a UEFA Super Cup and an Intercontinental Cup.

I met Del Bosque for the first time after he had been sacked as Real Madrid coach, having been judged not good enough to handle superstars like Beckham. I had been warned that Del Bosque was a retiring kind of guy who distrusted the media and valued his privacy. But a friendship I had struck up with some of the Real Madrid veterans provided me with a calling card. A visit to Del Bosque's spacious Madrid apartment, in a quiet residential block within a five-minute drive of the Bernabéu, revealed a sitting room complete with predictable totems of success – silverware and plaques, among them one naming him the best football manager in the world. But it was also taken up with simpler pursuits, like the computer course in Basic English belonging to his beloved youngest son who had Down's Syndrome, and surprising touches of humour such as a cartoon effigy of Joan Gaspart, one of the most disastrous presidents in the history of FC Barcelona, smiling like a Goya witch.

Del Bosque was sacked a day after winning his second league title as coach of Real Madrid, to add to two Champions League trophies, and a week after Beckham had been signed as part of club president Florentino Perez's *galacticos* policy. He was sacked because his low-key style did not fit the image of the star-studded Madrid globetrotters. But those who knew Del Bosque better had long recognised a coach with subtle skills of communication and bonding. 'He is very psychologically refined,' commented Real Madrid defender and Spanish international Sergio Ramos.

The man from Salamanca was, however, not a man without feelings. Del Bosque – a deeply committed family man who had devoted thirty-five years of his professional life to Real Madrid – never adapted to coaching in Turkey with Besiktas after leaving the Spanish capital, the deep hurt he had felt at being sacked by Perez replaced by the suffering of an exile. He lasted even less time in Turkey than Aragonés and returned to Madrid to be closer to the family that was the rock in his life.

With a personality that is rare in Spaniards who have reached high positions in the public eye, Del Bosque never once complained in public, nor lobbied for position at other people's expense, and unlike Aragonés he retained enduring support among the decision-makers of Spanish football and wide swathes of the media. Even before Aragonés was picked as national coach, Del Bosque had been considered for the top job. When Aragonés decided to quit, he had become the natural choice to succeed the combustible old man from Hortaleza.

The Spanish players had, in jest but with an edge of seriousness, sung, 'We won't play without Luis' on their way back from Vienna two years earlier having ended Spain's years of serial underachievement, and here they were being presented with someone who was the polar opposite in personality terms. But Del Bosque's stoic nature was a boon.

When he landed the top job, Del Bosque had neither the need nor inclination to change a football philosophy. To do that to *La Roja* in 2008 after Spain had finally achieved glory would have been heresy.

And yet Del Bosque had more Catalans and Basques than Castilians in his squad – and Catalans claim to have within them not just *seny* – sense and sensibility – but also *rauxa*, an uncontrollable emotion, an outburst, any kind of irrational activity, while the Basques are the enduring torch-bearers of *La Furia*, that fighting spirit on the pitch that Franco thought belonged to a quintessential Spanish trait of heroic conquest and crusade. Watching the Spanish squad in South Africa was to get a sense of all that, but in harmony.

As things turned out, the quiet-spoken, sincere and conciliatory Del Bosque turned out to be the perfect choice to strike a balance between the old and the new when he took over from the controversial and complex Luis Aragonés. Spain had just had their finest footballing hour but a queue was already forming of young players ready to replace the internationals who had just been crowned European Champions.

The Barcelona trio, Pedro, Sergi Busquets and Gerard Piqué, all came in for the first time. The Real Madrid legend Raul remained excluded. But Del Bosque presided over evolution rather than revolution. There was no dramatic axing of a Beckham-type figure that marked Steve McClaren's appointment as English coach. Del Bosque even managed to make the fiery Catalan Victor Valdés feel valued as third-choice goalkeeper. On form alone Valdés was an obvious choice, but many believed he would rock the boat if he were named in the squad but not picked to start. With Del Bosque's calming influence on deck, no one rocked the boat, and Valdés was impeccably behaved, despite watching the tournament from the bench. In keeping Casillas as his captain, Del Bosque managed to assure himself of someone who had the respect of the whole team, regardless of other players' club colours. A key axis linking the Real Madrid and Barça players was the long-term friendship and mutual professional respect between Casillas and Xavi, who had played together representing Spain since they were teenagers.

Del Bosque understood his players despite coming from a very different era. He was born into a post-war Spanish generation that while still in childhood had begun to glimpse the beginning of a better future, although being destined to remain forever conscious of the memories of the Civil War. Did he remember how isolated from the rest of the world Spain seemed when he was growing up in the 1950s? Del Bosque told me: 'Of course one felt it. I don't like to talk about this because it seems to identify one politically, but I remember my parents feeling very insecure about everything that was going on, speaking in whispers about certain subjects.'

Del Bosque then went on to tell me about his father. 'He was radical, he had progressive ideas. He was caught up in the Spanish Civil War, taken prisoner by the Franco forces and served a sentence. You see, he was a pure-blooded Republican. He worked as a clerk for the national railways. He used to talk to me to convince me that nothing of what he lived through should ever be repeated . . . I think we Spaniards of today are not sufficiently thankful to his generation. With every day that passes the frontiers are disappearing. A lot of those who lived the drama of the Civil War have died – that has helped heal the wounds.'

I asked him whether it was fair to go on typecasting Real Madrid as Franco's team. 'Not especially. Anyway, Real Madrid was a football team. It was outside politics. It's a simplification to call it pro-Franco . . . Real Madrid is pluralist, it's got a huge number of followers of all tendencies,' he answered.

Del Bosque thought much the same of the Spanish squad he forged, despite the enduring rivalries at club level. Bringing good football together – that was the hallmark of a Spanish team that had proved so successful in South Africa, with no sign of tension between the players of Barça and the players from Real Madrid.

In the run-up to the 2010 World Cup in South Africa, Del Bosque strengthened the selection process which had taken shape under Aragonés and included a majority of Barça players in his first-choice squad, believing that this core of hugely talented players – because of the work ethos, team spirit and style of play they had built up under Guardiola – would be pivotal in helping him build on the success of the 2008 European Champions.

Canaries-born striker Pedro was selected for the first time, joining Cesc Fàbregas – another product of the Barça youth team who was Arsenal's star player and captain – and David Villa, who was on the move from Valencia to FC Barcelona. Barça's midfielders Iniesta, Xavi and Busquets were also brought in along with defenders Puyol and Piqué, with Valdés, another Masia veteran, as one of the two reserve goalkeepers, along with Liverpool's genial extrovert Pepe Reina, *La Roja*'s unofficial cheerleader much liked by all the players.

The Spanish squad, while more dependent on the manpower

of FC Barcelona than at any stage in football history, and mirroring the club's style, nevertheless aspired to be truly representative of the nation's best. Thus Real Madrid's brilliant and popular goalkeeper, the serene and widely respected Iker Casillas, was named captain, and was joined in the squad by two of his most talented team-mates, Sergio Ramos and Xabi Alonso. Other notable stars included in Del Bosque's line-up was Liverpool's Torres – who was recovering from a knee injury – Valencia's Mata and Silva, Villarreal's Capdevila, Sevilla's Jesús Navas and Athletic's Fernando Llorente, all part of a new generation of highly motivated and highly skilled players who together were capable of producing football that was both entertaining and effective.

Few of the protagonists in South Africa in 2010 defied celebrity status with the ease of Vicente Del Bosque. A caricature of a pensionable Guardia Civil keeping a watchful eye from the dugout, the Spanish coach was overweight, balding and mustachioed. His team may have set pulses racing on the field, but in a football scene where the cult of the manager had been built on virtuoso La Liga performances from Helenio Herrera and Johan Cruyff to Pep Guardiola at Barcelona, and Jorge Valdano via Fabio Capello to José Mourinho at Real Madrid, Del Bosque had been respected rather than venerated, never generating a mass following. To fellow Spaniards he was a difficult man to get excited about. That was until Spain's victory over Holland in the World Cup final turned him into a national hero.

With their status as European Champions underlined by a strong performance in the qualifying rounds – Del Bosque's *La Roja* had suffered just one defeat in forty-nine games prior to the tournament – and another impressive year for Spanish club football (La Liga had long established itself together with

England's Premier League with a mass following among the global satellite TV audience), Spain arrived in South Africa as the bookies' favourite.

However, lingering doubts resurfaced about Spain on the eve of the first World Cup to be held on African soil, part of the more apprehensive pre-tournament reporting along with the warnings of threatened race riots and the potential spread of AIDS brought in by HIV-positive prostitutes. The ghost of Quixote tilting at windmills lurked in the background.

One undeniable fact about the World Cup raised questions about Del Bosque's ability to improve on Luis Aragonés' achievement of winning the European Championship. Only seven football nations had ever won it, and Spain was not on the list. Of the seven who were competing in South Africa, it was Argentina that was presented with the most tantalising options. The presence of Argentine coach Diego Maradona divided commentators between those predicting the final debacle in world football's most enduring personal tragedy and those hoping, as Diego himself hoped, for the realisation of a dream.

Sectors of the English tabloid press were predictably jingoistic in thinking that Capello's squad could do well, this time. More sober minds suggested that Germany was fielding a much rejuvenated squad with attitude and style. And then there was Brazil, France, Italy and Uruguay, not at their historic best, but each capable of springing a surprise.

If your prediction was based on heart as well as head then Spain seemed the most obvious candidate to join the list of World Cup winners. Against tough European competition, the nation prone to bad luck and cursed with the label of underachievers had finally prevailed, and this was a team that played with verve, skill and passion.

And yet the sceptics reared their head during Spain's less than impressive first two weeks in the tournament. Del Bosque was given a bad press after his team's shock defeat by Switzerland. The old man from Hortaleza led the charge. Aragonés accused Spain of lacking the conviction to seize the game from the opening second, of lacking speed off the ball, of not looking for space well enough. He was particularly critical of Del Bosque's decision to play both Xabi Alonso and Sergio Busquets in midfield, with both players often hanging back – especially Busquets, who is a defensive player. And he suggested that Casillas might have played better had he not been distracted by his ongoing love affair with Spanish TV sports commentator Sara Carbonero. 'The better team didn't win, just the better organised one,' Aragonés concluded.

It was not an entirely unjustified judgement on a stuttering, nervous start by *La Roja*. Del Bosque's measured response simply made Aragonés' outburst sound less a betrayal than an irrelevance. Refusing to share blame, Del Bosque spoke in the kind of conciliatory language that had evaded Spain for much of its history. 'Not one bad word will escape my mouth about him (Aragonés),' Del Bosque said. 'There is only one Spain – not one Del Bosque and another Aragonés one.' Nor did Del Bosque panic. He held a series of team meetings – none longer than twenty minutes – and he reinforced what he wanted from his squad, prompting defender Sergio Ramos to say how 'psychologically refined' Del Bosque is. Victory in the following matches allowed him to be judged more favourably.

'He has been right all along,' wrote *Marca*'s Emilio Contreras, 'in his blind faith in Iker (Casillas), in his gamble on the Xabi Alonso–Busquets partnership, in the freedom he has given Barça's Xavi, in his decision not to insist on starting with

Torres, in his ability to make all the players feel partners of a team's success.'

With *La Roja*, Del Bosque, in the eyes of his fellow countrymen, sprung much more than a pleasant sporting surprise. For a while he forged a rare national consensus in a country that for most of its history has struggled to agree on what constitutes the common good. Del Bosque, a former Real Madrid player and coach, was happy to have a big Barça presence in his team, in a generous tribute to the extraordinary achievement of Guardiola in building a team ethos and a style that players understood and were happy with. And he achieved what no other Spanish coach had ever done before him without resorting to the egotistical projection or tempestuous rages of an Aragonés or Mourinho. He demonstrated that he was a master tactician as well as a quiet, softly-softly manager who did not like hogging the limelight or indeed kissing his players in public.

Even in the presence of journalists and fans, away from the stadium, Del Bosque's performance showed a very down-to-earth humanity. Accompanied by his wife Mari Trini, and three children – two boys, Vicente and Alvaro, and daughter Gema – he conducted himself like an ordinary family man, taking souvenir snapshots of some of the players or getting his sons a signed shirt, between meals and training sessions. Among the few disciplines he imposed on his players at the training camp in Potchefstroom was a restriction on their use of the internet and mobile phones, and access to the social network, to minimise their exposure to the pressures of 24-hour news, excessive pursuit by fans, or the threat of hacking.

The university campus was billed by the World Cup hosts as a centre of excellence where the South African cricketers prepared for their big tours. But the Spanish players and journalists were taken aback at first by its isolation. Such perceived austerity suited Del Bosque, the man from Salamanca, down to the ground and did no harm. 'When we first arrived,' recalled Spanish journalist Santiago Segurola, 'I thought we had hit a scene out of *The Last Picture Show*. Coming from Spain, it struck me like a bleak Texas town going nowhere. But it was comfortable and there was soon a real spirit of cohesion in the camp, thanks largely to Del Bosque.'

La Roja was pursued by hundreds of journalists throughout the tournament, but no story ever emerged of disunity or rebellion within the squad. If no complaints about Del Bosque leaked from the dressing room it was because there weren't any, in striking contrast to the tension in other camps, not least France's and Argentina's. Del Bosque was not the controlling type but he was hugely respected.

And if Del Bosque himself showed remarkable self-restraint in not showing favouritism to any one player, it was because he had seen all the players he had picked increasingly doing what was expected of them, of 'sweating the shirt', a phrase he grew up with as a young defender at Real Madrid. Only Torres had evidently underperformed compared to his stardom at Euro 2008, but Del Bosque made a point of not holding this against him in public, blaming it instead on a struggle to return to full fitness after the previous season's injury, and holding him to a cameo role in key games.

Del Bosque had seen what the *galactico* era had done to Real Madrid and was not impressed by celebrity or superegos or wasteful luxuries. At Real Madrid it had taken a José Mourinho to impose a semblance of coherence and team discipline in a club whose performance in recent years had been undermined by players with massive egos, an interventionist president, and one of the biggest turnovers of managers known to top-flight club football. At FC Barcelona it had taken someone with the cultural and political roots of Guardiola to bring about one of the club's most successful eras ever – a winning streak achieved with such style, solidarity and dignity that it helped silence critics of the club's huge sponsorship deal with Qatar that the purists claimed had sullied Barça's identity. As it was, FC Barcelona put the deal to a democratic vote of its members, following a prolonged debate within fan clubs and in the media. Barça may have become a global brand but it had yet to lose its cultural identity.

The 2010 World Cup showed Del Bosque's ability to get players of extraordinary individual talent to work as a team. Del Bosque could afford himself a smile when Puyol's goal against the Germans in the semi-final provoked a genuinely heartfelt and shared celebration between FC Barcelona and Real Madrid.

The history of Spanish football is not short of magical moments, superstition and divine intervention. But on this occasion, Spain's good fortune turned on enlightened teamwork in perfect harmony with their coach. Spain made history by repeating themselves, conquering Germany as they had done in the Euro 2008 final. The winning goal came in the 73rd minute when Xavi found the advancing Puyol with a bending corner kick. The goal had been meticulously planned at half-time in a discussion between Del Bosque and Puyol. The FC Barcelona captain had suggested that Germany's vulnerability lay in its static defence against the dead ball and that what was needed was a surprise attack involving a combination tried and tested at FC Barcelona between himself and Xavi.

The 1–0 result understated the significance of *La Roja's*

achievement in beating a team that had come fresh from scoring eight times while knocking out Capello's England and Maradona's Argentina. Spain's play had proven itself to be both enjoyable and masterful. The victory over the hugely skilled and youthful German team – one of the resurgent powers of international football – proved critical. 'The match against Germany was the turning point. I felt we had lost our fear, and that we could win,' Del Bosque told me.

I had my second long meeting with Del Bosque in late spring 2011, almost a year on from his World Cup victory. This time he asked me to meet him not at his home but in the bar of one of Madrid's tallest five-star hotels, one of several iconic skyscrapers on the northern route out of Madrid built during the boom years. In my childhood in the 1950s this was open countryside. Now it was part of the urban sprawl of modern Madrid. From the initial effusive greeting by a posse of doormen to the no less reverential refusal of the barman to charge for the bill, Don Vicente was treated as a VIP. And yet but for the choice of venue Del Bosque came across as the same quiet Spaniard I had met some eight years earlier. The same moustache, the same very ordinary suit, the same incisive way of talking about Spanish football and its challenges. And yet here was the man who had not only been given a noble title as a Marquis by the King of Spain, but had also topped the nation's popularity ratings in recognition of his World Cup achievement.

Del Bosque reflected with typical generosity towards others and was self-deprecating about his own role in making good things possible. He paid tribute to past managers like Aragonés, to Guardiola's Barça, to Iker Casillas, 'a great and natural captain' and all the other players. He identified two key points in the tournament. The first was when the squad had kept united and their faith after losing their first game against Switzerland. The second was when Spain conquered Germany in the semi-final. He did not have a harsh word to say about the Dutch team that Spain faced in a bruising final.

This was not the Dutch as conceived by Cruyff, but almost a caricature of *La Furia,* brutal, determined, but lacking grace or skill. Nine months before the World Cup an advert showed Dutch captain Giovanni van Bronckhorst (ex-Barça), and star players Wesley Sneijder and Rafael van der Vaart (ex-Real Madrid) and other players training with the intensity of soldiers preparing for war. 'Tears of joy are made of sweat', ran a caption in the brilliant orange that had made Dutch football so legendary in the past. But as David Winner, the historian of Dutch football, commented: 'Individualism was dead, the collective was king, and results were all that mattered. And just in case we missed the message that lovable old Holland with its culture of charming football and losing had been kicked into the dustbin of history . . .' the advert sneered, 'A beautiful defeat is still a defeat.'

Such a lead-up only fuelled the intense interest in the final. For if Holland was ditching the 'beautiful football' of the Ajax glory days, it was facing in *La Roja* a Spanish team that owed their ethos, tactics and style of play to the legacy of Rinus Michels and Johan Cruyff, the fathers of 'total football' who carried it on at Barcelona. When Cruyff managed Barcelona he turned the Catalan giants into Europe's leading club and the standard-bearer for beautiful attacking football, in a position regained under Guardiola and mirrored, at national level, first by Aragonés and then by Del Bosque.

The final did not quite live up to expectations. The Dutch surpassed themselves in their aggression, and *La Roja* struggled to replicate the brilliance they had shown against the Germans. The ugliness of the Dutch game was epitomised by de Jong's surprisingly un-red-carded wild kick on Xabi Alonso's stomach early on in the game. But Spain prevailed over a Holland team that was reduced to ten men when the English referee, Howard Webb, eventually dismissed the defender John Heitinga in extra-time with a second caution in the 109th minute. Cesc Fàbregas, on as a substitute, fed Andrés Iniesta to score the winner seven minutes later.

As Iniesta celebrated before a TV audience of more than 750 million, the Barça star removed his shirt to reveal the message '*Dani Jarque siempre con nosotros*' (Dani Jarque always with us), to commemorate a player who had suffered a fatal heart attack after a pre-season game. Iniesta had never played club football with Jarque, who was a player with Espanyol, but both players had risen together through the Spanish national team ranks. The action earned Iniesta a bureaucratic yellow card, but his gesture proved a fitting act of human solidarity for *La Roja* at its moment of maximum glory. For up to that moment Spain had developed an exceptional, mesmerising style of play with supreme artistry on and off the ball that demoralised and exhausted the opponent. If there was a potential flaw it was that possession might turn into an end in itself. But Spain had scored, and conquered.

La Roja at Wembley, November 2011

Epilogue

It takes just under four hours to travel by car or train across Spain's southern territory, from the mines of Rio Tinto to Alicante on the southeast coast. To travel the distance recently was to be reminded of the extraordinary transformation of Spanish football from its early roots to its modern achievement.

It's taken Spain just over a century to shake off the complex of its colonial past in sporting terms. Spaniards learned their first lessons about football from the group of British managers and engineers who came to exploit their mines. But the roles have long reversed, with Spain looked up to, not just by Britain but by other countries from which it learned, as the dominant force of modern football, with *La Roja* drawing on players from the two strongest and globally most popular national club leagues, the Spanish La Liga and England's Premier League. The success of *La Roja*'s under-21 and under-19 squads – both European Champions in 2011 – and of its less fortunate under-20 side that showed itself the best team in its World Cup despite losing on penalties to Brazil in the quarter-finals – suggests the depth of a generational shift towards excellence.

Just how far things had changed was underlined by the continuing brilliance of Vicente Del Bosque's Spanish national squad in competitive games (non-friendly) in the run-up to the 2012 European Championships. Spain topped the list of all the teams that qualified for the finals in every statistical category, from passing and keeping possession to shots and goals scored.

It was in Alicante in October 2011 that Spain demolished Scotland with a typical display of creative ball control and general menace in attack. The magic of *La Roja*'s performance was epitomised by David Silva's perfect opening goal in a move that involved 42 touches, 94 seconds and all 11 Spanish players. Such is the quality of Spanish players, that Silva had had to fight hard for a place with the World and European Champions, despite comfortably establishing himself as one of the undisputed stars of the Premier League in his first two seasons with Manchester City.

Silva belonged to a generation of Spanish players who brought fluidity and the rare element of surprise to the game so that football became an intricate piece of choreography rather than a north-to-south battlefield. This one-for-all-all-for-one *tiki-taka* football was what had led Spain to victory in the European Championships in 2008 and in the World Cup in South Africa two years later. That this period also saw FC Barcelona laying claim to being the best club in the world with a memorable victory over Manchester United in the Champions League in 2011 was not purely coincidental.

In Spain, Silva shared a 'brotherhood' of style with Xavi, Cesc Fàbregas and Andrés Iniesta – all three of them Barça players. Of that other Barça player, Lionel Messi, it is worth noting that his star shone brightest at FC Barcelona rather than with his native Argentina. It was not just that lesser club teammates fed off him. He has also fed off and flourished thanks to the team ethos and strategies of the rest of Guardiola's boys.

Barça players formed a majority of *La Roja*. But this did not make the World Cup of 2010 any less of a triumph for Spain, which had not won any major football tournament since its gold medal in the Olympics of 1992. That date symbolised the emergence of a sporting ambition that had over the previous decades been sacrificed to bad management and even worse politics, with some bad luck thrown in. And lest we forget, *La Roja* counted on players from other Spanish clubs, not least Real Madrid, although the intensified rivalry between it and FC Barcelona provoked by Mourinho's coaching of the men in white threatened the national consensus patiently built up by Del Bosque. *La Roja* included players like Torres, Xabi Alonso, and Cesc Fàbregas, whose skills and physicality had benefited from the experience of playing in the Premier League. Coming to the UK at a young age, they were given the chance to play at the highest level and given immediate responsibility. They experienced a very different kind of football but managed to acclimatise, using the frenetic pace of the English game to their advantage. As Xabi Alonso told the *Guardian*'s Sid Lowe: "If in the middle of the frenetic pace of the Premier League, you're good enough to apply *pausa*, put the brakes on, feint and send the opponent flying ten metres past, that gives you a real advantage."

The history of football is littered with stories of teams being destroyed by the politics of the dressing room. Spanish clubs have not been immune to this and nor have Spanish national squads. But particularly during the Franco years it was the politics behind the dressing room that gave Spanish football its particular dynamic, not always in a positive sense. At club level, it fuelled intense competitive rivalry between two of the world's most powerful clubs, while failing to produce an agreed pattern of play at national level that could guarantee success.

It was the old mythologies of what constituted the true Spanish race that turned two earlier Spanish triumphs – the silver medal in the 1920 Olympics and victory over the Soviet Union in the European Nations final of 1964 – into legends of their time: trumpeted by government and fans as an example of *La Furia Española,* the Spanish Fury. But this had nothing to do with style or technique, still less team management, and everything to do with the delusion of a nation capable of conquering any enemy on account of its superior spirit. Hence the figure of Don Quixote that has loomed large over much of our narrative.

So has the bullfighting analogy. There was perhaps more than a touch of irony in that *La Roja*'s World Cup triumph should be followed within just over a year with the last bullfight ever to be fought in Barcelona, of all cities, as a result of a Catalan ban! But while Catalans, largely for political reasons, might have made their minds up about ending bullfights as a way of reaffirming an identity different from the rest of Spain, it is in the Catalan capital that in recent times one had seen the enduring similarities between the artistry of the greatest living *torero* and some of today's greatest footballers.

That the *torero* in question, José Tomas, suffered a near-fatal goring weeks before the World Cup in 2010, only to choose Barcelona's last bullfight for his most defiant comeback appearance, gives the analogy its poignancy. For Tomas was no El Cordobes, the manic Beatles-haired bullfighter of the 1960s who entertained mass tourism with his crude mimicry of courage and style – his graceless stunts included jumping like a frog in front of the bull. Tomas was a throwback to the golden age of bullfighting in the first half of the twentieth century when bullfighters did not fool with bulls but genuinely risked their lives with them (indeed some of them were killed in the process), while using their intricate technique to try to master and ultimately subdue the brute force of a bigger, weightier opponent, armed with horns sharpened like stilettos.

Similarities between bullfighting and Spanish football once belonged to the mythology of the Spanish character – of blood and guts and conquest as an end in itself, of death in the afternoon as the triumph of virility if not selfless sacrifice. But the spectacle of Tomas and *La Roja* took the analogy to another level. Both involved practitioners of relatively small stature, who were able to use their skill, courage and creativity to reduce a much greater physical force. These were poets in motion, as much as they were warriors.

It was during the 1950s that football as a mass sport overtook bullfighting as Spain's most popular entertainment, with fewer good *toreros* and a growing number of good football players. Traditionalists bemoaned the passing of true Spanish culture and the advent of the material world. In fact, national archetypes continued to straddle entertainment generally with Spaniards rather than foreigners caught up in the bullfighting analogy. (There have been non-Spanish bullfighters but none of them has been rated by the genuine bullfighting fans or *aficionados*.) In Spain it was the players of Real Madrid who have tended to indulge in bullfighting imagery, with Raul as the last great totem, representing as he did the essence of *La Furia* in which the ideal player was both *matador* and *toro bravo*, fearless in his pursuit of the opposition, ruthless and uncompromising when it came to the kill. At FC Barcelona Gary Lineker was called *El Matador* because he knew when to take a goal opportunity when it presented itself near the penalty area, but he never himself claimed to want to be a bullfighter like Raul, who not only looked like one but also actually knew how to handle a cape like one, and did so in packed football stadiums, much to the delight of his fans.

The doctrines of *La Furia* led to successive Spanish national teams underperforming and underachieving. The adoption by *La Roja* of *tiki-taka* was thus not merely a shift in tactics but a change of identity from bull to *torero*, with the sound of *Olé* often accompanying the passing movements performed by Spain's international stars as if it were poetry in motion.

The feel-good factor generated in most parts of the country by the World Cup victory of *La Roja* translated into a more enduring popular support for the Spanish national team than at any time in history, not just because of its success but also because of the quality of it – the talent of its players, the beauty of how they played, and the image of togetherness they and Del Bosque conveyed, even if the old rivalries at club level between FC Barcelona and Real Madrid in particular were fuelled by the arrival in Spain as Real Madrid's manager of José Mourinho – football's *agent provocateur*.

Politically there was little to link the renewed sense of patriotism that *La Roja*'s continued run of success in 2011 generated with ETA offering to lay down its arms in the Basque Country, or the political resurgence of the centre-right Madrid-headquartered People's Party. The wise, consensual, seemingly uncorrupted Del Bosque continued to be one of the most popular figures in Spain – in stark contrast to most of Spain's discredited politicians – but remained strictly a football man with no political ambition.

Investment in youth training and the development – almost production line – of Spanish football players capable of commanding worldwide respect was one of the few good-news stories that Spain had to offer amid the political and economic doldrums fuelled by the euro crisis.

So how long can the success of Spanish football last? Just over a decade ago, it was France, one of only three teams (the others being West Germany and Spain) to hold both the World Cup and European Championship simultaneously, that was raising similar expectations with its Clairefontaine football academy and other training programmes. France was eliminated from the 2002 World Cup in the group stage and although there was a brief revival in the 2006 World Cup, where they were runners-up to Italy, it went downhill in subsequent years. Other countries like Holland and Brazil that can claim to have created some of the best football of the post-war era also failed to keep up the momentum. Teams lose their hunger after too much success. Some players age or lose form quicker than others. Inspirational managers and players find their legacy diminished with the passage of time. Transitions from one generation to the next can be mismanaged and all this can happen at club as well as national level. It's easier to quit than to succeed.

Much of the history of Spanish football is inevitably driven by the rivaly of FC Barcelona and Real Madrid – its politics, its players, its power, its stadiums, its huge fan base. Together in recent years they have been the beneficiaries of huge transfer investments, and the products of their youth academies (more so in the case of FC Barcelona) have evolved into a new generation of highly marketable stars. Looming large over the quality of *La Roja* is the brilliance of Spain's two biggest clubs that in recent years have surged past the rest of La Liga – and perhaps the world.

Such a duopoly – dominating as it does TV revenue,

sponsorship and the transfer market, and with a debt burden softened by the deeply entrenched political, banking and business support each club can rely on – risks turning La Liga into a duel between globetrotters.

But Spain has been happy for much of its history with having its two super-sides thrash it out, with opinion polls showing that nearly 60 per cent of Spaniards have Real Madrid or FC Barcelona as their favourite club, while a minority support one or the other when their team isn't playing. Undoubtedly this has something to do with each club's quality of play and global projection. It may also reflect the fact that the two clubs have between them come closest to accommodating a national mood.

I would like to believe that this journey through Spanish football is far from over, and that the dynasty of *La Roja* could last a decade or more. Certainly the success of Spain's youth teams and the strength in depth of its major clubs suggests the future could be as bright as the present. But then could I be tilting at windmills?

Euro champions, again: Torres and Mata celebrate Spain's winning
goal against Italy in Euro 2012

Postscript

Euro 2012: *La Roja* makes history

La Roja prepared for the opening Group game of Euro 2012 against Italy with the weight of precedent stacked against it. No national team in modern history had managed to follow up victory in a European Championship and a World Cup with a third consecutive major tournament win. Not since Uruguay took the Olympic title in 1924 and 1928, then added the inaugural World Cup itself in 1930, had any country laid claim to a similar achievement, and that was in the days when football had yet to become the competitive, globalised game it is today.

Form suggested that Spain were in with a chance of doing well, although their ability to clinch the trophy was being questioned. Since winning the World Cup, *La Roja* had maintained an unbeaten record in nineteen competitive games, displaying their trademark skill and flair, of quick passing, possession football. However, the recent defeat of both FC Barcelona and Real Madrid in the Champions League semi-finals, at the hands of Chelsea and Bayern Munich, showed that Spain's two leading clubs, from whom *La Roja* drew many of its players, were not invincible. Indeed such defeats threatened to demoralize *La Roja* along with the shock resignation of FC Barcelona's manager Pep Guardiola, who had been a huge influence on the club and players that formed the backbone of the national team. Moreover, there had been two gruelling seasons during which the historic rivalry between the two clubs had reached a new intensity. As one of Spain's leading football commentators, the former Real Madrid coach and player Jorge Valdano, told me: 'I felt Spain was in a worse physical shape than during the World Cup . . . the Barça and Real Madrid players were physically and emotionally drained.' Nor did it help that two key players behind *La Roja*'s World Cup victory, leading goalscorer David Villa and pivotal defender Carlos Puyol, were unable to play through injury.

For those in the Spanish squad, the political and economic context in which the Championship was being played presented a particular challenge. The national euphoria that had been generated by the World Cup victory had dissipated as Spain, heavily in debt, recording the highest ever levels of unemployment, and poorly governed by the recently elected centre-right Popular Party, sank deeper into its worst political and economic crisis in living memory. Spain may have become the Eurozone's A&E patient, but its football was still in apparent health and something that the rest of the world looked up to.

On 1 June 2012, days away from the start of the Euro 2012 tournament, the embattled Spanish prime minister, Mariano Rajoy, joined in a photo-opportunity with the Spanish team and coach Vicente Del Bosque. He hoped success for *La Roja* might help lift his country's deep gloom. 'Us Spaniards need some happiness in these complex and difficult times we live in,' Rajoy said.

It was seen by his opponents as a cynical attempt to use *La Roja* to divert attention from his own failings as a leader. Del Bosque, a man of principle whose trade unionist father had been imprisoned by Franco, refused to lend himself to such a ploy. He responded: 'We are used to pressure, we will defend the title, and we are champions of the world, but winning this tournament will not solve the problems of this country.' In other words, while *La Roja* might transcend politics, it would not lend itself to political manipulation.

Del Bosque could have done without Rajoy's intervention. As he told me in a long conversation we had after Euro 2012: 'I said what I said to try and restore a sense of realism. We footballers can represent our country but our job is not to solve its problems. What is important is that people who are suffering feel they are being told the truth by their leaders. As for our team, it can serve as an example of solidarity. The flag we wave belongs to everyone.'

Del Bosque's riposte to Rajoy sprang also from other doubts that privately haunted him. As he told me at the point he had just officially renewed his contract as coach with the Spanish federation until after the 2014 World Cup, he was himself privately prepared for the possibility that Spain would not progress beyond the quarter-finals and that he would quit if, as he expected, he subsequently lost the country's support.

As things turned out, Del Bosque unwittingly courted a national debate over his tactics. He took a risk in Spain's opening game of the championship against Italy by starting with a formation without strikers, using Cesc Fàbregas as a 'false' No. 9, pushing him into the advance role usually played by Messi at FC Barcelona. *La Roja* had a reputation not just for controlling the ball but for scoring well-crafted goals. For a while Del

Bosque's Spain managed to do neither, as it faced an Italy playing with a creative attacking style that took the Spanish coach by surprise. 'It proved a very uncomfortable game for us because Italy did not play as they had traditionally played,' Del Bosque recalled. With Italy undermining Spain's intent to pass them into submission, but also outplaying them, Del Bosque's selection decision seemed flawed as Antoni Di Natale opened the score sheet with a goal for the Azzurri in the 61st minute. But then Fàbregas equalized and *La Roja* rallied.

Next, Del Bosque brought out Torres, hoping that the striker might find it in himself to help create or score a winning goal in the last quarter of the game. Weeks earlier, Torres had scored the final goal in Chelsea's Champions League semi-final victory over FC Barcelona. More recently he had shown himself fit and in positive spirits in the training sessions leading up to Euro 2012. Del Bosque was aware that Torres' form was still well below that which he had shown in the last European championship – when he had scored a match winner against Germany – and during his first season at Liverpool, but was prepared to believe that playing him once again in *La Roja* would motivate him in a way that Chelsea FC had apparently failed to do for most of the previous season.

From the moment he appeared, Torres created chances and put Italy under pressure, with Spain taking back control of the match. But his failure to exploit several scoring opportunities served to underline the extent to which he was lacking his previous edge. What we saw was a Torres with the capacity to disrupt the opposition almost with immediate effect but lacking that edge that made him such a powerful force in Euro 2008, and seemingly doubting himself too much to strike effectively. Torres had taken to looking up to the heavens and pleading. I suspect he was asking God to give him speed as well as luck. Doubt is a terrible thing for any striker to have. By contrast, Spain's best player and the man of the match was Andrés Iniesta, who was hugely creative in midfield and a constant challenge to the resilience of Italy's defence. He would later be nominated for the player of the tournament.

Many managers would have thereon preferred to leave Torres on the bench for the rest of the tournament, but the next match against Ireland, who were the weakest side in the tournament, lacking overall skill and with a style less sophisticated than that of a below-average Premier League side, was one that Torres could score goals in. And so it proved. Torres repaid his manager's faith in him by contributing two goals to a 4–0 final score that highlighted the extent of Ireland's total submission by a much superior side. It was the first time Torres had scored in a competitive fixture for Spain since netting twice against Liechtenstein in September 2010, and it promised a recovery of sorts. Torres looked both determined and happy for the first time since his goal against Barça in the Champions League semi-final. Other goals in the match were scored by Silva, 'effortlessly', as one blogger put it 'while the Irish defence all performed their charades for the word hapless'. Then Torres was taken off in the 73rd minute and replaced by Fàbregas, who went on to score the fourth. While Ireland's defeat by Spain saw them make an early exit from the tournament, it left *La Roja* embroiled in a conspiracy theory. So close together on points were Spain, Croatia and Italy in the group that the conspirators (mostly Italians) fuelled the suggestion that Spain and Croatia would agree to play for a 2–2 draw in the their game simply to ensure their progress into the next round, and the elimination – along with Ireland – of Italy, who were now regarded by Del Bosque as one of the strongest teams in the competition. Not only was there no evidence to support such a plot, but any suggestion of its existence was quickly dispelled by the way the Croatia–Spain game turned out.

If from the outset Spain seemed to lack their usual sparkle and fluffed too many passes, it was partly their own fault for coming out and thinking not of themselves as champions but of Russia, a team who showed real promise in their opening game, but subsequently exited from the championship, showing their true mediocrity by losing to a poor team.

By contrast Croatia were not a corrupted team. They came out and did exactly what they said they would do to frustrate and disarm the Spaniards, building up solid lines of defence, pressing and taking their chances with an occasional counter-attack. They could have, at one point, been leading Spain by two clear goals had it not been for the brilliance of Casillas, the only Spanish player, with the exception of the wing-back Jordi Alba, to really give it his best in response. The young Catalan-born Alba, only recently selected for the national squad, may have been one of the positive revelations of the tournament – but for Del Bosque he was a story foretold. Alba had caught Del Bosque's eye during an impressive performance he had given in a friendly game against England at Wembley a few months earlier. His pace, ball control, his skill both in defence and in attack, along with his ability to link in with the midfield, reminded Del Bosque of Roberto Carlos during the Brazilian's heyday at Real Madrid. 'When we were in the Austrian camp getting ready for Euro 2012, I told him, "You are going to be the best left back in the tournament", and I told him that not just to give him confidence, but because I was convinced it would prove so.'

Credit in that match also went to Del Bosque for bringing on Navas to replace a thwarted Torres so as to stretch the Croatian defence when it was already tiring and forcing a number of threatening corners, before scoring the winning goal. The goal, when it came in the final minutes, involved probably the first piece of successful creative play by *La Roja* in the whole match: Fàbregas (another late substitute) exploiting a gap in the Croatian defence, passed to Iniesta, who, after drawing out the goalkeeper, passed it to Navas for a final tap-in, in a characteristically faultless interchange of passes.

The goal brought cathartic scenes among the Spanish fans, who had looked increasingly tense and gloomy as the match proceeded, suspecting that just one Croatian goal would mean the end of the tournament for them just as surely as Don Quixote breaking his lance on a windmill. When the final whistle went, Del Bosque looked like a man who had been made to suffer for ninety minutes, and his players seemed shattered. The BBC commentator at one point blamed the heat – an absurd suggestion given the high temperatures Del Bosque's players are used to playing back in their native Spain in spring, summer and early autumn. The players were as shocked as their manager at how close they were to defeat, and all because they did not play as they knew they could – so much better than that night.

The Spanish media, stirred up by among others, Jose Mourinho, meanwhile continued to call for a change in tactics. Criticism was based on the view that Spain's game, for all its technique, had lacked resolution in overpowering and destroying the enemy. And even the flair seemed to be missing. With the exception of the match against the Republic of Ireland, Del Bosque's team had failed to entertain. Setting aside moments of brilliance, the ball had not flowed with its characteristic fluidity; the organisation of the team had been well short of perfect choreography. Boring, some commentators ventured.

Del Bosque resisted laying the blame on Torres, or any other individual player for that matter. It was a collective failure not to have won with more conviction. But *La Roja* was strong enough to bounce back. And it did, beating France in the quarter-final with two goals by Xabi Alonso (one a penalty), the first time in any competitive game Spain had ever beaten *Les Bleus*. The key was *La Roja*'s control, achieved with dominance of midfield, with Fàbregas once again selected over Torres, and the greater use of the fullbacks, notably Alba and his cutting-edge attacks, like the one that contributed to the first goal in the nineteenth minute.

And yet the problem of being champions is that you are expected to play as champions in every game, as if players were gods, not mere mortals subject to bad moods, bad luck and periods of mental and physical pain, which may be hidden from the public but which Del Bosque knows about and throws into his calculations. 'Coming to the tournament as champions was handicap rather than benefit. No one [since Uruguay] had done three in a row – there must have been a reason for that. To keep a winning team at a competitive level over such a long period of time was not easy', he told me weeks after the championship was over.

Against Portugal in the semi-finals, *La Roja* succeeded in reducing the best player in the tournament to his worst. Ronaldo played selfishly and inaccurately, his performance marked more by negative theatrics than by genuine skill. Alongside this narcissist, the majority of the Portuguese team played a battle plan set under advice from Mourinho,

Spanish football's *agent provocateur,* which certainly worked in neutralizing the effectiveness of *La Roja's* third striker Álvaro Negredo, who was brought on as an alternative to Torres and the unused Llorente. The Portuguese tactics would have undermined a lesser team. *La Roja* for a while lost its rhythm, its passing and possession losing its apparent capacity to remain fluid and deliver. But then, somewhat belatedly in extra time, it rallied and played some of the best football in the tournament. In the penalty shoot-out Spain had luck on its side. Portuguese coach Paul Bento took the decision not to use Ronaldo as an early kicker. By stark contrast Del Bosque ordered his players taking into account a premonition had by Cesc Fàbregas, the Barça and former Arsenal player. 'We had him on the list as second, but he insisted on being fifth. He was convinced because of a winning penalty he had taken against Italy in Euro 2008 that he would do it again.' And so it happened. During the Spanish celebrations, Ronaldo was caught on Portuguese TV mouthing: 'It's an injustice, it's an injustice.' Ronaldo, until this match, had been the best player of the tournament. But Spain was the better team.

At the end of mass on the morning of the Euro 2012 final between Spain and Italy the Italian priest got me to identify myself as the only Spaniard before announcing to the congregation that the *Azzurri* would tonight 'crush' *La Roja*. I replied that Santiago (St James, Patron Saint of Spain) and the Virgin of Montserrat (patron of Catalonia) might have had their own communication from God and come up with a different prediction.

In truth I had no certainty which team had God on its side, although I did say a prayer for *La Roja* in thanks for its contribution to world football, and in the hope that its below-par performance in the tournament so far – a source of great delight to my aspiring nemesis Captain Terry, alias Carlos Oppe, a diehard Chelsea fan and critic of my blogs – would be remedied with victory over an Italy that had defied expectations and defeated Germany brilliantly in its semi-final match.

La Roja laid claim to being much more than a team. Since winning Euro 2008, they have, as a national squad, innovated in their style of playing and organisation, and in their attitude towards winning – both a system of play and philosophy. This was a national team that, like FC Barcelona at club level, has prioritised passing, possession and movement in all positions, but with midfield acting as the key lubricant of defence as well as conduit of attack. I use the word 'lubricant' as opposed to 'bastion', or 'wall', or 'rock' just as I describe *La Roja*'s players Xavi and Iniesta as bullfighters rather than bulls because of the intricacy of their close-play choreography.

This was not a team lacking in tall men, nor was it without spirit and courage, but it was a team that prioritised style over virility and aggression when it was in possession of the ball, and it was more often than not very good at not losing control. *La Roja* was above all a team ethos, a one-for-all-and-all-for-one philosophy, where each player was an essential element of the strategy, and the attack became the best defence. What marks out *La Roja*'s best goals is the intricacy of the build-up play involved. This was not a team that believed in winning at all costs, that the end justifies the means, but whose self-belief was predicated on the fact that victory is assured by holding the ball as long as possible, rather than going out and physically annihilate the opponent.

Of *La Roja*'s victory over Italy in the final of Euro 2012 much has been written already, and, having not kept silent myself during the tournament (in blogs, Twitter posts, articles and interviews), I would like to simply conclude with a few points. *La Roja* is much more than a football achievement. It is a political, social and cultural phenomenon that Spaniards should recognise and take pride in. A country that has suffered the humiliation of being reduced to one of the beggars of the euro crisis, and surrendering its sovereignty to the markets and Berlin, has produced something that in its excellence leaves all other countries in its shadow.

La Roja in the final of Euro 2012 simply showed what it can do best, and that is better than anybody else around the globe, past or present. Perhaps comparisons with teams in other periods in history are meaningless. Let us not forget that the Brazil of Pele ran out of steam after four years, and even Guardiola's Barça buckled before Mourinho's Real Madrid and a Chelsea with Mourinho's imprint written all over it.

True, during the finals, even Spain's most ardent *La Roja* fans found it difficult to keep an eye on the ball without reading the latest text messages from their increasingly desperate families and friends back home. Each year since the collapse of Lehman Brothers in 2008, Spaniards have braced themselves for another year of crisis, only to be reassured by politicians that the sacrifices of austerity would be rewarded sooner or later with an economic recovery. As the *FT's* Madrid correspondent Victor Mallet put it; 'Each year, the light at the end of the tunnel – as in the sardonic joke – has turned out to be the threat of an oncoming train.' By the summer of 2012, Spain was readying itself for the humiliating full bail-out Prime Minister Rajoy had always insisted was not needed.

True, as the *FT* pointed out, even in the depths of international despair about the Eurozone, Spain could still boast of some economic and political achievements. Exports and the tourism industry have been performing well, and a current account deficit that topped 10 per cent of GDP at the start of the crisis was heading towards equilibrium as the economy rapidly adjusted. Spanish democracy still functioned and, even if its politicians were unpopular, Spain was not yet ruled by a techno-crat imposed by Brussels, and, in the Basque country, ETA's 'definitive ceasefire' was holding after 800 killings in half a century.

Yet Spain, which had become accustomed to receiving praise for its rapid modernisation, cultural vibrancy and economic growth after the restoration of democracy in 1978, has become the butt of jokes around the world. Probably the lowest blow was a jibe from Richard Boucher, a US official at the Organisation for Economic Cooperation and Development, who said Spain today was 'only good for flamenco and red wine'. Thankfully he had not added, 'Spanish football'.

On the night *La Roja* won Euro 2012, as the players cele-brated their victory, we got a glimpse of players and fans at peace with themselves – tolerant in their celebration, united in self-belief that went beyond partisan interest. Two Barça play-ers placed a Catalan flag by the trophy, a Real Madrid player from Andalucia showed off his bullfighting passes, and a tall blond Spanish export who plays for Chelsea and has been saved from the narcissism of Beckham and Ronaldo showed off his two small children in red, like any proud dad, like one more Spanish fan.

'*La Roja* has a good meaning. Del Bosque told me 'It's a worthwhile message – it means unity.' From here on, Spaniards should expect better things from their politicians or else suggest that Del Bosque become prime minister.

Select Bibliography

José Manuel Alonso, *Athletic for Ever* (bbk 1998)

David Avery, *Not on Queen Victoria's Birthday* (Collins 1974)

Phil Ball, *Morbo* (WSC 2003)

Patrick Barclay, *Mourinho* (Orion 2011)

Fritz Baren & Henk van Dorp, *Ajax, Barcelona, Cruyff* (Bloomsbury 1998)

Carlos Moreno Benito, *Una historia de fabula* (Soubriet 2003)

Kepa Bordegarai, *Clemente* (Baroja 1985)

Jimmy Burns, *Hand of God: The Life of Diego Maradona – Updated edition* (Bloomsbury 2010)

Jimmy Burns, *Barça, A People's Passion – Updated edition* (Bloomsbury 2010)

Jimmy Burns, *When Beckham Went to Spain* (Michael Joseph 2004)

Jimmy Burns, *Spain: A Literary Companion* (John Murray 1994)

Tom Burns, *La Monarquia Necesaria* (Planeta 2007)

Lucia Cailoli, *Messi* (Corinthian 2010)

Raymond Carr, *Spain* (Clarendon Press 1966)

Jaume Collell, *Pep Guardiola* (Peninsula 2009)

Juan Carlos Cubeiro/Leonor Gallardo, *Mourinho vs Guardiola* (Alienta 2010)

Hunter Davies, *Postcards from the Edge of Football* (Mainstream 2010)

Miguel Angel Diaz, *Los Secretos de La Roja* (Cupula 2010)

Alfredo Di Stéfano, *Gracias, Vieja* (Aguilar 2000)

K-Tono Frade Hijo, *Rincones del 'Botxo'* (bbk 2010)

Eduardo Galeano, *Football in Sun and Shadow* (Fourth Estate 1997)

Ian Gibson, *Fire in the Blood* (Faber 1992)

Brian Glanville, *The History of the World Cup* (Faber & Faber 2010)

David Goldblatt, *The Ball Is Round* (Penguin 2007)

José Miguel González, *El Fútbol de Michel* (Pearson Educacion 2003)

Robert Graham, *Spain, Change of a Nation* (Michael Joseph 1984)

Christopher Howse, *Pilgrim in Spain* (Continuum 2011)

Henry Kamen, *Imagining Spain* (Yale 2008)

Simon Kuper, *Football against the Enemy* (Orion 1994)

Simon Kuper, *Ajax, The Dutch, The War* (Orion 2003)

Simon Kuper, *The Football Men* (Simon & Schuster 2011)

Carlos Levi, *Atlético de Madrid* (Sile 2003)

Javier Marías, *Salvajes y Sentimentales* (Aguilar 2000)

Tony Mason, *Passion of the People* (Verso 1995)

Elizabeth Nash, *Seville* (Signal Books 2005)

Alfredo Relaño, *El Fútbol contado con sencillez* (Maeva 2001)

John Robinson, *Soccer: The World Cup 1930–1994* ((Redwood Books 1997)

Miguel Gonzalez San Martin, *Cronicas del Athletic* (bbk 2008)

Miguel Gonzalez San Martin, *Los anos funámbulos* (bbk 2008)

Carlos Fernández Santander, *El Fútbol durante La Guerra Civil y el Franquismo* (San Martin 1990)

Orfeo Suárez, *Hablamos de Fútbol* (Unicef 2009)

Enrique Terrachet, *Historia del Athletic de Bilbao* (Lagran 1984)

Giles Tremlett, *Ghosts of Spain* (Faber 2007)

Fernando Torres, *My Story* (HarperSport 2010)

Jorge Valdano, *Suenos de Fútbol* (ElPais/Aguilar 1995)

Edwin Winkels, *De methode Guardiola* (Hard Grass 2010)

David Winner, *Brilliant Orange* (Bloomsbury 2001)

Paddy Woodworth, *The Basque Country* (Signal Books 2007)

Francisco Zambrano Vazquez, *Don José Perez de Guzman y su fandango* (Diputacion Badajoz 2008)

Media publications and websites: The *Guardian*, *El Pais*, *El Mundo*, *Hard Gras*, *The Times*, *New York Times*, *Telegraph* newspapers, the *Sun*, Mirror Newspapers, *Mundo Deportivo*, *Sport*, *As*, *Marca*, *La Vanguardia*, *Financial Times*, BBC and RTÉ.

Acknowledgements

This book would not have come about without my late parents Tom Burns and Mabel Marañón, the love of my immediate family Kidge, Julia and Miriam, and the enduring hospitality of my brother Tom and sister-in-law Dolores.

Warm thanks, too, to all those quoted in the book and others who also helped in different ways: Jon Agiriano, Paco Arenosa, Chencho Arias, Patrick Buckley, Juanjo Diaz, Regino Garcia-Badell, Emilio Butragueño, José Manuel Delgado, Juan Blas Delgado, Anna Eizaguirre, Richard Foreman of Chalke Authors, K-Tono Frade, Josep Fusté, Bruno Garteiz Gandarias, Rafael Garteiz Gandarias, Asis Garteiz Gandarias, Robert and Concha Graham, Jorge Gallardo, Alfons Godall, Iñigo Gurruchaga, Patrick Harverson, Andrew and Edwina Haynes, Jon Holmes, Graham Hunter, Pere Jansa, Jon Juaristi, Simon Kuper, Iñigo Lizarralde, Fidel Lopez Alvarez, Marjolijn van der Meer, Juan Milagro, José-Maria Minguella, Javi Navarro, Peter Nicholson, Carlos Oppe, Alice Owen, Philip Paddack, Chus Pereda, Sol Perez de Guzman, Frank Porral, Eduardo Prim, Luis Fernando Rojo, Cuqui Sarrias, Ulises Sanchez Flor, Santiago Segurola, Henk Spaan, Orfeo Suárez, José Ángel Sanchez, Manolo Sanchis, José Miguel Teres, Carlos Tusquets,

Jorge Valdano, Carlos Uribe, David White, Edwin Winkels, David Winner, Paddy Woodworth. *Gracias tambien* to Annabel Merullo and team at PFD, Mike Jones, Rory Scarfe, Ian Allen, and the team at S&S; and Carl Bromley and team at Nation Books in the US who made it all look better.

Index